Idiot's Little Guide to Word for Windows

(You mean I Spent All That Time Writing This Book, and You're Not Going to Read It?)

Scrolling Through a Document with the Keyboard

To Move . . .	Press . . .
Up or down one line	Up or down arrow key
Left or right one character	Left or right arrow key
One word left or right	Ctrl+← or Ctrl+→
Up or down one paragraph	Ctrl+↑ or Ctrl+↓
Up or down one screen	Page Up or Page Down
Top of the screen	Ctrl+Page Up
Bottom of the screen	Ctrl+Page Down
Beginning of the line	Home
End of the line	End
Beginning of document	Ctrl+Home
End of document	Ctrl+End
Toggle between two panes	F6
Move to the next cell in a table	Tab
Move to a previous cell in a table	Shift+Tab

Selecting Text with the Mouse

To Select This . . .	Do This . . .
Word	Double-click on word.
Sentence	Press Ctrl and click on sentence.
Line	Click in front of the line.
Multiple lines	Drag in the selection bar next to the lines.
Paragraph	Triple-click in the paragraph.
Column	Click at top of column.
Row	Click in front of row.
Whole document	Triple-click in the selection bar.

Get Out Your Tools!

Too many tools? Here's a quick description of the Standard toolbar buttons:

Icon		Function
	New	Opens a new document.
	Open	Opens an existing document.
	Save	Saves the document you're working on.
	Print	Prints the current document.
	Preview	Previews a document before printing.
	Spelling	Checks the current document for spelling errors.
	Cut	Removes text and stores it for placement elsewhere.
	Copy	Copies text for placement elsewhere.
	Paste	Inserts stored text at current location.
	Format Painter	Copies text formatting.
	Undo	Undoes the last action or command.
	Redo/Repeat	Repeats a previous action.
	AutoFormat	Formats a document automatically.
	AutoText	Inserts your favorite text or graphics.
	Table	Changes text to table style.
	Excel	Inserts an Excel table or graph.
	Text Columns	Formats document with newspaper-style columns.
	Draw	Displays the Drawing toolbar.
	Graph	Starts Microsoft Graph.
	Show/Hide Paragraph Marks	Displays hidden codes.
100%	Zoom	Changes your view of the current document.
	Help	Provides help on a part of the screen.

alpha books

Formatting Frenzy!

Be a formatting fool with the Formatting toolbar:

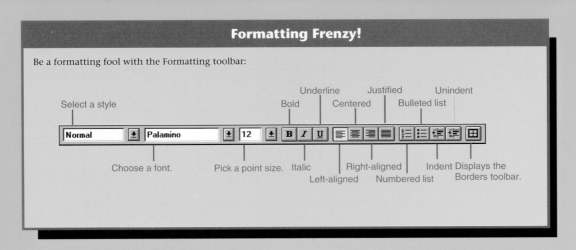

The Anatomy of a Ruler

Pleasure's hard to measure when you use the Ruler to change margins, indents, and to set tabs:

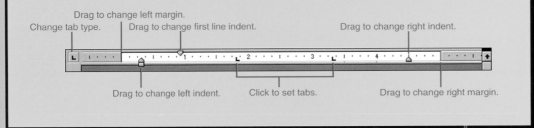

Formatting Text with the Keyboard

To Change Characters to:	Press This Key Combination:
Bold	Ctrl+B
Italic	Ctrl+I
Single Underline	Ctrl+U
Word Underline	Ctrl+Shift+W
Double Underline	Ctrl+Shift+D
Small Caps	Ctrl+Shift+K
All Caps	Ctrl+Shift+A
Hidden	Ctrl+Shift+H
Superscript	Ctrl+Shift+=
Subscript	Ctrl+=
Change the font	Ctrl+Shift+F
Change the point size	Ctrl+Shift+P
Make text one size bigger	Ctrl+Shift+>
Make text one size smaller	Ctrl+ Shift+<
Remove character formatting	Ctrl+Spacebar
Repeat formatting	F4

Formatting Paragraphs with the Keyboard

To Change Paragraphs to This:	Press This Key Combination:
Left-aligned text	Ctrl+L
Right-aligned text	Ctrl+R
Centered text	Ctrl+E
Justified text	Ctrl+J
Indent	Ctrl+M
Unindent	Ctrl+Shift+M
Hanging indent	Ctrl+T
Normal style	Ctrl+Shift+N
Change styles	Ctrl+Shift+S
Remove manual formatting	Ctrl+Q

by Jennifer Fulton

alpha
books

A Division of Prentice Hall Computer Publishing
201 W. 103rd Street, Indianapolis, IN 46290

To my sister Beth, whom I'm lucky to have as a sister and a best friend.

Second edition: I'd like to dedicate the second edition to my sister (of course), and to my new husband, Scott. I don't know what life has in store, but I know it will be so much nicer with you by my side. ILY4FR.

©1993 Alpha Books

International Standard Book Number: 1-56761-355-1
Library of Congress Catalog Card Number: 93-72390

96 95 94   8 7 6 5 4 3

Interpretation of the printing code: the rightmost number of the first series of numbers is the year of the book's printing; the rightmost number of the second series of numbers is the number of the book's printing. For example, a printing code of 93-1 shows that the first printing of the book occurred in 1993.

Screen reproductions in this book were created by means of the Collage Plus program from Inner Media, Inc., Hollis, NH.

Printed in the United States of America

Publisher
Marie Butler-Knight

Associate Publisher
Lisa A. Bucki

Managing Editor
Elizabeth Keaffaber

Development Editor
Seta Frantz

Production Editor
Linda Hawkins

Copy Editor
Barry Childs-Helton

Cover Designer
Scott Cook

Designer
Amy Peppler-Adams

Illustrator
Steve Vanderbosch

Indexers
Jeanne Clark and Craig Small

Production Team
*Gary Adair, Diana Bigham, Katy Bodenmiller, Ayrika Bryant, Brad Chinn,
Tim Cox, Meshell Dinn, Howard Jones, Wendy Ott, Beth Rago, Carrie Roth,
Marc Shecter, Greg Simsic*

*Special thanks to C. Herbert Feltner for ensuring the
technical accuracy of this book.*

Contents at a Glance

Contents

Part II: Document Beauty Makeovers   **127**

Introduction

You're not an idiot, but if Word for Windows makes you feel like one, you need a book that can help. What you don't need is a book that assumes you are (or want to become) a Word wizard. You don't need someone to tell you that Word for Windows is one of the most complex word processors around. (You've already learned that the hard way.) You're a busy person with a real life, and you're just trying to get a stupid letter, memo, or report written, spell-checked, and printed.

Why Do You Need This Book?

With so many computer books on the market, why do you need this one? Well, first off, this book won't assume that you know anything at all about how to use Word for Windows—or Windows itself, for that matter.

This book doesn't assume you want (or have the time) to learn everything there is to know about Word for Windows. The most common tasks are broken down into easy-to-read chapters that you can finish in a short time. Simply open the book when you have a question or a problem, read what you need to, and get back to your life.

How Do I Use This Book?

For starters, don't actually *read* this book! (At least not the whole thing.) When you need a quick answer, use the Table of Contents or the Index to find the right section. Each section is self-contained, with exactly what you need to know to solve your problem or to answer your question.

If you're supposed to press a particular key, you'll know it because that key will appear in bold, as in:

Press **Enter** to continue.

Sometimes you'll be asked to press two keys at the same time. This is called a *key combination*. Key combinations appear in this book with a plus sign between them. The plus means that you should hold the first key down while you press the second key listed. For example:

Press **Alt+F** to open the File menu.

In this case, you should hold the **Alt** key down while you press the letter **F**, and then something will happen. Alt is a pretty popular key; it's used with practically all the letters on the keyboard to do one thing or another (more on this later). The bold letter F that you see in the word File is there to remind you that you should press the letter F with the Alt key to open the File menu.

There are some special boxed notes in this book that will help you learn just what you need:

By the Way . . .
These boxes contain special hints from yours truly.

Put It to Work
These boxes provide safe ways to practice what you learn.

Easy-to-understand definitions for every computer term let you "speak like a geek."

Skip this background fodder unless you're truly interested.

Help when things go wrong.

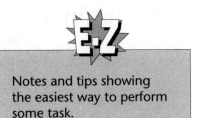

Notes and tips showing the easiest way to perform some task.

Other Special Treats

This book is so loaded with stuff, there are some things I almost forgot to tell you about:

Be sure to watch for the special "What's Wrong with This Picture?" sections; they highlight simple exercises that test what you've learned.

If you use Word 2.0, you won't feel like an idiot when you're using this book. Whenever something that's explained is different in your version of Word, you'll see this:

Watch for these boxes for helpful hints on using Word for Windows 2.0.

Acknowledgments

Again, thanks to everyone at Alpha Books who helped make this book a reality. It's nice to be part of such a great team.

In the first edition of this book, I thanked my fiancé, Scott, for his love and his patience. This book is now in its second edition, and his love is as strong as ever. By the time this book is published, I will be married to my friend, my compadre, my love—my Scott.

Trademarks

All terms mentioned in this book that are known to be trademarks or service marks are listed below. In addition, terms suspected of being trademarks or service marks have been appropriately capitalized. Alpha Books cannot attest to the accuracy of this information. Use of a term in this book should not be regarded as affecting the validity of any trademark or service mark.

CorelDRAW! is a trademark of Corel Systems.

DrawPerfect is a registered trademark of WordPerfect Corporation.

Lotus 1-2-3 is a registered trademark of Lotus Development Corporation.

Microsoft Excel, Microsoft Graph, Microsoft Windows, and Microsoft Word are registered trademarks and Word for Windows is a trademark of Microsoft Corporation.

PageMaker is a registered trademark of Aldus Corporation.

PC Paintbrush is a registered trademark of ZSoft Corporation.

Quattro Pro is a registered trademark of Borland International, Inc.

Ventura Publisher is a registered trademark of Xerox Corporation.

Part I
Dad Does Word Processing

My dad used to work at home a lot, and one day my brother Mike decided that Dad needed a computer, so he bought him one. After getting him started with a few basics ("Here's the keyboard; just type"), Mike left him alone. Later, Dad showed me a letter he'd printed: two paragraphs followed by four blank pages. Dad was very puzzled by this, so he asked, "Do you think it needs a new ribbon?" I could tell that Mike had left out some of the essentials.

That's the problem with most computer books today; they assume you know something, and they end up leaving out the essentials. In this section, you'll learn all those things Mike should have told my dad about using a word processor (including the fact that you shouldn't lean the manual against the Enter key or you'll end up producing four blank pages).

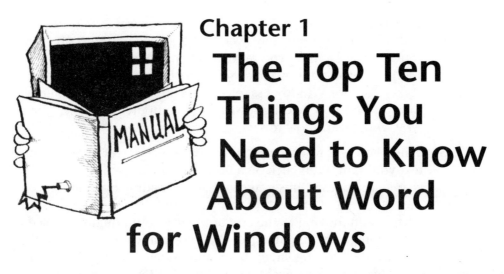

Chapter 1

The Top Ten Things You Need to Know About Word for Windows

Just like those other "notes" you used in high school to avoid *actually reading books*, here's a "Jennifer's Notes" version of the amazing facts you'll find within these pages. If you read nothing else in this book, for gosh sakes, read this!

1. **Word for Windows is a Windows program,** so you must know something about Windows in order to use it. If you're a stranger to Windows, read Chapter 3, and I'll introduce the two of you.

2. **Don't press Enter at the end of each line of text—only at the end of a paragraph.** If you're accustomed to using a typewriter, you're also used to returning the carriage to the left margin at the end of every line. Word processors are different; when you press Enter, you create a new paragraph. So how do you get to the next line if you don't press Enter? Well, as you type, words *wrap* between the left and right margins automatically. If you add or delete text in a paragraph, the existing text adjusts itself to fit the margins. Chapter 6 explains the ins and outs of typing text.

3. **Don't use the Spacebar to center text.** If you want your heading to be centered, don't use the Spacebar to move to the starting position. Instead, select *center alignment* (which centers any amount of text between the left and right margins). In Chapter 12, you'll learn how to set up centered, right-aligned, or left-aligned text.

4. **Save your work often.** Even a momentary power outage can make a simply horrible day even worse. When you turn off your computer, everything you're working on is erased from the computer's memory—so *save, save, save* it onto a disk! Better yet, make Word for Windows save your documents at timed intervals, so you won't ever be caught with your computer down. In Chapter 9, you'll learn how to save your documents.

5. **When you want to change how text looks, select it!** Select the text you want, then click on a button or use a menu command to change it. For example, you can select a heading by moving to the beginning of the text, pressing and holding the left mouse button, and moving to the end of the text to highlight it. Once the heading is highlighted (*selected*), you can choose commands to make the heading larger, bold, and underlined. In Chapter 6, you'll learn how to select text, and in Chapter 11, you'll learn how to make your text look the way you want it to.

6. **You can perform all your editing tasks faster and easier with a mouse than with the keyboard.** Just about any type of task (such as changing the look of text or saving or printing a document) can be done faster and easier with a mouse. With the toolbars, you click on a button to make changes or perform some task. You say you don't know how to use a mouse? Don't worry—you'll learn all about it in Chapter 3.

7. **What you see isn't always what you get.** The default viewing mode for Word for Windows is Normal. In *Normal mode*, you will not see pictures, graphs, and columns as they will appear when printed. Use *Print Preview mode* to view a document just before printing. Chapter 7 describes all the ways you can look at your document.

8. **Just 'cause you're a beginner doesn't mean you have to start at the beginning.** If you know what type of document you want to create (like a memo or a simple letter), let a Word for Windows *Wizard* do the work for you. Just open a new document, select a Wizard, and answer a few questions. With a wave of its wand, the Wizard will set up the pages with headings, page numbers, margins, and whatever's needed. With a Word Wizard, all you have to do is enter some text—and if you want help while you're entering it, the Wizard can help you there, too! Click your heels three times and jump to Chapter 8 for more info.

9. **Word for Windows lets you use all your Windows programs together.** Word for Windows can import part of a spreadsheet from any Windows program, such as Excel or Lotus for Windows. It can even create a link between your document and the imported item's native program, so that changes made to the imported item are reflected in your document automatically. Whew! In Chapter 21, you'll learn how to import data and pictures from other programs.

10. **Word for Windows lets you create your own style.** The *style* of a paragraph controls how it should look—its margins, alignment (such as centered), indentations, and so on. For example, you can create a Heading style that makes your headings bold and centered. By changing one of the style's settings, you change all paragraphs of that style—in one simple step. For example, if you changed the Heading style to include underline, then all headings within your document would change to bold, centered, and underlined. In addition, Word for Windows 6 comes with a collection of predesigned styles for you to choose from, or modify to fit your mood. If you prefer, you can even put Word on "automatic," and let it format your documents for you. Chapter 14 gives you the lowdown on styles—how to create them and how to use them.

What's New in Word for Windows 6.0

For those of you who've used a previous version of Word for Windows, here's a brief list of some of the many things that are new in Word for Windows 6.0:

1. **Super shortcut menus**—With a click of the right mouse button, bring up a convenient menu customized with commands that fit the current task. See Chapter 4 for more details.

2. **Multiple toolbars**—The Standard toolbar and the Ribbon (now called the *Formatting* toolbar) have given birth to a set of *toolbars*, customized to specific word processing tasks. Toolbars can now be positioned wherever you'd like. Adding new toolbars to the work area is easy through a shortcut menu. See Chapter 4 for the lowdown on toolbars.

3. **Make fewer mistakes**—With the new AutoCorrect feature, you can teach Word to correct your most common typing mistakes. See Chapter 6.

4. **Get repetitious**—AutoText lets you save often-used phrases so you can make them appear, error-free, with a few keystrokes. See Chapter 6 for easy how-to's.

5. **Locating a lost document** is even easier than before with the improved File Find. Find your way to Chapter 8 for more details.

6. **Making your document pretty doesn't take a lot of makeup**— Using AutoFormat, Word will improve the appearance of your document for you! If you prefer to do things your way, format (add bold, italics, etc.) yourself, then apply your choices to other text with the Format Painter. See Chapters 11 and 14—pretty soon!

7. **To template or not to template**—If you've used *templates* (mock documents you can use to construct your version of common documents such as business letters, memos, faxes, etc.) in earlier versions of Word, you're in for a nice surprise. Not only are the templates improved, but with Word Wizards, they're easier to use than ever before! See Chapter 17 for how-to's.

8. **Hey, Mr. Postman!**—Posting a letter to a long-lost love couldn't be easier than with Word's improved envelope-and-mailing-label system. See Chapter 18 for the complete mailing message.

9. **Pooped out on publishing?**—If you tried to use earlier versions of Word for desktop publishing (combining text with graphics), you'll be happy to hear that it's much, much easier. You can even create newspaper-style columns of different widths! See Chapter 19 for more on this late-breaking news story.

10. **Get graphic!**—Show how your Midwest region is leading the race for increased sales and productivity when you summarize your sums with a nice chart (graph). See Chapter 21 for details.

Chapter 2
A Kinder, Gentler Introduction to Word Processing

In This Chapter

- ☛ What is a word processor?
- ☛ Why learning to use a word processor is worth the time
- ☛ Things you can do with a word processor
- ☛ What is desktop publishing?

The Stone Age: Using a Typewriter to Record Thought

Back in the Stone Age of typewriters and correction fluid, the supposedly simple act of typing a letter or a memo was often thwarted by the ever-present red pen. Ogg would groan as his boss filled his freshly-typed pages with red lines, deletion marks, and new text. Ogg would then return crestfallen to his desk and retype the entire 10-page report. Poor Ogg—if only he'd had a *word processor*.

Word processor   A program that lets you enter, edit, format, and print text. A word processor can be used to type letters, reports, and envelopes, and to complete other tasks you would normally use a typewriter for.

What Makes a Word Processor So Great?

Admittedly, learning to use a word processor takes a bit more time than learning to use a typewriter, but look at the advantages: no more correction fluid on your fingers, no more sticky letter keys to unjam, no more platen grease smearing the sides of an important paper. Start using a word processor, and you'll quickly say "adios" to your typewriter. With a word processor, Ogg could have made all of his boss's changes, and been home in time for a hot bowl of woolly-mammoth stew—but no! Instead of chucking his typewriter into the nearest tar pit, Ogg retyped the entire report. With a word processor, Ogg could have:

- Inserted text into existing paragraphs, and watched in amazement as other text automatically moved down, while staying within the margins.

- Deleted text with the same ease as he inserted new text—other text would just "self-adjust" between the margins.

- Checked the report for spelling errors before printing it out.

- Easily centered his title, and added bold lettering to make it stand out.

- Added a big chart that made the report so nice-looking, his boss got a promotion—and Ogg got close-to-the-building parking privileges for his dinosaur.

- Printed out an extra copy of the report for his own files, instead of spending half the Stone Age waiting at the copier.

- Reused the same report next month, by changing some figures and replacing the word "March" with "April" throughout the report.

Without a word processor, Ogg probably spent the rest of his life retyping the same report—but not you! Armed with your Word for Windows program and this nifty book, you'll soon learn how to do all these things and more—but first, let's look at a typical day with a word processor.

A Day in the Life of a Word Processor

As you create your document in Word for Windows, you'll follow a basic pattern:

1. **Open an existing document, or create a new one.** You start your work session by typing text into a new document, or by editing an existing one. You'll learn about working with documents in Chapter 8.

2. **Type in some text.** This part of the process is easy; just type! Okay, there are some things you should know before you start typing, and you'll learn them in this chapter and in Chapter 6.

3. **Read what you've written, and make changes.** *Edit* your text until it's right: copy or move text from one place to another; delete or insert text to clarify a point. You'll learn some easy editing techniques in Chapter 6.

4. **Add pizzazz.** Improve the way your document looks with *formatting.* You'll learn how to format text in Chapter 11. To save time while formatting, create a *style* you can reapply over and over with a few short keystrokes.

5. **Spell-check your document.** Word comes with a *spell checker* that checks your words. You can also use the Word *grammar checker* to look for errors in context. Of course, nothing can replace the actual process of re-reading your text for sense, but these powerful tools help ensure that your documents look professional. You'll learn more about them in Chapter 16.

SPEAK LIKE A GEEK

Edit To make changes to existing information within a document. Editing in a word processor usually involves spell-checking, grammar checking, and making formatting changes until the document is judged to be complete.

Format Changing the look of a character (by making it bold, underlined, and slightly bigger, for example) or a paragraph (by centering the paragraph between the margins, or by adding an automatic indentation for the first line, for example).

Style A collection of specifications for formatting text. A style may include information for the font, size, typestyle (bold, italic, etc.), margins, and spacing of a section of text. Applying a style formats text to the style's specifications automatically.

6. **Save your document.** Once you're sure you have a document you like, you should save it. Actually, it's best to save a document often during the editing phase so you can't lose any changes. You'll learn how to save your document in Chapter 9.

7. **View your document before you print it.** Word gives you lots of ways to view your text, both as you are working, and right before you print your document. You'll learn all you need to know about viewing a document in Chapter 7.

8. **Print your document.** Nothing is better than holding the finished product in your own hands. You'll learn how to print your documents in Chapter 10.

Oggs and Ends of Using a Word Processor

Even Ogg had a few things to learn before he could use a word processor:

The thing you create with a word processor is called a document. "Document" is just a hoity-toity word for something like a memo, a letter, or a report. If you ask a PC guru for help, make sure you throw it in (if you can do an English accent, it's even better): "Pardon me, but I think I'm having trouble with this *document.*"

The cursor marks the place where text will be inserted. The *cursor* is a blinking vertical line that acts like the tip of a pencil; anything you type appears at the cursor. You'll learn more about the cursor as we go on. To be real cool, call the cursor by its nickname: *insertion point.*

What you see isn't necessarily what you get. The right-hand edge of your screen may not be the right-hand margin of your document. Word for Windows has several ways you can view your document on-screen; in one mode, the text is large and comfortable to work with, but you may not see the right-hand margin of your document when you work in that mode. You'll learn more about viewing modes in Chapter 7.

A dotted line marks the end of a page. Just cross over the dotted line when you see it; a dotted line tells Word for Windows where one page ends and another begins. If you add text above a dotted line, the excess text at the bottom of that page will flow onto the next page automatically.

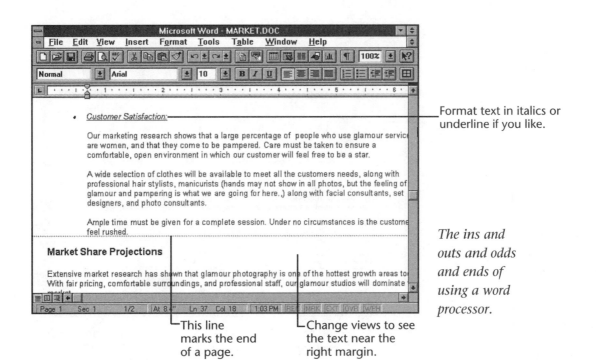

Format text in italics or underline if you like.

The ins and outs and odds and ends of using a word processor.

This line marks the end of a page.

Change views to see the text near the right margin.

So What's All This Fuss About Desktop Publishing?

"High-end" (in other words, expensive) word processors, such as Word for Windows, give you a lot of bang for your buck by including tons of features you'll probably use only occasionally. It's not that the people at Microsoft want to confuse you by including too much stuff; it's just that when you need to do something special with a piece of paper, they want you to be able to do it with Word for Windows, so you don't go off and try some other product. One of the special things you may want to do someday is *desktop publishing*.

Imported graphic

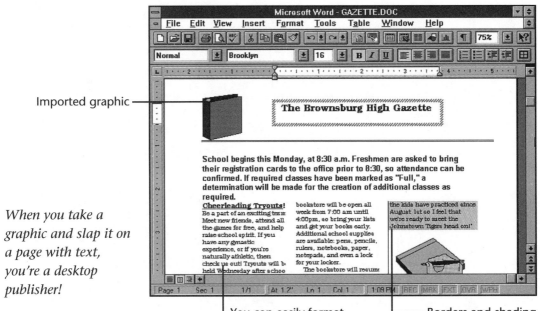

When you take a graphic and slap it on a page with text, you're a desktop publisher!

You can easily format your text in columns.

Borders and shading add pizzazz!

Desktop publishing (DTP) A program that allows you to combine text and graphics on the same page, and manipulate the text and the graphics on-screen. Desktop publishing programs are commonly used to create newsletters, brochures, flyers, résumés, and business cards.

Although you can do a few of the more popular desktop publishing chores (typing text in columns, placing graphics anywhere on a page, or adding borders and shading to emphasize certain words) in Word for Windows, if you want to do anything fancy, you should invest in a real desktop publishing program, such as PageMaker or Ventura Publisher. If you just can't wait to start your desktop publishing career, skip ahead to Chapter 19 for a lesson in creating newspaper-style columns, and Chapter 20 for instructions on how to manipulate text and graphics in Word.

The Least You Need to Know

It's a kinder, gentler world out there, thanks to word processors. Never again will you be faced with a dried-up bottle of White-out. And what's more, a word processor is so much faster than a typewriter when you need to:

- ☛ Insert and delete text from an existing document.

- ☛ Check for spelling and grammatical errors.

- ☛ Punch up your prose with bold, underlined, and italicized passages.

- ☛ Add pizzazz to your documents with charts and graphics.

- ☛ Print extra copies of your documents.

This page unintentionally left blank.

Chapter 3
For Those of Us Who Don't Do Windows

In This Chapter

- ☞ How to start Windows
- ☞ How to use a mouse
- ☞ The parts of a Windows window
- ☞ Moving windows around
- ☞ Closing windows
- ☞ Sizing a window so it's "just right"
- ☞ Exiting the Windows program

When I was first learning to use Windows, I felt overwhelmed. I'd never really used a mouse before, and all those boxes on my screen made me feel like a moving company. The only thought that kept me going was that (for the most part) I'd never have to see that ol' DOS prompt again. Also, I knew that once I learned how to use the mouse and manipulate windows, I'd know almost everything I needed to use *all my Windows programs*. So that's what you'll learn in this chapter—the basic stuff you'll use every day, in every Windows *program*—including Word for Windows.

SPEAK LIKE A GEEK

Monitor   A television-like screen where the computer displays information.

DOS prompt   An on-screen prompt that indicates DOS is ready to accept a command, and indicates where to type it in. The prompt looks something like **C>** or **C:\>**.

Program   A set of instructions written in a special "machine language" which the computer understands. Typical programs are word processors, spreadsheets, databases, and games.

OOPS!

If you type WIN and your PC just sits there doing nothing, first make sure you've pressed the **Enter** key. If nothing happens, then try typing **CD\WINDOWS**, press **Enter** and type **WIN** and press **Enter** again. If it still doesn't work, take two aspirin and see your PC guru in the morning.

A Logical Place to Start

I am occasionally hit by bouts of logic, and during a recent episode, it occurred to me that before I show you how to use Windows, I should show you how to start it. It's relatively easy:

Turn on your computer. Look for a switch on the front, back, or right-hand side of that big box thing. You may also have to turn on your *monitor* (it *looks* like a TV, but it gets lousy reception).

After you turn on your computer, Windows may start all by itself. If it does, pass Go and skip on down to the next section.

If you get a menu listing Windows as one of the options, press the number in front of the selection, then press **Enter**.

If instead you get a rather unassuming DOS prompt that resembles C> or C:\>, type:

```
WIN
```

and press **Enter**.

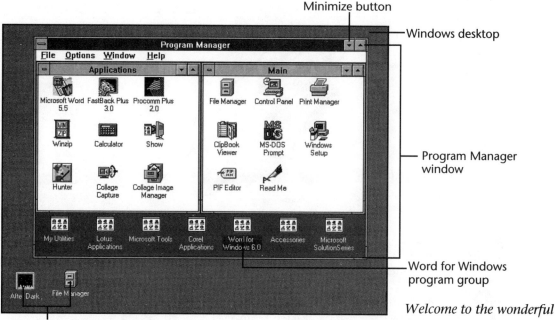

Minimize button

Windows desktop

Program Manager window

Word for Windows program group

Active programs minimized to icons

Welcome to the wonderful world of Windows.

Don't panic if your screen doesn't look exactly like mine; that's the point of Windows—you can customize it to work the way you do. When you start Windows, the main program, Program Manager, is usually open and ready to go. *Program Manager* helps you switch between programs and customize the way they work with Windows.

Making Friends with a Mouse

Using Windows (and Windows programs like Word for Windows) without a mouse is like trying to pull something out of the oven without mitts. It can be done, but why take the chance of getting burned? So play it smart; get a *mouse!*

The proper way to hold your furless friend.

Mouse   A device attached to your computer that moves an arrow (a pointer) around the screen. To move the on-screen pointer to the left, move the mouse to the left. To move the pointer to the right, move the mouse to the right, and so on.

Mouse pad   A small square of plastic or foam that the mouse rests on. A mouse pad provides better traction than the desktop, while keeping the mouse away from dust and other goop on your desk.

Point   To move the mouse pointer so that it is on top of a specific object on the screen.

To get to know your mouse quickly, here are some easy tips:

- Place the mouse in the middle of the *mouse pad,* with its cord extending away from you.

- Rest your hand on the mouse, with your palm at its base. Grip the mouse with your thumb and ring finger. When curled, your fingers should rest lightly on the buttons at the top of the mouse. Rest your index finger on the left mouse button and your middle finger on the right button. (If your mouse has a middle button, ignore it.)

- Move the little guy around. Don't be surprised if this feels a bit funny—remember what it felt like to drive a car for the first time? To me, it felt like the car would go completely out of control unless I held the wheel as tightly as I could. But you'll get used to your furless friend in no time.

- Practice moving the mouse on the mouse pad, to make the on-screen pointer point to different boxes and windows. (I know what your mother always told you, but in this case, it's polite to point.) If you move the mouse slowly, the pointer will move slowly, and about the same distance. If you move the mouse fast, the pointer steps on the gas and moves a greater distance on-screen.

☞ If you run out of mouse pad but you need to move further on the screen, just pick the critter up and place it back in the middle of the pad. When you lift the mouse, the pointer doesn't move; it's the roller on the bottom that moves it.

Right on the (Left) Button!

After you've moved the pointer on top of something on-screen, either click or double-click with the left mouse button (unless specifically told to use the right) to perform an action. Some actions require that you *drag* the mouse (no, not along the floor).

If you use Windows on a portable computer, such as a laptop, you may be using a "dead mouse"—but don't set any rat traps just yet! You don't move this kind of mouse, which is why it's nicknamed a "dead mouse." (Its real name is *trackball*.) A trackball has its roller ball on top, and you move the mouse pointer by moving the roller ball with your thumb.

Click   To move the mouse pointer over an object or icon, and press and release the mouse button once.

Double-click   To press and release the mouse button twice quickly.

Drag   To drag the mouse, first move the mouse pointer to the starting position. Now press and hold the left mouse button. Move the mouse to the ending position, and then release the mouse button.

By the Way . . .

As a general rule of thumb, you *click on* things to highlight or choose them, *double-click* to activate them, and *drag* to select them.

Put It to Work
Mousing Around

Try this quick exercise to practice using the mouse:
Point to the Program Manager's Minimize button. Move the mouse pointer so that it rests on top of the downward-pointing arrow. (Look back at the first figure in this chapter if you need help.)

Click on the Minimize button. Press the left mouse button once while pointing with the mouse to the downward pointing arrow. Clicking on the Minimize button chooses it, and the Program Manager becomes an icon at the bottom of the screen.

Point to the Program Manager icon. Move the mouse pointer so that it rests on top of the Program Manager icon (which appeared when you clicked on the Minimize button).

Double-click on the Program Manager icon to open it. Press the left mouse button two times quickly while pointing to the Program Manager icon. Double-clicking on the icon activates the Program Manager, and it reopens its window.

Now that you know how to use a mouse, you're ready to move on to something with a lot more buttons: *the keyboard.*

Playing with a Full Keyboard

Microsoft devised Windows and Word for Windows to work more easily with a mouse or trackball than with a keyboard. There are, however, some special key combinations that allow you to perform common tasks without using a mouse (though they force your hands into awkward positions). But personally, pressing multiple keys at the same time (such as Ctrl+Shift+P, a key combination that changes the size of your text) makes my hands ache, so I'm going to speak to you throughout this book as though you own a mouse. Windows without a mouse is about as pointless as lasagna without the pasta.

By the Way . . .

If you're allergic to mice—or if you are switching from a keyboard-intense word processor such as WordPerfect—you may prefer using the keyboard over using a mouse. So in Chapter 4, I'll show you how to use the keyboard to select commands. But you should still make an effort to learn to use the mouse for moving and copying text; it's the fastest and easiest way!

If you've ever used a typewriter, you'll notice that the computer keyboard is similar, but different. Don't let all those keys intimidate you—the keyboard is easy to use when you learn the functions of the keys.

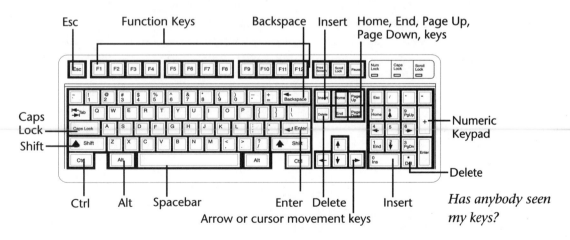

Has anybody seen my keys?

Here are the functions of some of the keys that are not so obvious:

Enter   In Word for Windows, you press the Enter key at the end of a *paragraph*, which is any grouping of words that should be treated as a unit—this includes normal paragraphs as well as single-line paragraphs (such as chapter titles, section headings, and captions for charts or other figures).

> ## By the Way . . .
> The Enter key is something that computer manufacturers like to hide by marking it with obscure symbols, such as a bent arrow pointing to the left, or by labeling it with "meaningful" words like *Return* (a holdover from the days of electric typewriters—a computer has no "carriage" to "return").

Esc   Called the *Escape key*, Esc is used to cancel commands or to back out of an operation in Word.

Function keys   These keys are sometimes called the *F keys* because they all begin with an "F." You'll find them at either the top or the left-hand side of the keyboard. Each program assigns its own special meanings to them. For example, in Word for Windows, F1 means Help, and F2 means Move.

Shift   Used just as it is on a typewriter, to type capital letters and special characters (such as #$%?>). In some programs, you can use the Shift key with other keys to issue commands with the keyboard. For example, in Word for Windows, Shift+F7 activates the Thesaurus.

Alt and Ctrl   The Alt and Ctrl keys are used like the Shift key; press them with another key to issue commands with the keyboard. For example, in Word for Windows, Ctrl+B bolds selected text, and Alt+F opens (selects) the File menu.

Caps Lock   This locks in the capital letters. Unlike the "Shift Lock" on a typewriter, however, you will not get ! when you press the **1** key (even with the Caps Lock on). To get ! when the Caps Lock is on, you must still press the **Shift** key and **1** at the same time. The same is true of @, #, and other special characters.

Backspace   Press this key to erase the letter or number to the left of the cursor. Use the Backspace key to erase all or part of a paragraph.

Arrow or cursor movement keys   Hmmm Kemosabe, the cursor go that way. (These keys will make the cursor move in the direction of the arrow.)

Spacebar   Use the Spacebar to insert a space between words and at the end of sentences. Don't be a space cadet and use the Spacebar to move the cursor—use the arrow keys or the mouse instead.

Insert (Ins)   If Insert is on (which is the default in Word for Windows), what you type is inserted between characters, beginning at the current cursor position. Press this key to switch to Overtype mode, and what you type will replace existing characters.

Delete (Del)   Deletes the character to the right of the cursor.

Home, End, Page Up, Page Down keys   Home moves the cursor to the beginning of a line; End moves the cursor to the end of a line; Page Down displays the next screen of text; and Page Up displays the previous screen.

Windows You Don't Look Through

The basic component of Windows is (not surprisingly) *windows*. Windows are boxes on your screen that you can open, close, move, resize, and otherwise manipulate to your heart's content—in Windows, you have total control of what's displayed on your screen. Let's open a window so we have something to look at:

Point to the Word for Windows program group icon. A *program group* is a special window that's used to group several applications together. For example, in the Word for Windows program group, you find two program icons: **Microsoft Word** and **Word Setup**. A program group *icon* is simply a program group that's been minimized (reduced to a small symbol on the screen).

Double-click on the program group icon to open the program group. Press the mouse button two times in quick succession, while pointing to the Word for Windows program group icon.

Maximize the word for Windows program group. Click on the **Maximize** button. The Word for Windows program group will grow to fill the Program Manager window; it will not fill the screen unless the Program Manager itself is maximized.

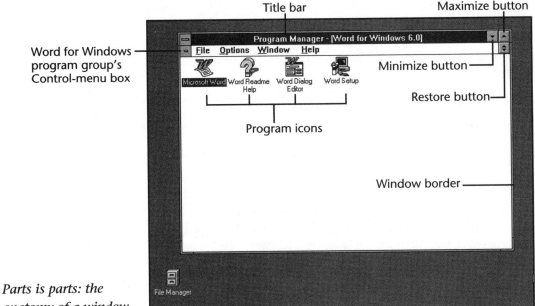

Parts is parts: the anatomy of a window.

Now that the window is open, let's look at its parts:

Title bar   This displays the title for the window.

Control-menu box   Every program group has one. Click here to display a menu with commands for resizing, closing, and moving windows.

Minimize button   Click here to reduce the window to an icon at the bottom of your screen.

Maximize button   Click here to increase the window to fill your screen.

Restore button   Click here to restore the window to its previous size.

Playing with Windows

In Windows, you can run multiple programs at the same time. For example, you can run a *spreadsheet program* and Word for Windows, and jump between the two whenever you wish. Each program you start has its own window, and that window will take up all or part of the screen, depending on how you size it. By manipulating your windows, you can see several programs at one time, and fly between them with the greatest of ease.

> ### By the Way . . .
> Why is the ability to run multiple programs such a big deal? With two programs running at the same time, it's easy to exchange data from one to the other. For example, you could compute the department budget in a spreadsheet program, and then copy that data into the department report you're writing in Word for Windows.

Changing the size of a window is easy. You can restore the Word for Windows program group to the size it was before you maximized it. Click on the **Restore** button now (the double-headed arrow) to restore the window.

You can maximize the window again by clicking on the **Maximize** button (the upward-pointing arrow). Go ahead and do that now.

If you click on the Restore button again, the window will be returned to its former petite self. Click on the **Restore** button and watch that weight come off!

You can minimize a window (reduce it to an icon at the bottom of the Program Manager window) by clicking on the Minimize button. Minimize the Word for Windows program group now by clicking on the **Minimize** button (the downward-pointing arrow).

You can open a minimized window by double-clicking on the window's icon. Go ahead and double-click—it'll make you feel good!

When you minimize a window, sometimes it plays hide-and-seek behind other open windows. If you can't find the Word for Windows program group after minimizing it, open the **Window** menu by clicking on it or by pressing **Alt+W**. When the menu is open, select the Word for Windows program group from the list by clicking on it or pressing its number.

A window cannot be bigger than the Program Manager window. If you look back at the last figure, you'll see that the Program Manager window does not fill my screen. (That gray background you see is the Windows *desktop*, and the Program Manager sits on top of it.) However, you can maximize your Program Manager window so it fills the screen; then any window that's maximized within it will also fill the screen.

Too Big or Too Small? Goldilocks Does Windows

If a window is too big when it's maximized, and too small when it's minimized, how do you resize a window so it's *just right?* Answer: you drag it!

Let's practice getting a window just the right size by playing with our Word for Windows program group. To resize a window, move the pointer very slowly to the window's edge. (The mouse pointer will turn into a double-headed arrow.) Now press the left mouse button and *hold it down*. While you're holding the mouse button down, drag the edge outward to make the window bigger, or inward to make it smaller. You'll see a ghostly image of the window edge as you drag. As long as you hold the mouse button down, you can play with the window's size as long as you want. When you've got the window "just right," release the mouse button.

If a window is maximized so that it fills your screen, you won't be able to resize it manually, because it won't have a border. (What a drag!) Instead, click on the **Restore** button to restore the window to its previous size, and then resize it manually if necessary.

Moving Day

Before I can start work, everything has to be in its proper place on my desk. I put my coffee cup to the left of my computer, and the mouse pad to the right; books and other reference items that I want to trip over throughout the day are placed on the floor.

When you work in Windows, you can move your windows around until you get everything in "its proper place." To move a window, you drag it by its *title bar* (the band at the top of the window that shows the program's name).

Let's practice on our Word for Windows program group. Point at the title bar at the top of the window. Then press the left mouse button and *hold it down*. While you're holding the mouse button down, drag the title bar around the screen (remember that you can't drag a program group off the Program Manager window). You'll see a ghostly image of the window as you drag. When you've found the window's new resting place, release the mouse button and voilà! the window's moved. (I wish sofas were as easy.)

If a window is maximized so that it fills your screen, you won't be able to move it around. (I mean, where would it go?) Instead, click on the **Restore** button to restore the window to its previous size, and then move it to wherever you'd like.

If You Feel a Draft, Close a Window

When you "close" a program group, it doesn't actually *close*—it is just gets minimized to an icon at the bottom of the Program Manager window. This makes closing a *program group* a harmless thing. (You'll learn later that closing a program *window* works differently, but let's take one thing at a time.)

To close a program group, you just double-click on the Control-menu box (which has a horizontal line on it; if you need help in identifying it, look back at the last figure). Try this now: double-click on the **Control-menu box** of the Word for Windows program group.

If you see a message that says **This will close your Windows session**, click on the word **Cancel**. You get this message when you close the Program Manager window, which tells Windows that you want to exit. (And you're not supposed to do that until the next section!)

Later, when we're working in Word for Windows, you'll have to be more careful. If you don't close a *program window* (that is, a window in which a program is running) correctly, you can lose the document you're working on.

When You're Done for the Day and You Want to Go Home

Here comes that logical side of me again. Since I started this chapter showing you how to get into Windows, I thought I'd end by showing you how to get out (how to *exit*).

To exit Windows, exit all your programs first. In other words, close all the windows that programs are running in. (This should be a moot point at the moment, since we didn't start any programs.) Then double-click on the Program Manager's **Control-menu box**. This will close the Program Manager window, which in turn, closes down Windows itself.

By the Way . . .

Here's an alternative procedure for closing a window: first, click once on the **Control-menu box**. The Control menu will open, displaying a list of choices. Click on the word **Close**.

A message will appear, telling you that you are about to end your Windows session. Translation: "Windows is about to close down for the night. Is this OK?" If it is, click on the word **OK**. If not, click on the word **Cancel**. If you click on **OK**, you'll exit Windows and return to either your really cool menu or the boring (yawn) DOS prompt.

The Least You Need to Know

Opening windows, closing windows—I'm pretty dizzy from all the stuff we covered in this chapter. Let's look at an instant replay:

☛ To start Windows, type **WIN** at the DOS prompt.

☛ Program Manager helps you switch between programs and customize the way your programs work with Windows.

☛ To click, press the left mouse button once.

☛ To double-click, press the left mouse button twice in rapid succession.

☛ To drag, move the pointer to the starting position. Then click and hold the mouse button. Drag the pointer to the ending position, and then release the mouse button.

☛ To maximize a window, click on the **Maximize** button (the upward-pointing arrow). To minimize a window, click on the **Minimize** button (the downward-pointing arrow). To return a window to its original size before it was maximized, click on the **Restore** button (the double-headed arrow). To adjust a window to a specific size, drag its edge.

☛ To move a window, drag it by its title bar.

☛ To close a window, double-click on the **Control-menu box** (located in the upper-left corner of every window).

☛ To exit Windows, double-click on the Program Manager's **Control-menu box**.

This page unintentionally left blank.

Chapter 4
Getting Off to the Right Start

In This Chapter

- ☛ How to start Word for Windows
- ☛ The basic parts of a Word for Windows screen
- ☛ Selecting commands
- ☛ Navigating a dialog box with ease
- ☛ Changing your mind and undoing a command
- ☛ Repeating a command
- ☛ Shutting down Word for Windows safely

Telling someone what to do is kind of fun. I think that deep down, we all want to be in charge of something. This is one of the things that I like most about using a computer—I get to tell it what to do.

The thing I like *least* about using a computer is learning how. Like most kids (and some adults) I know, computers love pretending *they don't understand*. So the trick to using a computer is to learn how to phrase things right. Once you learn that, a computer will do just about anything you tell it to (except the ironing—darn). In this chapter, you'll learn the simplest and quickest ways to tell Word for Windows what to do.

Launching (Starting) Word for Windows

The steps you use to "launch the Word for Windows rocket" are the same as with any application, so what you learn here, you'll use throughout Windows. As you go through these steps, just keep thinking, "I'm smarter than this stupid hunk of metal." Of course you are, but when I was a new user, it was helpful to remember that it was the computer that was stupid, not me. So here are the steps to start Word for Windows:

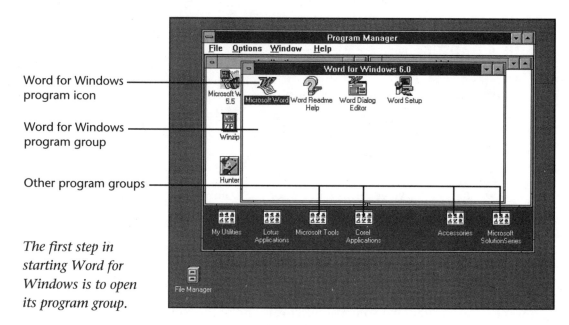

Word for Windows program icon

Word for Windows program group

Other program groups

The first step in starting Word for Windows is to open its program group.

First, open the Word for Windows program group. Hey, didn't you learn to do that in the last chapter? Good timing! (Just double-click on the **Word for Windows program group icon**.)

Next, double-click on the **Word for Windows program icon**. (Just move the pointer on top of the icon, and click twice real fast.) Word for Windows will start—one small step for the program, one giant step for us!

Tour de Word for Windows

Once inside the program, you'll notice some familiar friends: the Minimize, Maximize, and Restore buttons, the Control-menu box, and the title bar. Actually, you may think you're seeing double because you're seeing some things twice—but what you're really looking at is one window *inside* another. You see, the big window holds all the controls for the Word for Windows *program*, and the smaller window inside it holds the contents of the *document* (more on this in a minute). Let's look around and see what's new!

If you are using Word for Windows 2.0, it will start without a lot of fuss. If you are using Word for Windows 6.0, it displays a helpful tip when you start it. These tips are a nice way of learning about some of the shortcuts that Word gurus like to keep secret. You can prevent these tips from being displayed (gasp) by clicking on **S**how Tips at Startup. To follow the path to Word knowledge, click on **N**ext Tip. To OD on tips, click on **M**ore Tips. As if these options weren't enough, you can return to these tips at any time by selecting **Ti**p of the Day on the **H**elp menu (you'll learn how to select menu commands in just a minute).

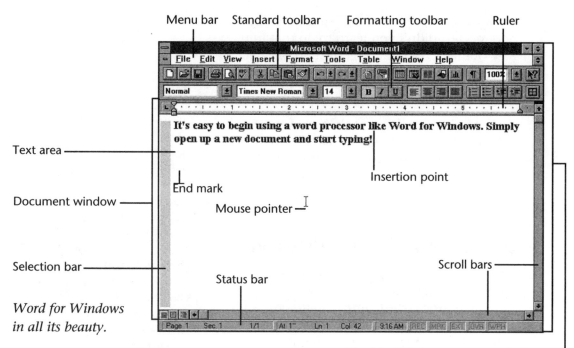

Menu bar   Standard toolbar   Formatting toolbar   Ruler

Text area

Insertion point

End mark

Document window

Mouse pointer

Selection bar

Status bar

Scroll bars

*Word for Windows
in all its beauty.*

Word for Windows program window

In Word for Windows 2.0,
the Standard toolbar is
called simply "the
Toolbar," and the Format-
ting toolbar is called "the
Ribbon." Additional
toolbars are not available
in Word 2.0.

Program window   This is the window that Word
for Windows runs in. Close this window, and you
close down (exit) Word for Windows. This window
frames the tools and the menus for the Word for
Windows program.

Document window   This window frames the
controls and information for the document file
being worked on. You can have multiple document
windows open at one time. (You'll learn how to
open multiple document windows in Chapter 8.)

Menu bar   Displays a list of menus that contain
the commands you'll use to edit documents.

Standard toolbar   Presents the most common commands in an easy-to-
access form. For example, one of the buttons on the Standard toolbar saves
your document when you click on it. There are many toolbars, each one
customized for particular tasks. You'll learn more about toolbars in this
chapter.

Formatting toolbar   A specialized toolbar that provides an easy method for changing the appearance of text: for example, adding bold and italic.

Ruler   Use this to set tab stops, indentations, and margins.

Scroll bars   Located along the bottom and right sides of the document window. You use scroll bars to display other areas of the document that are currently hidden (such as the next page).

Status bar   Displays information about your document.

End mark   This is Word for Windows' way of marking the end of the document; as you enter text, this mark will move down.

Selection bar   This *invisible area* runs along the left side of the document window, and provides a quick way for you to select a section of text to edit.

Text area   The main part of the document window; this is where the text you type will appear.

Insertion point   Vertical line that marks where text will be inserted into the document. To insert text in a different part of the document, move the insertion point there before you type.

When you work with Word for Windows, you use a default *template* (called NORMAL.DOT) that defines the working environment, such as margin settings, page orientation, and so on. The template also controls which menu commands are available, and what tools appear on the toolbar you're using.

Word for Windows comes with additional templates that you can use to create specialized documents, and if you are using one of these templates, your screen may look different from the ones shown in this book. Also, you may have additional commands available on the menus. To see which template you are using, choose the **T**emplates... command on the **F**ile menu. If it says **NORMAL** under Document **T**emplate, then you're using the default template.

Mouse pointer   This vertical line with curls at either end is also called an *I-beam*. The mouse pointer reflects the movement of the mouse. Move the mouse pointer to a particular spot within the text, then click (press the left mouse button), and you'll move the insertion point.

> ## By the Way . . .
> If you think that all these screen elements (such as scroll bars, toolbars, etc.) just get in the way, you're not alone. Lots of people prefer to enter their text in a nice, clean screen. If you're among them, flip to Chapter 7 to learn about Full Screen view.

Pull down   A *pull-down* menu contains the selections for a menu command. This type of menu, when activated, is pulled down below the menu bar, the way a window shade can be pulled down from the top of a window frame.

Menu, Please

Tucked away at the top of the Word for Windows screen, you'll see something called a *menu bar*. The menu bar is like a salad bar, except instead of choosing from carrots, mushrooms, and radishes, you choose commands.

The menu bar lists the main menus, such as **File**, **Edit**, **View**, and so on. Under each of these menus, there are additional selections, but you can't see them until you *pull down* (open) the menu. (Be patient; you'll learn how to pull down a menu soon.)

Reading the Menu

I have trouble understanding the menus in fancy French restaurants (I took Spanish), but I'm sure you'll have no such trouble with the Word for Windows menu system; it follows certain conventions that make it easy to understand:

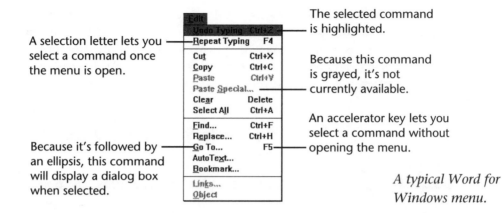

A selection letter lets you select a command once the menu is open.

Because it's followed by an ellipsis, this command will display a dialog box when selected.

The selected command is highlighted.

Because this command is grayed, it's not currently available.

An accelerator key lets you select a command without opening the menu.

A typical Word for Windows menu.

Grayed text   Commands that are currently unavailable will be grayed (and otherwise depressed) because you can't select them.

Selection letter   A single letter of a menu command which is underlined, such as the *F* in Find. While a menu is open, press the selection letter to select the command. In this book, selection letters appear as bold letters so you can find them easily.

Accelerator key   Sometimes called *shortcut keys*. Like selection letters, these can be used to activate the command with the keyboard. Unlike selection letters, however, accelerator keys work without opening the menu. Accelerator keys—which usually consist of a function key or a *key combination* (such as Ctrl+V)—are displayed next to the menu command. To use an accelerator key, press and hold the first key (in this case, **Ctrl**), and then press the second key (in this case, **V**).

To close a menu you opened by accident, press **Esc** or click anywhere in the document.

Dialog box   A special window or box that appears when the program requires additional information before executing a command.

Ellipsis   Three consecutive periods following the name of a menu command (as in the Edit Replace... command). When you select a command that has an ellipsis, a *dialog box* will appear, so you can provide more specific information before the command is executed. In this case, you would need to tell Word for Windows *what* to replace.

Take Your Pick: Selecting Menu Commands

Word 2.0 does not have shortcut menus. To select a command, click on it, or use the appropriate shortcut keys. *Warning*: Many shortcut keys listed in this book are different; Word 6.0 has substituted different shortcut keys for many of the **File** and **Edit** commands. Watch for additional notes like these throughout this book.

It's easy to select menu commands: just point to the menu name, and click. For example, click on the word File to open the File menu. While the menu is open, click once on a menu command to select it.

So that the keyboard doesn't get too jealous, I'll show you how you can use it to select commands. Press **Alt** and the selection letter to open a menu (for example, press **Alt** and F to open the File menu). Then press the selection letter alone to choose a command (for example, press **X** to select Exit).

What's Wrong with This Picture?

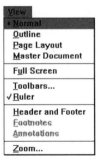

Can you decipher the meaning of the check mark in front of **Ruler**? And what's that dot doing in front of **Normal**?

Answer: The check mark is a standard way of letting you know an option is "on." The Ruler command is a *toggle* that can be turned off or on (picture a light switch). Select such a command when the check mark is displayed, and you'll turn it "off." By the way, when the **R**uler command is on, the Ruler appears on your screen. When it's off, the Ruler is hidden.

Now, what about that dot in front of the Normal command? Normal is just one way of viewing your document (you'll learn about the Page Layout, Outline, and Master Document viewing methods in Chapter 7). The dot tells you which viewing *mode* (method) you are currently using. If you were to select **P**age Layout from this menu, the dot in front of Normal would move to **P**age Layout.

If there is an accelerator key for a command, you can press its key combination to activate the command, instead of opening the menu. For example, to select the **Edit Paste** command, you can press the **Ctrl** and **V** keys at the same time.

To close a dialog box without choosing anything, just press **Esc**.

Talking to Your Computer with Dialog Boxes

When you select a menu command followed by an ellipsis, as in the File Print... command, a dialog box appears.

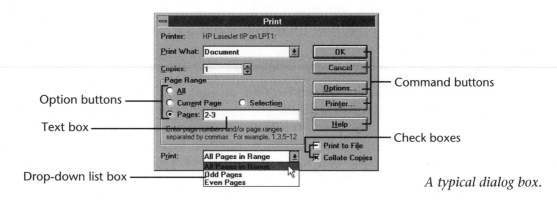

A typical dialog box.

A quick way to select some commands is to use a *shortcut menu*. A shortcut menu appears when you point at something on the screen (such as a toolbar, the ruler, or text) and click the *right* mouse button. The shortcut menu appears, listing commands that are specific to the object you are pointing to—for example, if you point at text and click the right mouse button, you'll get a shortcut menu with commands for copying, moving, and formatting text. Remember this slick click trick, because shortcut menus are fast, easy, and the best way to select commands. If you want to display a shortcut menu with the keyboard instead of the mouse, press **Shift+F10**. To close a shortcut menu without selecting a command, press **Esc** or click anywhere in the document.

Meet the characters that hang around dialog boxes:

List box   Presents a list of items to choose from, such as a list of files.

Drop-down list box   Like a normal list box, except that the list is not displayed until activated. The list is displayed under the main list item, much like a window shade.

Text box   Allows you to type information, such as the name of a file.

Check box   Used to indicate options that can be turned on or off, such as Collate Copies. When a check box is selected, an X appears inside it.

Option buttons   Used to select *mutually exclusive* options (options that you can select only one of), such as All, Current Page, or Pages. When an option button is selected, a dot appears inside it.

Command buttons   Perform some specific command, such as OK or Cancel. To make things fun, some command buttons (those darn ellipses again) cause additional dialog boxes to display—for example, the Options... button shown here.

Making the Right Choice

I like dialog boxes because they give me so many things to play with, such as list boxes and options buttons and the like. (I think it reminds me of all those pinball games I used to play as a child.) Anyway, here's how you flip all those "switches" and press all those "buzzers":

To move around a dialog box, click on any item to activate it; if you want to use the keyboard, press **Tab** until you get to the area you want. Use **Ctrl+Tab** to move between the tabbed sections of a dialog box. You can also press **Alt** and the underlined letter you see on the screen (for example, the *i* in Collate Copies) to move to a particular place within the dialog box. In this book, those underlined letters will appear as bold.

To display additional options in a list, click on the up or down arrow to scroll one item at a time and click on an item to select it. If you're using the keyboard, use the **arrow** keys to scroll through the list and to select an item.

To open a drop-down list box, click on the arrow to the right of the box. Click on an item to select it. With the keyboard, use the **down arrow** key to open the list box and to highlight an item.

To select an option button or check box, click on it to toggle the option on or off. With the keyboard, press **Tab** (as explained earlier) to move to the option button or check box area. Then use the **down arrow** to move to the option button or check box you want. Finally, use the **Spacebar** to toggle an option on or off.

To exit a dialog box, use a command button. You'll meet some standard command buttons while using dialog boxes (such as Cancel, which cancels the choices you have made in the dialog box and returns you to your program). If you want to close the dialog box and execute your choices, use the **OK** button. Sometimes there'll be a Close button, which retains the choices you made and closes the dialog box without executing your choices right now. If a command button name is followed by an ellipsis, choosing it will take you to an additional dialog box.

Dealing With Dialog Layers

As mentioned earlier, if you click on a command button with an ellipsis following its name (as in Options...), you're taken to an additional dialog box. I call these hidden dialog boxes "sub-dialogs." But sometimes there are so many options related to a particular command, you'll see a "filing system" of dialog boxes:

Additional sections that are available

Tabbed section currently being displayed

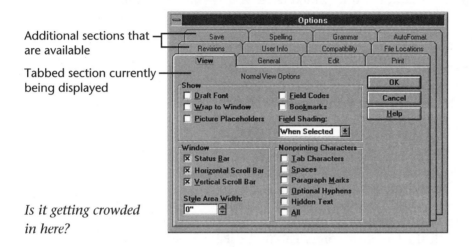

Is it getting crowded in here?

File this away for future reference: each of these tabbed sections is accessed through its *filing tab*. Just click on a tab to jump from section to section, selecting as many options as you want. (Keyboarders: press **Ctrl+Tab** to move from section to section.) When you're done, close the main dialog box by clicking on **OK**. To forget the whole thing (undo your choices) press **Esc** or click on **Cancel**.

Another way to find out about something is to point at it with the mouse. Go ahead and try it—move the mouse pointer over a button on the Standard toolbar (don't click, just point) and stop. Look down at the status bar, and you'll see a brief explanation. Pretty cool, eh?

I Think Icon, I Think Icon!

Toolbars are the quickest way for you to select the most common commands. When you start Word for Windows, two toolbars are displayed: the Standard toolbar and the Formatting toolbar. There are additional toolbars in hiding; you'll learn how to display them in just a minute. Each of the toolbars was designed with a specific task in mind, such as formatting text or creating a chart (you'll learn about each toolbar and what it does as we go along). The little squares that make up the toolbars are called *buttons* because they look as if you're "pressing" them down when you click on them with the mouse. They are also called *icons* because they contain little pictures that represent the task they perform.

> ## By the Way . . .
>
> If you're dying to know what every icon is for, turn to the front of this book and check out the reference card. It gives you the unfiltered, unauthorized life story of every button on the Standard and Formatting toolbars.

Getting What You Want

When you start Word for Windows, it displays the Standard and the Formatting toolbars. Don't worry—other toolbars are just a click away. Simply move the mouse pointer over one of the toolbars, and click the right button. Select a toolbar from the shortcut menu, and it appears! If a toolbar is already displayed, it'll have a little checkmark in front of its name. If you prefer the long way around, you can use the Toolbars command on the View menu to select the toolbars to display.

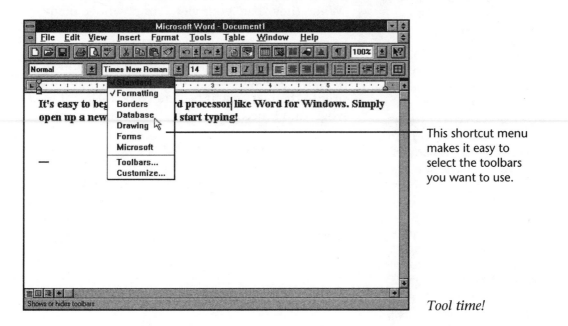

This shortcut menu makes it easy to select the toolbars you want to use.

Tool time!

You can customize any toolbar by adding buttons for the commands you use most often. From the **Toolbars** dialog box, click on **C**ustomize. Select a category, then choose a button. Drag the button out onto a toolbar. To remove a button, drag it off a toolbar.

When you customize a toolbar, it modifies the template you are currently working with, unless you select another template under the Save Changes In list box. (If you customize a toolbar when you are using the default template, NORMAL.DOT, then that toolbar will be changed *for all documents*.)

Let's say you often work with newsletters. You could create a template just for newsletters—which includes a customized Standard toolbar with the buttons you'll need. The template also stores page margins, column markers, and so on. If you create a newsletter template, not only will your toolbars be set up and ready to go, but so will your *document defaults* (such as one-inch margins and three newspaper-style columns)— you'll be all set to type this month's newsletter! Chapter 17 has all the details.

If you don't want to display any toolbars at all, that's cool. Just deselect them one at a time until they go away! Selecting a toolbar that's already displayed causes that toolbar to disappear. If you want all the screen elements to go away, you can select **Full Screen** view (which you'll learn about in Chapter 7). Unfortunately, the Full Screen option does not remove other annoyances such as the loudmouth at the copier, the person in front of you at the bank, or your boss (actually, my boss is very nice, and takes the time to read everything I write, which is why I added this disclaimer). But feel free to skip to Chapter 7 and give Full Screen view a try!

When Toolbars Bar Your View

When I go to a movie theater, nine times out of ten, the tallest person in the place will sit down right in front of me. (How do they do that? Do they have radar in their heads?) Anyway, you don't have to take that same stuff from your toolbars. When they "bar" your view, simply move them with the mouse. Here's how: click on the toolbar's title bar and keep on clicking (hold the left button down). "Barring" any problems, you can simply drag the toolbar wherever you want it. If you drag it into the text area, it becomes a box. Drag it to an edge, and it becomes a bar.

Still not satisfied? You can change the shape of a toolbar's box by dragging one of its edges. Click on an edge and hold, then drag until the box is the size you want. As you drag, you may see a ghost— that's the imaginary outline, and it's there to guide you.

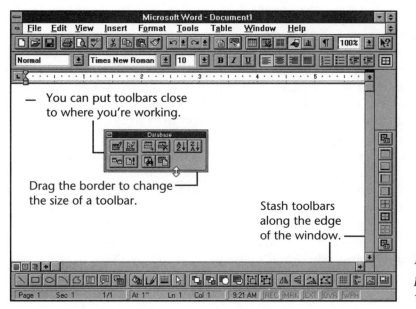

You can put toolbars close to where you're working.

Drag the border to change the size of a toolbar.

Stash toolbars along the edge of the window.

Drag 'em out and put 'em where you want 'em.

Good Friends to Know: Undo and Redo/Repeat

If a command is in progress, you can press **Esc** to cancel it. But what happens if you just finished deleting some text, and it was the wrong text? I can't tell you how many times I've done just that. Well, weep no more. You can restore your deleted text with a little magic button called *Undo*.

 Undo undoes your last few actions or commands. If for some reason your last actions can't be undone (such as saving a document), Undo becomes unavailable. How do you undo? To undo your last action, click on the **Undo** button on the **Standard toolbar**, or click on the arrow to select a previous action to

> **E·Z**
>
> You can display several toolbars at once by selecting **Toolbars** from the shortcut menu, then clicking on the checkboxes of the toolbars you want.

undo. (Refer to the reference card at the front of this book for the secret location of the Undo button.) If you're a keyboard connoisseur, press **Ctrl+Z** to activate Undo instead of using the mouse (you can also use the Undo command on the Edit menu).

To undo your undo (is there an echo in here?), click on the **Redo/Repeat** button, or use the arrow next to it to select a previous undo to undo. (My editors just loved that last sentence!) If you use the keyboard, just press **F4** to undo an undo. Actually, undoing an undo is not the only thing you can do with the Redo/Repeat button. Redo/Repeat lets you repeat your last action or command. For example, suppose you've just changed some text so that it's bold, underlined, and 2 inches from the left margin. You can repeat this same sequence of commands on another section of text by using the Redo/Repeat command. Redo/Repeat also duplicates typing, whether it's words or paragraphs. Now here's where I get to repeat myself: to use Redo/Repeat, click on the **Redo/Repeat** button, or press **F4**.

Exit, Stage Right

Here I am with another logic attack: since I began this chapter showing you how to start Word for Windows, I thought I'd end by showing you how to *stop* it. The technical name for stopping a program is called *exiting*. Here's what you do:

First, save whatever you're working on. If you don't, it won't be there when you come back. Computers are very literal, and unless you tell them to save something for you, they don't. You'll learn how to save your documents in Chapter 9.

Exit, stage right. Here you can exercise your own sense of style, because there are a multitude of ways to stop a program:

- ☞ Select the Exit command from the File menu or press **Alt+F4**.
- ☞ Double-click on the **Word for Windows Control-menu box**.
- ☞ Click once on the **Word for Windows Control-menu box**, and then select the Close command.

☞ Turn off the computer. Turning off the computer without exiting a program (in this case, two programs: Word for Windows, and Windows itself) is the computer equivalent of *taking a hammer and bashing yourself over the head.* When you wake up, you're probably not going to remember what hit you, and neither will the computer. If you turn off a computer without first saving your work, it's gone. So, don't turn off a computer until you see the whites of DOS' eyes: the DOS prompt.

☞ When you've exited your program properly (see my diatribe above on how NOT to exit a program), you can probably turn off your computer. How can you tell if it's okay to do that? Look for the DOS prompt (it looks something like C> or C:\>). If you see a menu, choose an exit option to return to DOS, and then turn off the computer.

The Least You Need to Know

Just about everything in this chapter is the least you need to know when using *any* Windows program, such as Word for Windows. Most of these are what I call my Windows life-skills:

☞ To start any program (such as Word for Windows), open the program group it's located in, and double-click on the program's icon.

☞ To select a menu command with the mouse, open a menu by clicking on the menu name, and then click on the command you want.

☞ To select a menu command with the keyboard, open a menu by pressing **Alt** and the selection letter. Select the command you want by pressing its selection letter.

☞ To select an item in a dialog box with the mouse, just click on it. Click on the down arrow to open a drop-down list box, and click on an item to select it. Clicking on an option button or a check box toggles it on or off.

continues

continued

☛ To select an item in a dialog box with the keyboard, use the Tab key. To move between tabbed sections of a dialog box, use **Ctrl+Tab**. Use the **arrow** keys to select an item from a list. Use the **Spacebar** to toggle option buttons and check boxes on or off.

☛ 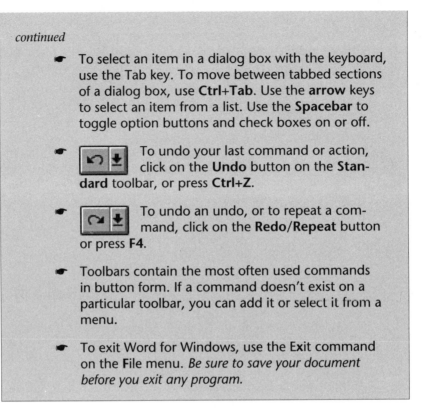 To undo your last command or action, click on the **Undo** button on the **Standard** toolbar, or press **Ctrl+Z**.

☛ To undo an undo, or to repeat a command, click on the **Redo/Repeat** button or press **F4**.

☛ Toolbars contain the most often used commands in button form. If a command doesn't exist on a particular toolbar, you can add it or select it from a menu.

☛ To exit Word for Windows, use the **Exit** command on the **File** menu. *Be sure to save your document before you exit any program.*

Chapter 5

Getting a Little Help from Your Friends

In This Chapter

- ☞ How to get help when you need it
- ☞ Using the Help index
- ☞ How to complete a Word tutorial

You never know when you'll need help, so getting help when you need it is what this chapter is all about. Help in Word for Windows is as varied as the people who use it. You're sure to find help in some form that you'll like.

Getting the Help You Need

Help for Word for Windows is available 24 hours a day by pressing **F1**. Help is *context-sensitive*; which in English means that Help pays attention to what you're doing, so when you press F1, it takes you to a section that explains that specific task. For example, when you use the command to save a document, a dialog box appears, asking for more information (such as a name for the file). If you don't know what to do, just press **F1**, and you'll be taken to the section in the Help system that talks about saving your document.

To get help with an area of the screen in Word 2.0, press **Shift+F1** and click on an object.

To jump directly to specific help on a particular command or an element of the screen, click on the **Help** button, then click on the object or command. If you're a keyboarder, press **Shift+F1**, then move the on-screen arrow to the screen element, and press **Enter**.

Jump topic   A word with a solid underline, appearing within a Help window. Clicking on a jump topic carries you to the How To window on that topic.

Jump term   A word with a dotted underline, appearing with a Help window. Clicking on a jump term will cause a quick definition to appear.

If you're wondering about a particular toolbar button, move the mouse pointer over it, and a brief description will display on the Status Bar. For help with a menu command, highlight the command with the **arrow** keys, and you'll again see a description on the Status Bar.

How Can You Find the Answer, When You're Not Sure of the Question?

When you're not sure what to do or where to start, use the Help menu. To open the Help menu, click on it or press **Alt+H**. When the Help menu is open, you'll have many things to choose from:

Contents   Here tasks are organized by topic. Use this option when you know generally what you want to do, or you want to access any of the subsections of Help (such as the reference, examples and demos, or technical support areas).

Search for Help On   This option is perfect when you know what you need help on.

Index   Here, tasks are organized alphabetically. This option is similar to Search, but best when you aren't sure what to call something.

Quick Preview   These tutorials are great for the first-time user. If you're new to word processing or to Word for Windows, these lessons will get you up to speed fast.

Examples and Demos   These tutorials are perfect for after you have learned the basics. The most popular Word for Windows tasks are presented here, in a hands-on style that lets you practice the commands without affecting your document.

Tip of the Day   Use this option to redisplay the tips that appear each time you start Word for Windows.

WordPerfect Help   Switching from WordPerfect? Use this Help command to get you up and running in Word.

Technical Support   Get answers to the most-often-asked questions.

About Microsoft Word...   Displays licensing information. Click on System Info to see how much *memory* and *hard disk* space you have left.

Let Your Fingers Do the Walking: Getting Around Help

If you're just sitting in your document, wondering how to add a page number (or some such), you can go directly to the Help contents—or you can search for the topic "page numbers" by accessing the index, or by using the Search for Help On command. It doesn't matter how you get there—once you get within the Help system, there are some things you need to know about how to get around.

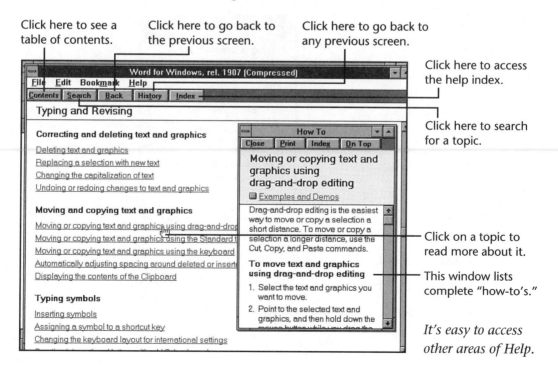

Click here to see a table of contents.

Click here to go back to the previous screen.

Click here to go back to any previous screen.

Click here to access the help index.

Click here to search for a topic.

Click on a topic to read more about it.

This window lists complete "how-to's."

It's easy to access other areas of Help.

SPEAK LIKE A GEEK

Memory An electronic storage area inside the computer, used to store data or program instructions temporarily when the computer is using them. The computer's memory is erased when the power to the computer is turned off.

Hard disk A non-removable disk drive that stores many megabytes of data. Because it is fixed in place inside the computer (see *fixed disk drive*), it performs quicker and more efficiently than a floppy disk.

You'll be presented with a lot of choices as you try to find information on the topic you're interested in. With a mouse, simply click on something to choose it. With the keyboard, press **Tab** until you highlight your choice, and then press **Enter**. To access one of the buttons along the top of the Help window, press **Alt** plus the underlined letter. For example, to begin a search, press **Alt+S**.

To scroll through long lists, click on either arrow on the scroll bar, or press **Page Down** to go forward in the list, and **Page Up** to go back.

Some How-To's on How To

When you select a topic within Help, a How To dialog box will appear. When it's got something to show you, an Examples and Demos button will display at the top of the window. Otherwise, you've got a few standard buttons to choose from:

A recipe for moving text.

Close   Click here to close the How To window.

Print   Click here to print out the instructions for this topic.

Index   Here's that ol' index button again!

On Top   This button's a cool one (in my humble opinion). If you've ever used a Windows program before, one of the most frustrating things is that as soon as you locate something in the Help system, and you click within the document window so you can try it out, the Help window goes away. This button keeps the How To window on top of all the other windows on your screen. Of course, sometimes this is not a great thing. But if the How To window gets in your way, move it by dragging the title bar. Or you can simply close the thing. If neither one of these options suits your fancy, click on this button to make the How To window fall behind the other windows on your screen.

Searching for Help in All the Right Places

If you know what you're looking for, you can search for a particular topic. With the Help index, you can page through an alphabetical listing of Help topics until you find the one you want. If you like life in the fast lane, use the Search for Help on command (or click on the Search button within a Help window), and the hunt is on!

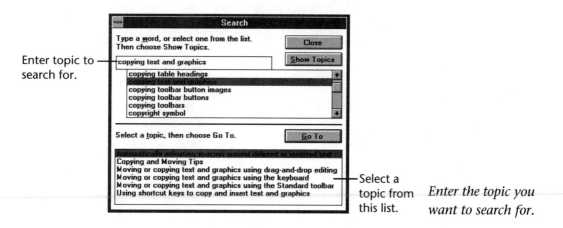

Enter topic to search for.

Select a topic from this list.

Enter the topic you want to search for.

Just type in the word you want to look up, and press **Enter**. Related topics appear at the bottom of this dialog box. Select the topic of your choice by double-clicking on it, or by using the **arrow** keys to highlight it and pressing **Enter**.

Put It to Work

Marking Frequently Used Topics

You can mark the Help topics you use most frequently by placing a *bookmark* there. (Think of this as putting a paper clip on a favorite page in a book.) Once you have a favorite topic displayed:

1. Open the Bookmark menu. Press **Alt+M** or click on the menu to open it.

2. Choose **Define**. Press **D** or click on **D**efine.

3. If you want to change the title of the topic to something you prefer, type the topic's new name. Then press **Enter** or click on **OK**.

To get to a bookmark, open the **Help** menu by pressing **Alt+H** or by clicking on **Help**. Then select Bookmark by pressing **Alt+M** or by clicking on the menu. When the Bookmark menu is displayed, click on a bookmark, or use the **arrow** keys to select it.

Class Act: Using a Word Tutorial

Word *tutorials* take you step by step through various lessons as you learn specific Word tasks: think of them as one of those PBS do-it-yourself shows, but without the tools. You can complete a Word tutorial by using the mouse or the keyboard. First, choose either Quick Preview or Examples and Demos from the Help menu.

```
┌─────────────────────────────────────────────────────┐
│ ─        Word for Windows, rel. 1907 (Compressed)   ▼ │
│ File  Edit  Bookmark  Help                            │
│ ┌────────┬────────┬──────┬─────────┬───────┐         │
│ │Contents│ Search │ Back │ History │ Index │         │
│ └────────┴────────┴──────┴─────────┴───────┘         │
│   ▦                                                   │
│      Examples and Demos                               │
│                                                       │
│    ▣ Getting Started        ▣ Page Design and Layout │
│    ▣ Typing and Editing     ▣ Frames and Graphics    │
│    ▣ Proofing               ▣ Working with Long Documents│
│    ▣ Formatting Text        ▣ File Management         │
│    ▣ Formatting Paragraphs  ▣ Using Word in a Workgroup│
│    ▣ Styles                 ▣ Mail Merge              │
│    ▣ Tables                 ▣ Automating Your Work    │
│    Bitmap to come                                     │
│                                                       │
└─────────────────────────────────────────────────────┘
```

Move through each tutorial at your own pace.

Click on a demo to select it, or press **Tab** to highlight the demo you want, then press **Enter**. Quick Preview does everything for you; just click on Next or press **Enter** to move to the next screen. When the demo's over, select another one, or click on Return to Word (or press **Alt+R**).

Examples and Demos provide basic how-to's on Word's features, and demos if you want them. Again, click on a topic to select it, or press **Tab** to highlight the topic and then press **Enter**. Each topic has several features you can learn more about; click on a feature to select it, or press **Alt** plus the underlined letter. To have Word demonstrate the feature for you, click on **Demo** or press **Alt+D**.

The Least You Need to Know

"Help" me review what we learned in this chapter:

- To get help while in Word, press **F1**.

- To get help with a part of the Word screen, click on the **Help** button or press **Shift+F1**.

- You can search for a topic by choosing the **Search for Help On** command, by clicking on the **Search** button, or by pressing **Alt+S** from within a Help window. When the Search window is displayed, type the name of the item you want to search for, and press **Enter**. Select a topic with the **arrow** keys or the mouse, and away you go!

- Keep the How To window visible by selecting the **O**n Top button.

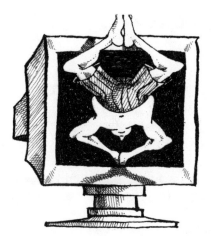

Chapter 6
Diving into a Document

In This Chapter

- ☛ Some simple rules for entering text
- ☛ Moving that darn insertion point
- ☛ Selecting the text you want to edit
- ☛ Inserting and deleting text
- ☛ Inserting text automatically
- ☛ Copying and moving text

Well, congratulations. You've made it to Chapter 6. Sorry about all that preliminary stuff; it seems there's always something you have to learn before you really "get down to work." Anyway, getting down to work is what this chapter is all about—how to enter text (and how to change it once it's been entered).

Dancing Fingers: How to Enter Text into a Word Document

Word wrap With word wrapping, words are automatically advanced to the next line of a paragraph when they "bump" into the right-hand margin. Likewise, you can insert words into the middle of a paragraph, and the rest of the paragraph will be adjusted downward automatically. If you change the margins, paragraphs will adjust automatically.

When you start Word for Windows, it places your cursor automatically at the top of an empty document window, so that you are ready to start entering text. (The *insertion point* is a blinking vertical line that acts like the tip of a pencil; anything you type appears at the insertion point.) To enter text into a document, simply start typing. As you type, your words will appear on the screen, like words from a typewriter. Unlike using a typewriter, however, *you should not press Enter when you reach the edge of the screen.* (Make hip and syncopated mouth noises as you read the following line.) Word-for-Windows-will-advance-your-text-automatically-to-the-next-line-at-the-appropriate-point. This is called Word Rap; I mean *word wrap*. With word wrap, you just type, and the words take care of themselves. When you get to the end of a complete paragraph, *that's* when you press **Enter**.

By the Way . . .

The horizontal line you see on-screen is the *end-of-file marker*. It appears at the bottom of your file. When you start a document, there aren't any words yet, so the end-of-file marker is at the top. As you insert text, it will move down the page. You shouldn't try to delete the end-of-file marker, but it's certainly safe (and advisable) to *ignore it*.

But What If I Make a Mistake?

Correcting typing mistakes in Word for Windows is easy. Simply press the **Backspace** key to back up and erase text, or select unwanted text (selecting text is covered in the next section) and remove that text by pressing the **Delete** key.

Using a Word Processor: Some Rules of the Road

Using a word processor is different from using a typewriter in many respects. So before you take Word for Windows out for a test drive, here are some rules of the road:

Don't press Enter/Return at the end of every line. I've said it before, but it's worth saying again: when you use a typewriter, you press the carriage return at the end of a line so you can move down to the next one. When you use a word processor and your text bumps into the right margin, the word processor grabs the last word on that line and places it at the beginning of the next line automatically. Press **Enter** *only when you reach the end of a paragraph, or to insert a blank line.* If you want to divide an existing paragraph into two, move the cursor to the dividing point and press **Enter**. To put two paragraphs back together, move to the first letter of the second paragraph and press **Backspace**.

Use the Spacebar to insert a space between words or sentences. Don't use the Spacebar to move the cursor from place to place in a document. (You'll learn how to move the cursor in the next section.)

Press Tab (not the Spacebar) to indent the first line of a paragraph. Spaces are not just blank holes on the page; they are characters. Depending on the size of the characters you're using throughout your document, your paragraphs can come out looking uneven if you use the Spacebar to align them. Using the Tab key allows Word for Windows to line up paragraphs for you.

You can teach Word for Windows to correct your most common typing errors so you won't have to use your Backspace key too often. If you're prone to typing "teh" instead of "the," for example, you can have AutoCorrect catch your mistakes before you even notice you've made them! You can also use AutoCorrect (and a similar feature, AutoText) for shorthand text entry—for example, you could set it up so you type *bc* and Word inserts *Balcom Corporation* into your document. Learn the how-to's later in this chapter.

Paragraph   Any grouping of words that should be treated as a unit. This includes normal paragraphs as well as single-line paragraphs, such as chapter titles, section headings, and captions for charts or other figures. When you press Enter/Return in Word for Windows, you are marking the end of a paragraph.

A dotted line marks the end of a page. Just ignore the dotted line when you see it; it's there to tell Word for Windows where one page ends and another begins. If you add text above a dotted line, the excess text at the bottom of that page will flow onto the next page automatically. You can force the end of a page (before its time) by pressing **Ctrl+Enter**. When you do this, the dots multiply (get more dense) to show that this is a forced page break.

Magic Trick: Moving the Insertion Point Without Entering Text

As you type, the little insertion point, or cursor, moves along with you, like a happy puppy at your heels. But suppose you want to insert (or delete, or copy, or move) a word in a previous paragraph? Do you have to back up using the Backspace key and erase everything you've done, so you can retype that sentence? The answer is a welcome "No."

What you do instead is move the insertion point. To move the insertion point with the mouse, just click on the spot where you want it to go. (If you need to move through your document to get to the right spot, see the next chapter for some hints on *scrolling*.)

For People Who Let Their Fingers Do the Walking

Sometimes I hate to have my fingers leave the keyboard just to use the mouse, because they always land back on the wrong keys and I end up typing garbage. Here's how you can move the insertion point, and not your fingers:

To Move . . .	Press . . .
Up or down one line	Up or Down arrow key
Left or right one character	Left or Right arrow key
One word left or right	Ctrl+ either the Left or Right arrow key
Up or down one paragraph	Ctrl+ either the Up or Down arrow key
Up or down one screen	Page Up or Page Down
Top of the screen	Ctrl+Page Up
Bottom of the screen	Ctrl+Page Down
Beginning of the line	Home
End of the line	End
Beginning of document	Ctrl+Home
End of document	Ctrl+End

By the Way . . .

You can return to any previous editing spot by pressing **Shift+F5** as many times as necessary.

Selecting Text

As you edit your documents, you'll probably begin by modifying only certain sections of text. For example, you may want to move a sentence from the beginning of a paragraph to the end. You can move, copy, delete, and replace text by selecting it and then performing certain commands.

Mousing Around

To select text with the mouse, place the mouse pointer on the first letter in the text to be selected, then click and hold. Drag the mouse until you reach the end of the text you want to select. Release the mouse button, and the text you selected will be highlighted in reverse video.

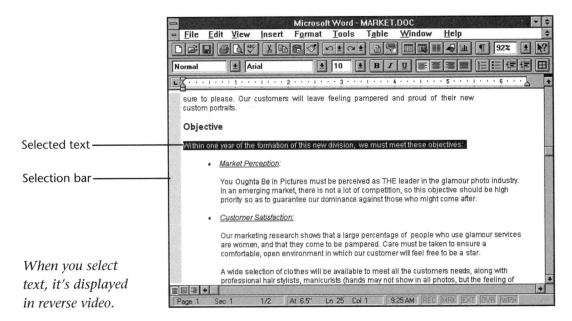

Selected text ——

Selection bar ——

When you select text, it's displayed in reverse video.

If you find this method of selecting text a *drag*, here are some shortcuts you can use when selecting text with the mouse:

Text to Select	Action
Word	Double-click on the word.
Sentence	Press the **Ctrl** key and click on the sentence.
Paragraph	Double-click in the *selection bar* next to the paragraph, or triple-click inside the paragraph.
Multiple paragraphs	Double-click in the *selection bar* next to the first paragraph, then drag.

Text to Select	Action
Line	Click in the selection bar next to the line.
Multiple lines	Drag in the selection bar next to the lines.
Column of text	Press **Alt** and drag until the column is high-lighted.
Whole document	Triple-click in the selection bar.

To extend your text selection to include more than one word, sentence, or paragraph, simply drag the pointer. For example, to select several words, double-click on one word and drag the pointer over the rest of the words you want to select.

Surf's Up, Grab Your Keyboard, and Come On!

Your keyboard is beginning to think I don't like it, so I'll show you how to select text with the keyboard too. First, move the insertion point to the first letter in the text to be selected, and press the **Shift** key. Then, with the Shift key depressed, use the **arrow** keys to reach the end of the text you wish to select. Release the Shift key, and the text you selected will be highlighted in reverse video.

While selecting text with the keyboard, you can use any of those movement keys we discussed a few pages back. For example, to move to the next word, you press **Ctrl+→**. To *select* a word, press **Shift+Ctrl+→**. To select text to the end of the paragraph, press **Shift+Ctrl+↓**, and so on. If you want to select the entire document, press **Ctrl+5** (use the 5 on the numeric keypad).

Some of these selection shortcuts are different for Word 2.0. For example, to select multiple paragraphs, click in the selection bar beside the first paragraph, then drag. To select an entire document, press **Ctrl** then click inside the selection bar.

To select any amount of text, hold the **Shift** key down, click at the beginning of the selection, then click to mark the end of the selection.

Change Your Mind?

Select the wrong text? Don't worry—just press an **arrow** key or click anywhere in the document. You can also select other text instead.

Insert mode The default typing mode for most word processors and text editors. When you are in Insert mode, the characters you type will be inserted to the right of the insertion point (cursor).

Overtype mode The opposite of Insert mode. When you are in Overtype mode, the characters you type will replace existing characters in the document.

In with the Good: Inserting Text

Text is always inserted into a document beginning at the *insertion point* (cursor). To move the insertion point, simply click at the point where you want to begin inserting text, or use the arrow keys.

When you type text into a document, Word assumes that you want to *insert* new text, and not type over existing text. Therefore, Word automatically uses *Insert mode*, in which the text you type appears at the insertion point, and all existing text is pushed to the right. However, if you want to type over existing characters, you can switch to *Overtype mode*.

To toggle between Overtype and Insert mode, press the **Insert** key. When you are in Overtype mode, **OVR** appears at the bottom of the screen on the Status bar. Remember that the default is Insert mode; when you place the insertion point in text and start typing, words are inserted at that point. To type over (re-place) existing text, use OVR mode (overtype).

Well, thank goodness we got through that! From now on, the only mode I want to think about is apple pie *à la mode*.

Out with the Bad: Deleting Text

Deleting text is the opposite of inserting. To delete a section of text:

☞ Select the text you wish to delete.

☞ Press the **Delete** key.

You can also delete text as you type by backing up with the **Backspace** key. If you want to delete text and then add it back (in a different place in the document), you *move it*. Moving text is covered in the next section.

But I Didn't Mean to Delete That!

 Everyone has a right to change their mind (being a woman, I feel I have more right to do that than anyone else). If you find that you've deleted some text you meant to save, select Edit from the **Main** menu and choose Undo. As long as the Undo command is not grayed (meaning that you can't select it), you'll undo your most recent action. You can also click on the **Undo** button on the **Standard** toolbar to undo your previous action. It's never too late to change you mind; click on the arrow next to the **Undo** button to select any of several prior actions to undo.

Copying and Moving Text

Copying and moving text is often the key to "fine-tuning" a document. Because of this, the techniques you'll learn in this section will be the ones you'll probably use the most. When text is copied or moved, the Windows *Clipboard* is used.

Copy Cat!

To copy text, "copy" these steps: first (using the methods you learned earlier in this chapter), select the text you want to copy. Then open the Edit menu and choose Copy. The text is copied to the Clipboard.

SPEAK LIKE A GEEK

Clipboard   The Windows Clipboard is a special area inside your computer where data is stored temporarily as it is moved or copied from one place to another. Think of the Clipboard as a kind of invisible way station for data. Using the Clipboard area, a Windows program, such as Word for Windows, can copy or move data within the same document, from one document to another, *or from/to another Windows program.*

Next, move the pointer to the place where you want to insert the text, and click to establish the insertion point. Open the Edit menu again, and this time choose Paste. The text is copied from the Clipboard into the document at the insertion point.

Copying in the Fast Lane

There are some shortcuts you can use to save time copying:

 To copy text, select it and press **Ctrl+C**, or click on the **Copy** button on the **Standard** toolbar.

 To paste text, press **Ctrl+V** or click on the **Paste** button.

When you copy or move text, Word automatically removes extra spaces which you might have selected accidentally—as long as the option **S**mart Cut and Paste is on. To check, open the **T**ools menu and choose **O**ptions. Click on the **Edit** tab, and make sure that Use **S**mart Cut and Paste is selected.

To place the same section of text in multiple areas of a document, simply repeat the Edit Paste command. The contents of the Clipboard are never erased (until you exit Windows); instead, they are overlaid. As long as you have not copied something else to the Clipboard with the Edit Copy command, whatever you copied originally is still there, waiting to be pasted over and over again. You can also copy text with the *drag-and-drop method*; see "By the Way" coming up in this section.

Moving Day

Moving text is very similar to copying. Move along with me here: first (using the methods you learned earlier in this chapter), select the text you want to move. Then open the Edit menu and select Cut. The text is moved to the Clipboard.

Then move the pointer to the place where you want to insert the text, and click to establish the insertion point. Open the Edit menu again, and choose Paste. The text is moved from the Clipboard into the document at the insertion point.

Get a Move On with These Fast Techniques

Here are some shortcuts you can use to save time moving text:

To move (cut) text, select it and press **Ctrl+X**, or click on the **Cut** button on the **Standard** toolbar.

To paste text, press **Ctrl+V** or click on the **Paste** button on the **Standard** toolbar.

When you use the **Cut** command, the selected text is removed from the document and placed on the Clipboard. If something else is copied to the Clipboard before you finish moving the text, the text you selected to be moved will be lost.

By the Way . . .

When I want to move text to a place I can see on-screen, I just drag-and-drop text where I want it to be. To move text with the mouse, first select it, and then click and hold the left mouse button. The cursor will change to an arrow with a little rectangle below it. Drag that pointer to the place where you want to insert the text, and then release the mouse button. The selected text is moved to the insertion point. (Incidentally, you can *copy* text instead by pressing **Ctrl** as you drag.)

I Like Spike!

If you need to make major changes to your document by moving several sections of text to one spot, save time with *Spike*. Here's how it works: first, select an item to move. To move the item into Spike, press **Ctrl+F3**. Repeat this process as much as you need to, gathering up

You can move several sections of text in one step with Spike. See the upcoming section for details.

In Word 2.0, to copy the contents of Spike without emptying it, type the word **spike** and press **F3**.

If you use AutoCorrect to create typing shortcuts, you will not have any control over when those substitutions are automatically made for you. If you want to control when text is inserted, use AutoText instead. Both features let you type a minimum amount (such as the letters *bc*), but with AutoText, the substitution doesn't happen *until you initiate it*. You'll find out more about AutoText in a minute.

pieces you want to move. Unlike the Clipboard, your next selection is added to the existing text in Spike, instead of replacing it. Once you have all the text you want to move within Spike, place the insertion point wherever you'd like, then press **Ctrl+Shift+F3**. This will empty Spike, placing its contents at the current location.

If you don't want to empty Spike (because you need to insert its contents in more than one place, for example), type the word **spike** at the insertion point, and click on the AutoText button or press **Alt+Ctrl+V**. The contents of Spike are placed at the insertion point, but Spike is not emptied. With this method, you can copy the contents of Spike to several locations within the document.

Taking a Typing Shortcut

Word offers many options to reduce the amount of time you spend typing the same stuff over and over. For example, suppose you have three clients to whom you send lots of correspondence. Typing *Big Blathering Bogus Corporation* throughout a letter can be very detrimental to the digits. Using Auto-Correct, you can create a substitution so all you have to type is **bc**, and Word will automatically substitute **Big Blathering Bogus Corporation.**

Word comes with a beginner's set of shortcuts built in. To add your own, type the text you want to save, then select it. If you want your text saved with special formatting (such as bold), apply that formatting before you select the text. After selecting the AutoCorrect entry, open the Tools menu and select AutoCorrect.

Make sure that the Replace Text as You Type checkbox is selected (if it's not, then AutoCorrect is turned off). Under Replace, enter a shorthand name for your text. For example, type **bc**. The name you enter cannot have any spaces in it. Click on the Add button, then click on **OK**.

To test out your new entry, type **bc** followed by a space. Watch as Word changes *bc* into your substitution, **Big Blathering Bogus Corporation**.

Controlling Automatic Substitutions

To control when substitutions are made, use AutoText. You can also save graphics with AutoText—for example, you could save your company name and logo, and use it as a common letterhead (you'll learn how to import *graphics* such as logos, etc. in Chapter 21). To save your AutoText entry, enter it into your document, and then select it. Once you have the AutoText entry selected, click on the **AutoText** button, or choose Edit AutoText.

Under Name, type a shortcut name such as **logo**. Word makes your AutoText shortcut available to every document you create, but if you want to save it to a particular document template, enter the name of the template under Make AutoText Entry Available To. (A *template* defines the Word environment by establishing margin settings, page orientation, and so on. Word for Windows comes with templates you can use to create specialized documents, or you can create your own templates. See Chapter 17.) Click on the Add button and you're done.

To use your new AutoText entry, place the cursor wherever you'd like, then type the name of the entry. For example, type **logo**. Click on the **AutoText** button again (or press **F3**), and the substitution is made automatically.

The Least You Need to Know

Editing is the most important processing you do when creating any kind of document, so here's a quick review of what you'll need to know to make your documents perfect:

- ☛ Text is always inserted at the cursor, otherwise known as the insertion point. To type over existing text, press **Insert** to turn on Overtype mode (and do the same to get back to Insert mode).

- ☛ To move the insertion point with the mouse, just click on the place where you want to move it.

- ☛ To enter text using a word processor, don't press Enter—except at the end of a paragraph. Don't use the Spacebar—except once between words, and once or twice between sentences. Use the **Tab** key, not the Spacebar, to indent paragraphs.

- ☛ To end a page before it is full, press **Ctrl+Enter**.

- ☛ To select text with the mouse, press and hold the mouse button (the left one, unless the right is specified), and drag the mouse over the text. To select text with the keyboard, press and hold the **Shift** key as you use the **arrow** keys to highlight the text.

- ☛ To delete text, select it and press **Delete**.

- ☛ To copy text quickly, select it and press **Ctrl+C** (or use the **Copy** button). Paste text in a new location by pressing **Ctrl+V**, or by clicking on the **Paste** button.

- ☛ To move text quickly, select it and press **Ctrl+X** or use the **Cut** button. Paste text into a new location by pressing **Ctrl+V**, or by clicking on the **Paste** button.

- ☞ Use Spike to move several sections of text to one location. First, select each section of text and press **Ctrl+F3** in turn. When you're ready to place the text, press **Ctrl+Shift+F3**.

- ☞ To create typing shortcuts, use AutoCorrect. To control substitutions, use AutoText. To insert an AutoCorrect entry, simply type its name. To insert an AutoText entry, click on the **AutoText** button.

This page unintentionally left blank.

Chapter 7
A Different Point of View

In This Chapter

- ☞ The many ways you can view your document
- ☞ Viewing your document before you print
- ☞ Moving back and forth through a document

This chapter is all about points of view: what you see on your screen when you look at your document, and—more importantly—*what you don't see*. There is a perfect document view for each of the tasks you are trying to accomplish: editing (Normal view), reorganization (Outline view), manipulating graphics or pictures (Page Layout view), or preparing to print (Print Preview).

If you need to create complex documents such as multipart reports, you can combine each separate report as a *subdocument* within a *master document*. A master document allows you to work within a single document window, where you can view overall structure of the combined subdocuments. By breaking up a long project in this way, Word for Windows keeps each subdocument to a manageable size; restructuring the project takes minutes instead of days. When working within a master document, use Master Document view.

Before we get to the main topic in this chapter (changing your view), let's cover something a bit easier—*scrolling*.

Scroll To move text up/down or right/left on a computer screen.

Scroll bars Located along the bottom and right sides of the Document Window, you use scroll bars to display other areas of the document.

Scroll box Its position within the entire scroll bar tells you roughly where you are within your document.

Taking Your Document Out for a Scroll

When I'm editing, I tend to move around the document a lot: making changes, reading, and rereading, until I find just the right words or just the right look. Such jumping around is called *scrolling*. You can move through a document (scrolling) by using a mouse or the keyboard.

The fastest way to scroll through a document is with the mouse and the scroll bars. You'll find the *vertical scroll bar* lurking along the right-hand side of the document window. This scroll bar looks like an elevator shaft with a tiny elevator suspended in it. That "elevator" is called the *scroll box*, and it helps you know where you are. For example, if the scroll box is close to the bottom of the scroll bar, then you're almost at the end of your document.

Keep in mind that scrolling with the mouse simply changes the part of the document you're looking at. If you want to start editing, click within the document to move the insertion point. If you missed the award-winning documentary "Magic Trick: Moving the Insertion Point without Entering Text" when it was on PBS, see Chapter 6 for a quick review.

You'll also see a scroll bar along the bottom of the window; it's called the *horizontal scroll bar*, and it tells you where you are in relation to the margins of your document. Here's how to take your document "out for a scroll."

Scroll box

Vertical scroll bar

Horizontal scroll bar

Scroll arrows

You move through your document with a scroll bar and a mouse.

To Move . . .	Click . . .
Up or down one line	On the up or down arrow of the vertical scroll bar.
Left or right	On the left or right arrow of the horizontal scroll bar.
Up or down one screen	Above or below the scroll box in the right-hand scroll bar.
A portion of the document length	On the vertical scroll box, and drag it up or down a proportionate amount.
A portion of the document width	On the horizontal scroll box, and drag it left or right a proportionate amount.
In Normal view, past the zero mark on the Ruler	On the left arrow on the horizontal scroll bar, while holding down the Shift key.

I know it's weird that the Page keys don't move you one whole *page* in your document (like from page 1 to page 2), but the computer's "page" is its screen, so that's why the keys work that way.

Working in a screen without the normal distractions of a menu bar, scroll bars, etc., can be a relaxing and speedy experience, since Full Screen mode requires less time to update than other modes. If you're a fast typist (or you simply hate clutter), Full Screen mode is for you.

If you want to have your cake and eat it too, you can still enjoy the benefits of Full Screen mode without removing *all* the clutter. Simply click on the **Full Screen** button, and select the toolbars you wish to display when in Full Screen mode. You can arrange these toolbars to suit your taste; see Chapter 4 for help.

Most Windows programs do not display the scroll bars unless some portion of your document is not being displayed (if the right margin is hidden, for example, you see a horizontal scroll bar you can use to scroll right). Word for Windows does not follow this unwritten rule; instead, it displays both the horizontal and vertical scroll bars at all times, unless you turn them off.

Anyway, back to what I was saying: to turn the scroll bars off, open the **Tools** menu and select **Options**. Click on the **View** tab. In the Window area, use the horizontal or vertical scroll bar check boxes to toggle the scroll bars on or off. When you're done making your choices, click on **OK**.

Scrolling with the Keyboard

To scroll through a document with the keyboard, simply press **Page Down** to move one screen forward in the document. Press **Page Up** to move one screen back. You can get nowhere fast by scrolling one line at a time with the Up and Down arrow keys.

Unlike when you use the mouse with the scroll bar, scrolling with the keyboard *does* move the insertion point, so you don't have to unpack your editing bags when you get there—you're ready to edit.

What's Wrong With This Picture?

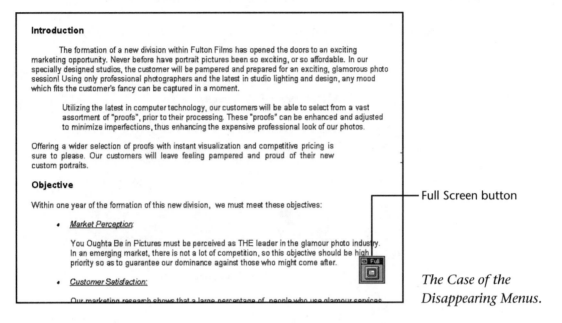

Introduction

The formation of a new division within Fulton Films has opened the doors to an exciting marketing opportunity. Never before have portrait pictures been so exciting, or so affordable. In our specially designed studios, the customer will be pampered and prepared for an exciting, glamorous photo session! Using only professional photographers and the latest in studio lighting and design, any mood which fits the customer's fancy can be captured in a moment.

Utilizing the latest in computer technology, our customers will be able to select from a vast assortment of "proofs", prior to their processing. These "proofs" can be enhanced and adjusted to minimize imperfections, thus enhancing the expensive professional look of our photos.

Offering a wider selection of proofs with instant visualization and competitive pricing is sure to please. Our customers will leave feeling pampered and proud of their new custom portraits.

Objective

Within one year of the formation of this new division, we must meet these objectives:

• *Market Perception:*

You Oughta Be in Pictures must be perceived as THE leader in the glamour photo industry. In an emerging market, there is not a lot of competition, so this objective should be high priority so as to guarantee our dominance against those who might come after.

• *Customer Satisfaction:*

Our marketing research shows that a large percentage of people who use glamour services

Full Screen button

The Case of the Disappearing Menus.

Take a good look at this picture. Can you list everything that's missing?

Answer: If you said the scroll bars, the menu bar, the toolbars, the status bar, and the Ruler, you're right. If these things are just a collection of junk that gets in the way of your typing, get rid of them! In Word for Windows, you have the option of removing everything from the screen so you can do your typing in peace. This option will be especially welcome if you switched from WordPerfect, where the normal operating environment does not include any clutter.

So, whether you're a former WordPerfect user, or you just want to give this a try, here's what you do: open the View menu and select Full Screen.

To return to "normal" clutter, click on the **Full Screen** button, or press **Esc** anytime you want.

A Word Horse: Normal View

The default viewing mode for Word for Windows is a little word-horse (or work-horse) called (aptly enough) *Normal*. Normal view is the best all-purpose view mode for working. But even Normal view is not totally "normal"; it has some interesting quirks that you should be aware of.

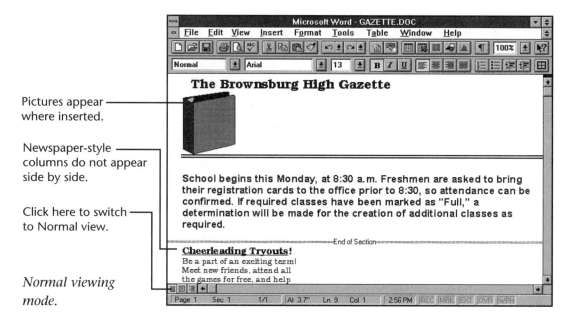

Pictures appear where inserted.

Newspaper-style columns do not appear side by side.

Click here to switch to Normal view.

Normal viewing mode.

Newspaper-style columns do not appear side by side as they will appear on the printed paper. Instead, they appear as one continuous column. You'll learn how to create *newspaper-style columns* in Chapter 19.

Pictures and text that you've placed in frames will appear where they are first inserted into the document, not where they will be when printed. You'll learn how to work with *frames* in Chapter 20.

When you add headers, footers, or footnotes, you work in a separate dialog box,
outside of the regular document. You'll learn
more about *headers and footers* in Chapter 13.

Switching to Normal View

To switch to Normal view from some other
view, just click on the **Normal** button (located
on the horizontal scroll bar), or open the View
menu and select Normal. Pretty easy, huh?

How to Speed Up Normal View

As you move back and forth through your
document, the computer is constantly redrawing what is being displayed on your screen.
Think of trying to do a pencil sketch of a
tennis match: although a computer is very
fast, if your document contains complex
graphics (pictures) or other detailed information, this redrawing process can take longer
than you'd like.

While using Normal view, you can speed up
the redraw process by utilizing *draft font*. Just
open the Tools menu and select Options.
Click on the View tab, and select the Draft
Font check box.

To enter Full Screen mode
in version 2.0, use the **Tools
Options** command. Under
Category, select **View**.
Choose the **Full Screen**
option and click on **OK**. To
exit Full Screen mode, press
Esc. If you don't have this
option, shame, shame.
When you register your
copy of Word, they send
you periodic updates for
free! Anyway, this option
existed beginning with
version 2.0b. (This is way off
the subject, but to see what
version you have, open the
Help menu and select
About...).

To change to **Draft** mode in
version 2.0, open the **View**
menu and select **Draft**.

Just a Little Reorganization

When you need to move several sections of a long document, use Outline
view. When you work in Outline view, you'll see just the section headings
of your document. You can change the headings themselves, or copy,
move, and delete their associated sections.

Switching to Outline View

To change to Outline view, click on the **Outline** button on the horizontal scroll bar, or open the **View** menu and select Outline. To change your view, adjust heading levels, and move headings or other text, you can select buttons on the Outlining toolbar.

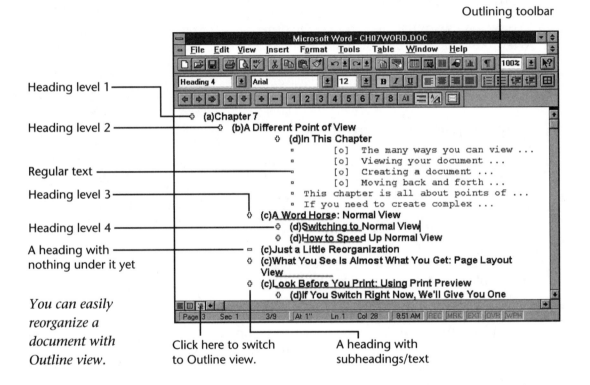

Outlining toolbar

Heading level 1

Heading level 2

Regular text

Heading level 3

Heading level 4

A heading with nothing under it yet

You can easily reorganize a document with Outline view.

Click here to switch to Outline view.

A heading with subheadings/text

Outline view is great for working with the structure of a long document. Although you can enter regular text while in Outline view, switch to Normal view if you want to change the formatting of individual paragraphs.

Creating a New Outline

To create a new outline, switch to **Outline** view and start typing the first heading. To type a lower level heading (such as Heading 2 for example), press **Tab** or click on the **Demote** button (right arrow). To type a higher-level heading (to type a Heading 1 after entering a Heading 2, for example), press **Shift+Tab** or click on the **Promote** button (left arrow). To type a paragraph of regular text, click on the **Demote to Body Text** button (double right arrow).

By the Way . . .

Use Outline view to create your outline first, then switch to **Normal** view to enter your text. Although you can enter text in Outline view, it's pretty cumbersome and difficult to manage.

SPEAK LIKE A GEEK

Newspaper-style columns Columns similar to those found in newspapers. Text flows between invisible boundaries, down one part of the page. When the text hits the end of a column, it wraps to the top of the next.

Frames Small boxes in which you place text or pictures so you can maneuver them easily within your document.

Headers and footers A header is text that can be reprinted at the top of every page, and a footer is text that can be reprinted at the bottom.

Changing Your Point of View

After you've created your outline—and maybe even entered some text—you can use Outline view to control the level of subheadings, and the amount of the underlying text that you see. To expand a heading so you can see the subheadings, select the heading by clicking on it, then click on the **Expand** button (plus sign). To collapse a heading so you do not see subheadings, select the heading and click on the **Collapse** button (minus sign). To see only the first line of each exposed paragraph, click on the **Show First Line Only** button.

You can also expand and collapse a heading by double-clicking on its plus sign within the outline.

To expand or collapse the entire outline, click on the **All** button. To expand the outline to a particular heading level, click on the appropriate number. For example, to expand an outline to heading level 3, click on the **3** within the **Outlining** toolbar.

Getting the Outline Just Right

When I start out to write a book (or anything else, for that matter), I try to get organized by creating an outline right off. Then I proceed to ignore my outline and write what I want. Okay, it's not really that bad, but I find that during the course of creating any long document (such as a chapter, report, or manual), that changes in the structure of the original outline are inevitable. (At least that's what I tell my editor!)

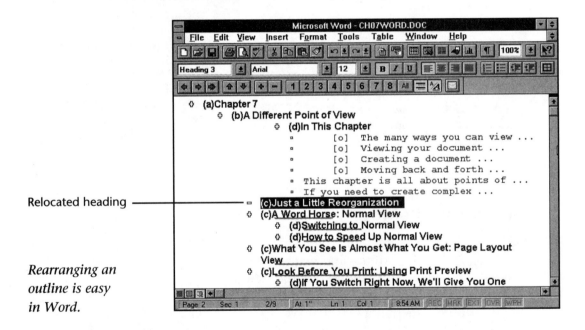

Relocated heading ———

Rearranging an outline is easy in Word.

Word makes changing your outline easy to do. To change a heading's level, use the Demote and Promote buttons. For example, to change a Heading 3 to a Heading 4, click on the **Demote** (right arrow) button. To change a Heading 3 to a Heading 2, click on the **Promote** button (left arrow).

To move a heading and all of its underlying text, use the Move Up and Move Down buttons. For example, to move a heading (and text) up in the outline, click on **Move Up** (up arrow). To move the heading down in the outline, click **Move Down** (down arrow). You can move a heading (and its text) anywhere in the outline by clicking on its plus sign and dragging it to its new location. To move just the heading (and not the text), expand the heading by double-clicking on its plus sign, then select just the heading and drag it to its new location.

What You See Is Almost What You Get: Page Layout View

If you've been working in Normal view and you want to see such things as columns, graphics, or headers as they will appear when printed, switch to **Page Layout** view.

You can print the outline of your document at any time, simply by switching to **Outline** view and selecting the **File Print** command. You'll learn more about printing in Chapter 10.

By the Way . . .

Word has a similar viewing option called *Print Preview*, which you'll learn about later in this chapter. While you can continue editing in Print Preview, it is much more difficult. You should probably limit your use of Print Preview to global, page-shattering changes like margin settings, or as a last-minute check right before printing. More extensive changes to your document are easier to perform in Page Layout or Normal view.

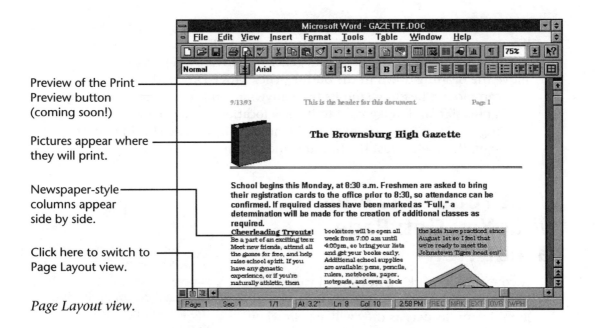

Preview of the Print Preview button (coming soon!)

Pictures appear where they will print.

Newspaper-style columns appear side by side.

Click here to switch to Page Layout view.

Page Layout view.

No viewing mode is perfect—but don't worry, there is an appropriate mode for each task you are trying to accomplish. Here are some quirks about the Page Layout view that you should be aware of:

Use this mode to work with frames. You'll see the text and graphic "boxes" as they'll appear when printed, so you can use this mode to create, edit, and resize frames.

When you scroll your document, you can move through the document one whole page at a time if you want. Just click on the double-up or double-down arrows on the vertical scroll bar.

When working with headers, footers, and footnotes, you work in the document, not in a separate box as you do in Normal view.

Making the Switch to Page Layout View

Make the switch—here's how: just click on the **Page Layout** button on the horizontal scroll bar, or open the View menu and choose **Page Layout**.

Look Before You Print: Using Print Preview

In version 2.0, Page Layout mode does not display line numbers (like those used in legal documents) and lines between columns. Instead, you should use Print Preview to view these items.

Print Preview, like Page Layout view, displays *everything* as it will print. If you like what you see in Print Preview view, you can print your document by simply clicking on the **Print** button.

If you're using Word 2.0, you will not be able to edit (make changes) in Print Preview. Use Page Layout mode instead.

Although you can use Print Preview to make editing changes, it's difficult. That's because normally, in Print Preview, it's too difficult to see what you're doing. There's all this really teeny text, you see, that looks like a three-thousand-year-old excavated mosaic from the Libraries of Alexandria. If you insist on making last-minute changes to your document, you can use Word's *Magnifying button* to enlarge the text temporarily so you can edit. (You'll learn how to perform this magic trick in just a minute.) The process of editing in Print Preview is rather clumsy, so you should probably limit your use of Print Preview to making broad changes, such as margin settings.

If You Switch Right Now to *Print Preview,* We'll Give You One Month's Free Service . . .

To switch to Print Preview view, just click on the **Print Preview** button (we "previewed" it earlier under the Page Layout section), or open the File menu and select Print Preview. (I bet you thought I was going to say open the View menu!) You can also press **Ctrl+F2** to preview a document.

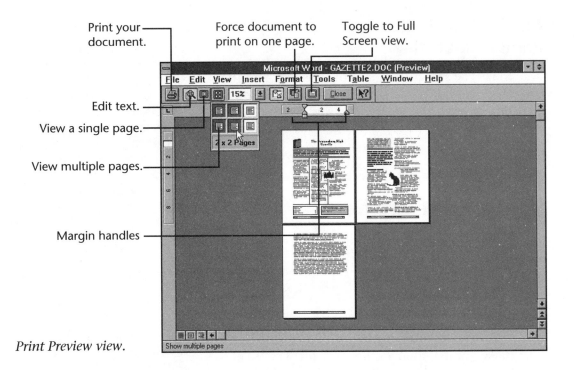

Print your document.

Force document to print on one page.

Toggle to Full Screen view.

Edit text.

View a single page.

View multiple pages.

Margin handles

Print Preview view.

You can do several nifty things in Print Preview, as you can see by this figure. Some buttons are easy to use (for example, to print, just click on the button!); others deserve a better explanation. To edit text, click on the tiny magnifying glass, then click within the document. After you've been zoomed to the indicated area, click on the **Magnifying** button again—the cursor changes into a regular mouse cursor, perfectly designed for editing. Edit to your heart's content, then click on the magnifying glass again—and the text area again—to return to regular Print Preview (teeny tiny print).

If you want to see multiple pages at once, Word is pretty accommodating. Just click on the **Multiple Pages** button and highlight the number of pages you want to see (from one to six). Click on the **Single Page** button to return to the regular view. If you hate things getting in your way, click on the **Full Page** button to remove screen clutter such as the rulers. Click on it again to return to regular Print Preview.

To return to whatever view you were using before you previewed, click on Close. You can change to any other view by clicking the appropriate button on the horizontal scroll bar.

Changing Margin Settings in Print Preview View

This is one of the few changes you might want to make while in Print Preview view, so I thought I'd give it special treatment in its own section. To change the margins, drag a *margin handle* to its new location (point at the margin handle, then press and hold the left mouse button as you move the mouse). As you drag, you'll see an "invisible" guideline to help you get it right. When the margin's set, release the mouse button, and the text will adjust automatically (ah, the wonders of word processing!).

By the Way . . .

You can use this same technique to change the margins within Page Layout or Normal view. Make sure the **Ruler** is displayed by selecting it from the **View** menu. Then grab a margin handle and drag it to its intended resting place.

Magnifying What You See

Sherlock Holmes would have loved this option. In all views, you can adjust the page display as if you were holding a magnifying glass to the screen. You can choose from several magnifications in the *Zoom drop-down list box* (located on the Standard toolbar described below. It's elementary, my dear Watson:

200, 150, 100, 75, 50, 25, 10   Select a percentage, and the page will be reduced or enlarged to that portion of its normal size. For example, if you select 200, the page will appear twice its normal size. Choose 50, and it will appear half its normal size.

Page Width   Choose this option to see both margins of your document on the screen (text fills the screen from side to side). I call this the "Large Print" view; it's great for people like me who have trouble seeing words after working at a computer all day.

Whole Page   Choose this option if you want to see an entire page of your document on the screen.

Two Pages   Get two pages for the price of one with this option.

You can also select your own custom percentage by using the Zoom command on the View menu. Just click on the commands (or press **Alt+V** to open the View menu), then press **Z** for Zoom.

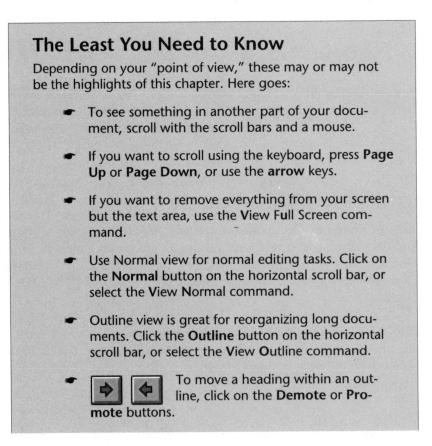

The Least You Need to Know

Depending on your "point of view," these may or may not be the highlights of this chapter. Here goes:

- ☞ To see something in another part of your document, scroll with the scroll bars and a mouse.

- ☞ If you want to scroll using the keyboard, press **Page Up** or **Page Down**, or use the **arrow** keys.

- ☞ If you want to remove everything from your screen but the text area, use the View **Full Screen** command.

- ☞ Use Normal view for normal editing tasks. Click on the **Normal** button on the horizontal scroll bar, or select the View **Normal** command.

- ☞ Outline view is great for reorganizing long documents. Click the **Outline** button on the horizontal scroll bar, or select the View **Outline** command.

- ☞ To move a heading within an outline, click on the **Demote** or **Promote** buttons.

☞ To change an outline heading into text, click on the **Text** button.

☞ To display lower levels in an outline, click the **Expand** button. To hide lower levels, click the **Collapse** button.

☞ Page Layout view is great for working with graphics, headers and footers, and newspaper columns. You can see everything as it will look when you print it, and you can still make changes to your document. Click on the **Page Layout** button on the horizontal scroll bar, or select View Page Layout.

☞ Use Print Preview just prior to printing, or to make broad changes, such as margin settings. Select File Print Preview.

☞ **100%** Want to see something close-up? Select an option on the **Zoom** drop-down list, or use the Zoom command on the View menu.

This page unintentionally left blank.

Chapter 8
Juggling Documents

In This Chapter

- ☞ Creating a new document
- ☞ Opening an existing document
- ☞ Returning to a previous editing position within a document
- ☞ Finding little lost documents
- ☞ "Paneless" ways to work with multiple documents
- ☞ Working in two places in a document at the same time

Maybe it's not so wonderful to have to juggle changing priorities and multiple projects, but at least Word for Windows works the way we really do: that is, *on more than one thing at a time*. As you work in Word for Windows, you'll find yourself opening old documents and starting new ones. You may even want to have several documents showing on your screen at the same time, or two parts of the same document. This chapter will show you how to do all this and more.

Starting A-New

When you first start Word for Windows, it assumes you want to start something new, so it accommodates you by giving you a blank screen. But what do you do when you've just finished one document, and you want to start "a-new"? How do you get an empty window so you can start typing?

Well, you've got two options:

☞ Open the File menu and select the New command. Just click to open the menu and select the command, or press **Alt+F** and then N. A dialog box will open. You can basically ignore this box and press **Enter**, unless you want to base your new document on a template other than the Normal template.

☞ Click on the **New** button on the **Standard** toolbar or press **Ctrl+N**. This is the quickest method if you want to base your new document on the Normal template. If you want to select another template, you must use the New command on the File menu.

TECHNO NERD TEACHES

When you work with Word for Windows, you use a default *template* (called NORMAL.DOT) that defines margin settings, page orientation, and so on. Word for Windows comes with additional templates (see Chapter 17) that you can use to create specialized documents, such as memos, proposals, overheads, faxes, and mailing labels. If you want to use one of these specialized templates, use the **File New** command.

What's Wrong with This Picture?

Yvonne wants to create a memo using the MEMO2 template, so she clicks on the New button on the Standard toolbar to start a new document. What did Yvonne do wrong?

Answer: She should have used the New command on the File menu, and selected the **MEMO2** template from the dialog box that was displayed. When she clicked on the New button on the Standard toolbar, Word assumed that she wanted to use the NORMAL template to create a new document, and it didn't display the dialog box.

Documenting Your Documents

When you start a new document (or anytime thereafter) you can add document summary information which will make it easier to locate that document later on. With the **Summary** option, you can record the document's title, author (that's you!), subject (such as Sales Report), keywords (such as *sales*, *1993*, *first quarter*), and comments. From the **New** dialog box, simply click on **Summary** or press **Alt+S**. Complete as much as you'd like, then click on **OK** or press **Enter**.

When you start a new document, you can let a *Word Wizard* do most of the setup work for you. See the section on Word Wizards coming up later in this chapter.

Summary Info	
File Name: Document4	**OK**
Directory:	**Cancel**
Title: November Book Sales Report	**Statistics...**
Subject: Alpha Book Sales	**Help**
Author: Jennifer Flynn	
Keywords: November, Alpha, Sales	
Comments: Great sales month. Sent extra copy to Jan Storm for publication.	

Here's your chance to make a statement.

If you've already started a document, you can still add a summary. Just open the File menu and select Summary Info. Whenever you want, you can use the Find File command (explained later in this chapter) to locate a document based on its summary.

You won't have to go to so much trouble to document your documents in Word 2.0. Simply start a new document, and the Document Summary box will appear. If you need to view it again after starting a document, select the Summary Info command on the File menu.

Help Me, Mr. Wizard!

Word Wizards set up a new document's margins, fonts, and headings in a series of easy steps. Use Word Wizards to create any of several standard documents, including business letters, memos, reports, and even fax cover sheets. Here's how:

Open the File menu and select New.   With the keyboard, press **Alt+F**, then **N**.

Choose your Wizard!   Click on a Wizard to select it from the template list, and then click on **OK** (or use the **Down arrow** keys to highlight one, and press **Enter**).

Follow the on-screen instructions.   Just follow along. Click on an option to select it, or press **Alt** plus the underlined letter. When you're done with one screen, move on—click on Next or press **Alt+N**.

Now you're finished!   Click on Finish or press **Alt+F**. If you want additional help completing the document, select Yes, display Help as I work.

Put It to Work

Let's create a sample document using one of the Word Wizards. First, open the **File** menu and select **New** (keyboarders, press **Alt+F**, then **N**).

Select **Award Wizard** from the template list by clicking on it (or highlighting it with the **arrow** keys). Press **Enter** or click on **OK**. Select any style you want by clicking on it (or by pressing **Alt** plus the underlined letter). Continue to the next screen by clicking on **N**ext or pressing **Alt+N**.

We want this award to print in landscape, so we'll leave that option as is. We don't have any special bordered paper, so we'll leave that option alone too. Click **N**ext or press **Alt+N**.

Type the name of the person you're giving this award to (such as your spouse or significant other). Enter a title for the award, such as **The Greatest Guy (or Gal) in the World**. Click on **N**ext or press **Alt+N**.

Enter your name and proceed to the next screen. Under Presented by, enter something like **Committee of People Who Should Know**. On the next screen, enter today's date and some additional text, such as **Because of the unselfish love he gives me**. Click on Finish, or press **Alt+F**. Wow! You've just created a cool award in just minutes instead of hours! Try out some of the other Wizards—I think you'll be equally pleased. In the next few chapters, you'll learn how to save your new document and print it.

Document Déjà Vu: Opening an Existing Document

Word remembers the last four (or more) documents you worked on, so you can get to them easily. So if the document you want to work on (open) is a recent one, it'll be displayed at the end of the File menu. To open it, open the File menu and click on the document you want, or press the number next to the document name. (I use this method to open existing documents more often than any other method.)

> You can have Word for Windows display more than the last four documents at the end of the File list. Use the **Tools Options** command. Click on the **General** tab or press **Ctrl+Tab** to select it. With the Recently Used Files list, you can choose to display up to nine files.

If you haven't worked on a document in a while, you'll have to open it the long way.

Enter name of file to open or select from list.

Change directories.

Locate a lost file.

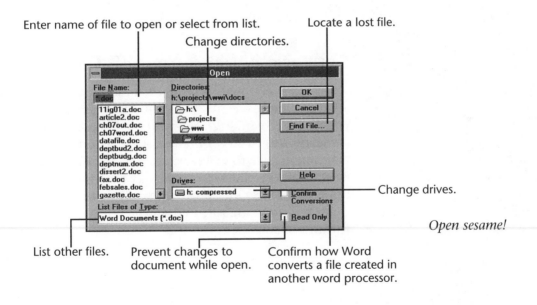

Change drives.

Open sesame!

List other files.

Prevent changes to document while open.

Confirm how Word converts a file created in another word processor.

Open the File menu and select the Open command, or press **Ctrl+O**. To use a mouse, click on the **Open** button on the **Standard** toolbar. Another one of those boxes will appear (oh, goody). Either type the name of the file you want to open, or (using the scroll bars or the **Up** or **Down arrow** keys) scroll through the list.

When you open a foreign-format document (such as a WordPerfect file), Word attempts to convert it. Expect to lose some formatting; no conversion process is absolutely perfect.

Disk drive A type of computer storage device. Think of a disk drive as a cassette recorder/player. Just like a cassette player, a disk drive can record data on a magnetic disk and play back the data. Most computers have two types of disk drives: a *hard disk drive*, which stores vast amounts of data on permanently mounted disks, and a *floppy disk drive*, which records smaller amounts of data on portable disks.

Directory You often need to store related files in separate directories on the disk. Think of your disk as a filing cabinet, and each directory as a drawer in the filing cabinet. By keeping files in separate directories, it is easier to locate and work with related files.

If you can't find your file, change to a different drive or *directory*. (To move to Directories with the keyboard, press **Alt+D**; to move to Drives, press **Alt+V**.) Select a different *disk drive* from the drop-down list box by clicking on the **down arrow** and then clicking on a different drive. If you need to change to another directory, click on that directory.

If you're trying to open a document that was created in another program (such as WordPerfect), select a file type from the drop-down list box by clicking on the **down arrow** and then picking a type. If your file type is not listed, select **All Files**.

To protect this document against accidental changes, use the Read Only check box. When you're done making choices, select **OK** to open the file

Get Back to Where You Left Off

A real nifty feature of Word for Windows is its ability to locate the place in your document where you were last working. (Now if it could only find my keys.) After you open an existing document, you can go back to where you left off by using Go Back. Just press **Shift+F5**. (You may remember this from Chapter 6.) By using this handy feature, you can return to your last three editing positions within the document.

Help! I Lost My File!

If you're having trouble locating an old document, don't worry—be happy! Word has a nice command called Find File that'll do *most* of the work of locating a file for you (okay, you *do* have to tell it what to look for).

First, wait 24 hours to be sure that the file is really missing and hasn't just run away. (Okay, I'm just kidding.) Then open the File menu and select the Find File command—or (if you're in the Open dialog box) click on the Find File button or press **Alt+F**.

Enter a filename here.

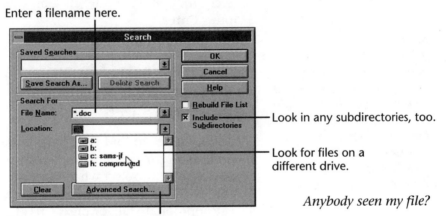

Look in any subdirectories, too.

Look for files on a different drive.

Anybody seen my file?

Select complex search criteria.

Follow these steps to locate your missing file:

File Name   If you know the name of the file you want to search for, enter it here. If you're not sure of the spelling, use a question mark in place of a single character, such as CHAPTER?.DOC. (Word automatically enters *.DOC for you; files you save with Word usually have a .DOC extension.) You can use an asterisk to replace multiple characters, as in CH*.DOC or M*.*. You'll learn more than you'll ever want to know about file names in Chapter 9.

Location   This controls which disk drive and directories are searched. Click on the **down arrow** (or press the **Down arrow** key) and select a drive letter. If you want Word to search in a particular directory, type it after the drive letter. For example, to search in a directory called JENNY, type **C:\JENNY.** You can have Word search subdirectories (directories within the one you selected) by clicking on Include Subdirectories, or by pressing **Alt+B.**

Initially, a preview of your selected file will display in the box to the right. If you'd like to see the document's summary or file information, use the drop-down list box to select the appropriate option. To tell Word more information about the lost file, click on Advanced Search or press **Alt+A.** (You'll learn more about advanced searches in the next section). If you're done, click on **Close** or press **Enter.**

Although they appear in different places, all of the items listed here are displayed in the Word 2.0 File Find box. One item to note: the easiest way to locate files in a different directory is with the **E**dit Path button. Simply select a drive and directory from the drop-down list boxes.

Just the Facts, Ma'am: Telling Word Additional Stuff to Search For

In your quest to find your file, you can select *complex search criteria* with the Advanced Search button. Select whatever options you can: to move from section to section, click on the appropriate tab, or press **Ctrl+Tab.** To select an option, click on it (or press **Alt** plus the underlined letter).

Under the Location tab, you can select multiple directories to search. Simply select a directory, then click on the Add button or press **Alt+A.** You can access directories on a network drive by clicking on Network or pressing **Alt+N.**

Under the Summary tab, you can specify the title, subject, keywords, or author (you entered these in the Summary Info box you complete when you start a new a file). You can also search for text within a document.

Under the Timestamp tab, you can locate a file based on who created it (or made the last changes to it). You can even locate a file based on the time or date it was created or last changed.

> ### By the Way . . .
> When I'm searching for files based on date or author name, I like to change the sort options for the file list—and you can too. Just use the **Commands** button in the Find File dialog box, and select Sorting to sort the file list by file name, author, creation date, save name, save date, and file size.

Once You've Found a File, Never Let It Go

Some enchanted evening, you may find your strange file, you may find your strange file across a crowded disk . . . but what can you do with a file once you've found it? Well, just about anything. You can open, print, copy, and delete any files you locate using File Find File. Here's how.

After conducting your search and finding some lost files, select a file or files in the Listed Files box. Use the **arrow** keys or click on a file to select it. To select multiple files with the mouse, hold down the **Ctrl** key as you click on a file name. To select multiple files with the keyboard, press **Shift+F8**, and then use the **arrow** keys to highlight a file. With a file highlighted, press the **Spacebar** to select it.

Then select the option you want. To open the selected files, click on the Open button (or press **Alt+O**). To perform other commands, click on the Commands button (or press **Alt+C**), then select Open Read Only, Print, Summary, Delete, Copy or Sorting. If you're copying files, enter the directory to which you want to copy the files.

What's Wrong with This Picture?

Bob wants to print two files, BUDGET.DOC and APRSALES.DOC. He opens the File menu and selects the Print command. Then he tries to select both files for printing. What did Bob do wrong?

Answer: Nothing much—he just used the wrong command. Word is perfectly capable of printing several documents in a row while you go get some coffee. Bob should have used the Find File command on the File menu to select his two files. After clicking on the Command button and selecting Print, Bob's off to the break room in no time!

A Paneless Way to Work with Multiple Windows

You can open up to nine documents at one time, with each of your "children" running around in its own document window. You can open them one at a time throughout a work session, or you can open several files at once by using the Find File command as explained earlier.

Once several documents are open, you can copy or move text between them, or simply refer to one document as you edit another. You can scroll through each document, and make changes as you would at any other time. However, you can only make changes to one document at a time—the *active document*.

Active document   The document you are currently working in. The active document contains the insertion point, and if more than one document window is being displayed on-screen, the active document's title bar appears darker than those of the other document windows.

Doing the Document Shuffle

Normally, the active document takes up the entire screen, but you can split the screen equally among all active documents by opening the **Window** menu and selecting Arrange All. Jump between documents using one of these two methods:

Use the Window menu. Open the Window menu and select the document from the list displayed at the bottom.

OR

If more than one window is displayed on-screen, click inside a window to make it active. You can also press **Alt+F6** to move back and forth between windows.

You close document windows in the normal way, by saving the file, then closing the window. You'll learn how to do this in the next chapter.

Looking at Two Parts of the Same Document Is Not a Pane

Sometimes you want to work in two sections of the same document at the same time. For example, if you wanted to move or copy text within a long document, scrolling back and forth would be a waste of time. Instead, just split the document window into two *panes* (two sections).

You can resize and/or move document windows to get them "just right." If you need a quick review, see Chapter 3.

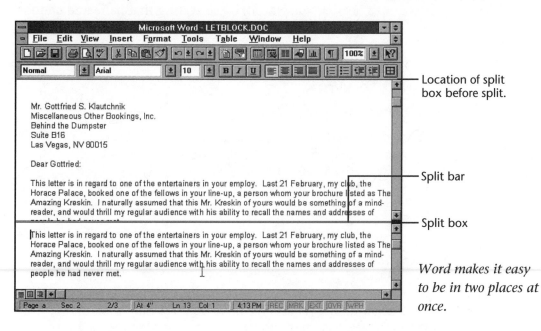

Location of split box before split.

Split bar

Split box

Word makes it easy to be in two places at once.

If you've got a mouse, just double-click on the **split box**. This splits the window into two equal panes. If you want to adjust the sizes of the windows, drag (click the left mouse button and hold it down as you move the mouse) the split box to the desired size. To return to a single window, double-click on the split box again.

To split a window with the keyboard in Word 2.0, open the **Window** menu and select **Arrange All**. This splits the window into two equal-sized panes. To adjust the size of the panes, press **Alt** and the **hyphen** (-). Select Split, and then use the **arrow** keys to move the split bar. Press **Enter** when you are through.

If you want to use the keyboard, open the **Window** menu and select the **Split** command, or press **Alt+Ctrl+S**. Press the **Up** and **Down arrow** keys to adjust the size of the split windows, and press **Enter**. To return to a single window, open the **Window** menu and select the Remove **Split** command.

To move between the two panes, click inside a pane to make it active, or press **F6** to toggle back and forth. You can get really fancy and select different views for each pane (see Chapter 7 for more information). You can remove the Ruler from the second pane (if it's displayed) by activating that pane and choosing the **View Ruler** command.

Put It to Work

Working with a Long Document

Let's practice some of the techniques we learned in this chapter by using one of the standard documents Word comes with, the SAMPLE1.DOC. This document is used with the Word tutorials. While we're working with it, we won't make any permanent changes, so you'll still have a chance to use it later.

First, let's open it. I'm taking a wild guess, but I'm going to assume that you haven't been working on this file lately, so we won't find it listed at the end of the **File** menu. This means that we're going to have to open the file manually, with the **File Open** command. Click on the **Open** button on the **Standard** toolbar, or press **Alt+F** and then **O** to select the **Open** command.

One of those wonderful boxes appears. The SAMPLE1.DOC file is in the \WINWORD6\WORDCBT directory, so if you see it listed, select it. If you're not in the right directory, we're going to have to change to the \WINWORD6\WORDCBT directory, so hang on. Either scroll through the **Directories** list to locate \WINWORD6\WORDCBT and then click on it, or press **Tab** until **Directories** is highlighted, and then use the **Down arrow** key to change to the \WINWORD6\WORDCBT directory.

Now that you're in the right directory, select the SAMPLE1.DOC file. Choose **OK** to open the file. Now we're getting somewhere! Let's split the window in half:

Double-click on the **split box**, or use the S**p**lit command on the **W**indow menu.

Now let's practice moving back and forth:

Click on either pane to activate it, or press **F6** to toggle back and forth.

You can practice copying text between the two panes, but be sure *not* to save the file. When you're ready to unsplit the window, double-click on the **split box** again, or open the **W**indow menu and select the Remove S**p**lit command. To close up, double-click on the **Control-menu box**, or press **Ctrl+F4** to close the window.

The Least You Need to Know

Congratulations! You now have your Document Doctorate. Let's review what you learned:

- ☞ To open a new document window, click on the **New** button on the **Standard** toolbar, or use the **File** New command.

- ☞ To open an existing document, click on the **Open** button on the **Standard** toolbar, or use the **File** Open command.

- ☞ To return to the last editing place in a document, press **Shift+F5**.

- ☞ If you can't find a document, use the **Find File** command on the **File** menu (or within the Open dialog box). You can find a file in many ways: by name, by contents, and by date, just to name a few.

- ☞ Once you've found a file or files, you can open them, copy them, print them, or delete them. You can also preview their contents or their document summary before using them.

- ☞ You can open up to nine documents at the same time. To move to another document window, open the **Window** menu and select the document you want. If more than one window is displayed on the screen, you can click on a window, or press **Alt+F6** to make another window active.

- ☞ You can work on two sections of the same document by splitting the window into panes. Double-click on the **split box**, or open the **Window** menu and select the Split command.

- ☞ To adjust the size of the two panes, drag the split bar.

- ☞ To move between the two panes, click inside a pane to make it active, or press **F6** to toggle back and forth.

Chapter 9

Saving Your Docs for a Rainy Day

In This Chapter

- ☞ How to save a new document
- ☞ Valid names for your files
- ☞ Saving all your files with one step
- ☞ Creating a copy of a document
- ☞ Saving your documents automatically
- ☞ Closing document windows

Save a document, save a life. Okay, maybe it's not that dramatic, but by saving your documents often, you can save yourself a lot of time and trouble if something happens to your computer (such as a power failure).

If you don't want to bother with remembering to save files often, you can configure Word for Windows so it saves your files at regular intervals. If it makes things easier for your computer, you can also have Word keep track of all the changes you make to a document, and save just those changes at *periodic intervals*.

> **By the Way . . .**
>
> I like that term "periodic intervals," don't you? I try to use it often to make me sound smart: "In the morning, I need coffee at *periodic intervals*." Feel free to try it yourself: "Before I found this wonderful book to help me, I used to toss my computer against the wall at *periodic intervals*. Now I toss my computer manual."

When Should I Save a Document?

You'll always want to save your document prior to exiting Word for Windows (because otherwise, it's a goner!). But you may also want to save the document periodically during a long work session.

Any time is a great time to save your documents, but I like to save them just before I attempt some complicated task, and again when I finish that task correctly. I also save documents just prior to printing.

Knowing that you should save your documents frequently is one thing; remembering to do it is another. You can configure Word for Windows so that it saves your work for you at (ahem) periodic intervals. Stay tuned; you'll learn how later in this chapter.

File DOS stores information in files. Anything can be placed in a file: a memo, a budget report, or even a graphic image (like a picture of a boat or a computer). Each document you create in Word for Windows is stored in its own file. Files always have a *filename* to identify them.

A Document by Any Other Filename Would Still Spell As Sweet

Shakespeare would argue that there's not much in a filename, but I have to disagree. Naming your documents so you can identify them easily is an important time-saver when it comes time to locate them. DOS must agree with Shakespeare, though, because it gives you very little room to be informative when naming your *files*.

Each filename has a first and a last name. The last name (called the *extension*) helps to identify the file's type. Word for Windows uses the extension *.DOC* to identify your files as documents. You give your documents their first names, which can be as long as eight characters. Let me give you some examples:

93BUDGET.DOC

TO_DO.DOC

4THQTR.DOC

COVLETTR.DOC

WHATS_UP.DOC

RESUME.DOC

You can use letters and numbers, and even an underscore as a substitute space (you can't use actual spaces), but you can't go over eight characters. Don't worry about the extension; Word for Windows adds the .DOC extension for you.

Now that you know how to name your files, let's get down to the business of saving them.

What's Wrong with This Picture?

Joey wants to give his document a descriptive filename. The document is a sales report for the Northwest Region, so he types NORTHWEST.DOC. What's wrong with this picture?

Answer: Joey used too many letters; he can only use eight characters (excluding the three-character extension). Joey decides to call the file NW SALES.DOC instead. Now what's wrong with this picture?

Answer: Joey forgot that you can't use spaces in a filename. Joey can really use some help. Can you choose a valid filename from the list below?

NWSALESDOC

NW_SALES.DOC

N.W.SALES.DOC

Answer: NW_SALES.DOC is the only one that's valid. It has eight characters exactly (including the underscore). NWSALESDOC doesn't work because Joey didn't put the period in before the .DOC extension, so Word thinks that NWSALESDOC is the filename, and it's too long. N.W.SALES.DOC doesn't work because you can only have one period in a filename, and it goes right before the extension, as in .DOC.

There's a First Time for Everything: Saving a Document

Saving your document for the first time is a little bit more complex than saving it later on, because you must answer some basic questions (such as "What do you want to call this thing?") before Word can save your work. Here's the play-by-play:

First, select File from the main menu and choose Save, or press **Ctrl+S**. If you want to use a mouse, click on the **Save** button on the **Standard** toolbar. Then type the name for your file. Remember not to use more than eight characters. Also, you don't have to add the .DOC extension—but if you do, separate it from the filename with a period, as in CH09.DOC.

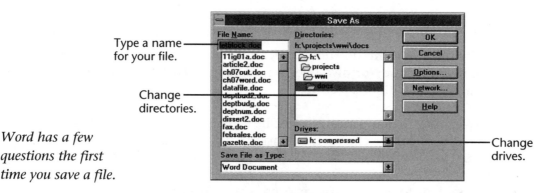

Type a name for your file.

Change directories.

Word has a few questions the first time you save a file.

Change drives.

If you want to save your file in a different drive or directory, select a different disk drive from the drop-down list box. If you need to change to another directory, click on that directory or press **Alt+D**, and then use the **Down arrow** key to select the directory.

If you want to save the document for use with another program, you may want to change the *file type*. Select a file type from the Save File as **T**ype drop-down list box.

If a file with the name you want to use already exists, Word will ask whether you want to replace the existing file. If you don't, type a different filename.

Know Your Options

There are many file-save options you should get to know. From the **Save As** dialog box, click on Options or press **Alt+O**. To select an option, click on it, or press **Alt** plus the underlined letter. Here's the lowdown on what all these options are for:

You can change these options at any time by opening the **T**ools menu, selecting the **O**ptions command, and choosing the **Save** tab.

Always Create Backup Copy   This option saves a copy of your original unchanged file with the extension *.BAK*. Useful if you need to change your mind about some changes you've made.

Allow Fast Saves   This option saves only the changes to a file, instead of the entire file. With this option, saving a file often is a quick and easy process. As a precautionary measure, periodically the entire file is saved, even when this option is in effect.

Prompt for Summary Info   If you're like me, when you start a new document, you just want to get started, so you don't stop to complete the document summary box. This option reminds you to fill it in when you save the file for the first time.

Prompt to Save NORMAL.DOT   NORMAL.DOT is the Normal template file. With this option on, you'll be prompted before changes are saved to the Normal template.

Save Native Picture Formats Only   This option saves graphic files imported from a Macintosh computer in Windows format. Using this option reduces the document's file size.

Embed True Type Fonts   "True-ly" a cool option for those of us who use fonts to dress up our documents (see Chapter 11 for more on fonts). With this option, the True Type fonts you use are incorporated into the document, so they will display even when the document is opened on a system that doesn't have that particular font. Without this option, the other system is forced to find a likely substitute, and that can affect the total look you were trying to achieve when you selected the original font in the first place.

Save Data Only for Forms   This option saves the data you keyed into a Word form in a format that's compatible with common database programs.

Automatic Save Every _____ Minutes   You won't have to worry when a storm shuts down your computer's power if you've saved your data recently. But if you're the kind of person who gets so involved in working that you forget to save, you may want to have Word save your changes automatically. Use this option to put Word on "automatic." Type the number of minutes you want Word to wait between automatic saves. You can enter any number between 1 and 120, but I recommend 10 or 15 minutes.

File Sharing Options   To protect your document against changes, use this option. You can make this document *password protected* (no one can open the document without the password of up to 15 characters), and/or *lock it for viewing only* (others can open the document and view it, but they can't change the text). You can choose **Read-Only** Recommended, which means that a person can open and edit your document, but they will see a message advising them not to make changes.

By the Way . . .

Once you protect a document, no one but you can make changes to it. How does Word distinguish who you are? Well, when a document is saved, an author's name is inserted into the Summary Info box and stored with the file. When you open a protected file later, Word checks the name in the user information area against the summary information. You can change the name of the Word "user" by opening the **Tools** menu and selecting **Options**. Select the **User Info** tab, then change the name and click on **OK**.

By the way, if you are the author of a document, you always have full access to it—so, if you want to "unprotect" the document later on, you have the right to do so. Just use the **File Save As** command, click on the **Options** button, and change the password protection.

Whew. Now that you're done, press **Enter** or click on **OK**, and Word for Windows returns you to the Save As dialog box. Press **Enter** or click on **OK** again, and Word saves the document with the name you specified.

Put It to Work

 Now you can save that award-winning document you created in the last chapter. (If you skipped the *Put It to Work*, do not pass Go or collect $200!)

With the document open, click on the **Save** button on the **Standard** toolbar, or press **Ctrl+S**. Enter a name for the file, such as **SCOTTAWD.DOC**. In the next chapter, we'll print our award.

Saving It All

You can save all your open documents in one fell swoop by using the Save All command on the File menu. Using this command saves other files (such as customized dictionaries) as well.

Don't leave document windows open if you're done with them; they just add to screen clutter and make it more difficult to work. (I'm writing this as I search for a disk under tons of paper and other stuff on my desk. I thought you'd appreciate the irony.) Close document windows when you're through (after saving them first, of course!). Also, if you continue working on your document after saving it, remember to save the file *again* before you exit Word or close the document's window.

To close a document's window, save the document first (okay, enough already!), then open the **File** menu and select **Close**, or double-click on the document's **Control-menu box**.

Saving Once, Saving Twice

After a file has been saved for the first time, whenever you use the **File Save** command or the Save button, your document is simply saved to the disk with the same name you used when you first saved it. This process updates the existing file with the changes you've made.

But what if you're creating a revision to a document, and you want to save this version under a new name? To save a document under a different filename, you need its birth certificate, Social Security card, several IRS tax forms, and the Save As command.

First, select File from the main menu, and choose the Save As command. If you want a quicker method, simply press **F12**, and a dialog box appears. (Do *not* use the Save button on the Standard toolbar, because it just saves the file without allowing you to make any changes.) Don't think you've gone crazy; this is the same box that appears when you first save a file. Why should Word use two boxes when one will do?

Next, type the new name for your file. Remember not to use more than eight characters. Also, you don't have to add the .DOC extension, but if you do, separate it from the filename with a period, as in CH09.DOC.

If you want to save this copy of your file in a different drive or directory, select a different disk drive from the Drives drop-down list box. If you need to change to another directory, click on that directory or press **Alt+D**, then use the **Down arrow** key to select a directory.

Since this is the same dialog box, if you want to save this copy for use with another program, protect your document against changes, or unprotect it, follow the directions given earlier. When you're done, press **Enter** or click on **OK**, and Word for Windows saves the document with the name you specified.

You can make copies of several files at one time with the Find File command. Refer to Chapter 8 if you need a refresher.

Before closing a document, you should save it. When you exit Word for Windows, all files are closed automatically, so you should save your files before you quit.

Closing a Document and Going Home

My mom was always yelling at us to close the door: "Do you think I want to heat the outside?" Along that same vein, you should close document windows after you're finished working with them. Of course, you probably won't have your mother to remind you, but remembering to close windows when you're through will eliminate clutter and make it easier for you to work.

Be careful not to double-click on the bigger square just above the document window's Control-menu box; that will cause you to exit Word for Windows.

To close the active document window, double-click on its **Control-menu box** (that's the square with a dash in it, in the upper left corner of the *document* window). If you are using a keyboard, press **Ctrl+W** to close the active document window.

If you have more than one document open, the other windows will be unaffected by your actions.

The Least You Need to Know

As we bring this chapter to a "close," let's review what we've learned:

- ☛ Always save your documents before exiting Word for Windows, and before and after any complicated task. It's also a good idea to save your document prior to printing.

- ☛ Filenames consist of up to eight characters, with a three-character extension. Word for Windows documents use a .DOC extension, as in CH09.DOC.

- ☛ To save a document, click on the **Save** button on the **Standard** toolbar.

- ☛ You can save a copy of your current document under a new name with the Save **As** command on the **File** menu.

- ☛ To set up Word for Windows so it saves documents automatically, use the **O**ptions button within the **Save As** dialog box, or open the **T**ools menu, select the **O**ptions command, and choose the **Save** tab.

- ☛ You can close a document window after you've saved the file, and get it out of your way. To close a document window, double-click on the window's **Control-menu box.**

Chapter 10
Hold the Presses, It's Time to Print!

In This Chapter

- ☛ Printing your document
- ☛ Selecting certain pages or text to print
- ☛ Printing just the current page
- ☛ Printing multiple copies of a document
- ☛ Changing the orientation of the printed page
- ☛ Printing an envelope
- ☛ What to do when your printer is having a bad day
- ☛ Selecting the printer to use

There's nothing better than holding the result of your hard work in your own hands. After I've wrestled with Word for hours trying to get a document to look exactly the way I want, I get this overpowering feeling to jump up and say, "See? I did this!"

You might be experiencing something like this now, since your document is just about ready to print. In this chapter, you'll learn how to do just that, and if you experience any problems along the way, there's a troubleshooting section at the end of the chapter to help you out.

A Sneak Preview Is a Good Idea Before You Print

Before you print your document, you should look at it in Print Preview or Page Layout view. These two viewing modes show you what your document will look like when printed, so you can make sure that everything is the way you want it *before you print*. In Print Preview, it's a bit more difficult to make text changes, so choose the viewing mode that best suits your needs. If you need a re-"view" of viewing modes, see Chapter 7.

The Printed Word

It's always a good idea to save a document before you print it, in case you run into printer errors or other problems. Click on the **Save** button on the **Standard** toolbar, or use the Save command on the File menu. (You can also press **Ctrl+S** to save the current document.)

Printing the active document is easy if you want to print the entire document, and you want only one copy of it. Later in this chapter, you'll learn how you can be selective in what you're printing. But for now, let's start with the basics.

To print a document with the mouse, just click on the **Print** button on the **Standard** toolbar. The active document will start printing according to the *print defaults*—Word's out-of-the-box settings which specify printing just one copy of the entire document. If you want to print more than one copy (or less than the entire document), you'll need to use the File **Print** command described next.

OOPS!

If you need to stop the print job while Word for Windows is still processing it, press **Esc**. If the printer runs out of paper, a dialog box will appear and tell you so. You'll be able to choose Retry or Cancel. Load more paper, then choose **Retry**.

To print the current document using the keyboard, select the **Print** command on the File menu, or press **Ctrl+P**. A dialog box appears when you use this command, allowing you to change the print defaults (such as the number of copies you want). In later sections of this chapter, you'll learn what each of these options is for—but if you just want to print one copy of the entire document, press **Enter** and that's it!

If you have problems printing, check out the troubleshooting section later in this chapter.

> ## Put It to Work
>
> If you've been following along for the last two chapters, then you've created a mighty fine award for someone special, and you've saved it. The only thing that's left now is to print it.
>
> With the document open, click on the **Print** button on the **Standard** toolbar, or press **Ctrl+P**. There you go!

Printing Part of a Document

You can print only certain pages in a document if you want. For example, maybe one page was misprinted and you want to reprint it with corrections, or perhaps you need only one section of a complex document. Here's what to do.

You can print several documents, one after the other, using the Find File command. See Chapter 8 for the lowdown on this nifty option.

Select the Print command from the File menu. (Do not use the Print button on the toolbar; by default, it prints *all* the pages of a document.) Surprise! It's a box.

Enter the page numbers to print.

You can print only part of a document if you want.

To print selected pages using Word 2.0, enter the beginning page number in the **F**rom box, press **Tab**, then enter the ending page number in the **T**o box. You cannot print non-consecutive ranges in Word 2.0.

If you have a printer that allows you to select the number of copies to print on some kind of control panel, you may want to use that option instead of having Word print your copies for you. When Word prints multiple copies, it reprocesses the document over and over, using more time than your printer would to print the same number of copies.

First, click on Pages or press **Alt+G**. Now you need to do some typing. Type a single page number (such as *2*), a page range (for example: **5-7**), or a combination of the two separated by commas (for example: **3,5-7**). When you're done, choose **OK**.

As an alternative, you can print the current page by choosing Curr**e**nt Page or pressing **Alt+E**. You can print selected text by highlighting it first (see Chapter 6 for a review) and choosing Selectio**n**, or by pressing **Alt+N**.

I'll Take Two!

If you need more than one copy of your document, Word can print it for you, and save you time standing in the copier line.

Start out by selecting the **Print** command from the File menu. (Do not use the Print button on the toolbar; by default, it prints only one copy of a document.) When that dialog box appears, type the number of copies you want under Copies. If you're using the keyboard, press **Alt+C** to move to Copies, and then type your number.

If you choose Collate Copies, Word for Windows not only slices and dices, but it collates, too—by printing all of one copy first, and then all of the next. When you're completely finished, choose **OK**.

The Great American Landscape Mode

You can print your document in *Portrait* mode or *Landscape* mode.

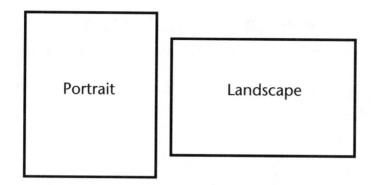

To change the orientation of pages within your document, just follow along with me.

First, open the File menu and choose the Page Setup command. Keyboarders: press **Alt+F**, then **U**. Next, click on the Paper **S**ize tab. If you're using a keyboard, press **Alt+S**.

Now it's time to pick a page orientation. Click on either the Portrait or the Landscape option button. If you're using a keyboard, press **Alt+I** or **Alt+C**. Then, in the Apply To drop-down list box, select a portion of the document that you want this change to affect. You can choose from options such as Whole Document, Selected Text, and This Point Forward. For example, if you have a table on page two that you want to print in Landscape mode, but you want the rest of the report printed in Portrait mode, simply move the insertion point to page two, and select **This Point Forward**. If your report has a page three, move to page three, switch back to **Portrait** orientation, and again select **This Point Forward**. When you're finished, choose **OK**.

Portrait orientation   Your document is oriented so that it is longer than it is wide, as in 8½ by 11 inches. This is the normal orientation of most documents.

Landscape orientation Your document is oriented so that it is wider than it is long, as in 11 by 8½ inches.

To print an envelope in Word 2.0, simply click on the **Envelope** button located on the **toolbar**, or use the Create Envelope command on the Tools menu.

If your address appeared in the return area, it could be that you've done this before, and saved it (Word remembers your return address after you enter it just once). Another explanation is that you entered the address under the **User Info** tab with the **Tools Options** command.

The Envelope, Please

Word makes it incredibly easy to prepare an envelope for a letter. The only thing that you'll find hard about this is getting your printer to print the darn thing—so I'll give you some tips in a moment. First, the easy part.

If you've included more than one address in your letter, start out by selecting the delivery address. If you didn't include an address in your letter (or if you included *just the delivery address*), that's okay—just skip this step.

Select the Envelopes and Labels command on the Tools menu (for keyboard, press **Alt+T**, then **E**). When the dialog box appears, if you didn't select an address earlier, you'll have to type one in the Delivery Address box.

Next, enter your return address by clicking in the Return Address box or by pressing **Tab**. (Your address may have appeared already; I'll explain how this magic trick was done in just a moment.) The first time you use this option, Word will ask whether you want to save the return address. Click on Yes or press **Enter** to save it. If you have special envelopes and you don't want to print a return address, then use the **Omit** check box. If you're using a keyboard, press **Alt+M** to check this box.

Before we print our envelope, let's check some of the options. Click on the Options button or press **Alt+O**. If you want, you can change the *font* for both the delivery and the return address. Click on the appropriate option, or press **Alt+F** for the delivery address, and **Alt+O** for the return address. (You'll learn more about fonts in Chapter 11.)

Finally, check the envelope size. Make sure that the correct size is selected in the Envelope Size box. To change sizes, click on the **down arrow** to open the list box, or press **Alt+S**. Select an envelope size by clicking on it (or highlighting it with the **arrow** keys and pressing **Enter**).

If you need to verify the *feed options* (the method used to insert the envelope in the printer), click on the Printing Options tab or press **Ctrl+Tab**. Select an appropriate option, and click on **OK** or press **Enter**.

You can print it now, or you can print it later. If you want to print the envelope now, use the **Print** button (if you're using a keyboard, press **Alt+P**). Use the Add To Document button to print the envelope later, at the same time you print the document (to print just the envelope at some later date, print page **0** only). Click on the button or press **Alt+A** to add the envelope to the document.

Font   Any set of characters which share the same *typeface* (style or design). Fonts convey the mood and style of a document. Technically, font describes the combination of the *typeface* and the *point size* of a character, as in Times Roman 12-point, but in common usage it describes only a character's style or typeface.

Some Quick Tips for Printing Envelopes

If you have a laser printer:

- ☛ You pretty much need a special thing called an *envelope feeder*. If you don't have one, check your manual for instructions on how to feed an envelope in some kind of "straight-through" path that bypasses the nasty twists and turns that normal paper takes through your laser.

- ☛ Check your manual to see if the envelope is supposed to be inserted in the center of the feed slot or against one edge (lasers vary on how they want this done).

- ☛ Most important of all: don't skimp on quality. Buy envelopes that are made for a laser. Other envelopes practically melt from the heat, and really gum up the works (if you don't mind the pun).

If you have a dot-matrix printer:

- ☛ Line up the left edge of the envelope against the left edge of the paper feed.

- ☛ Move the tractor feed so the top edge of the envelope is even with the print head. Word will move the envelope up about a half inch before it prints anything, so don't worry that your address will fall off the edge.

Printer Jams and Other Problems You Might Encounter

There is probably nothing more frustrating than coaxing a reluctant printer to spit out some text. After putting all your hard work into creating the perfect report, the last thing you want to deal with is a problem printer. If you encounter problems, check the printer cables to be sure they're plugged in tight, and verify that the printer is on and on-line (look for a button labeled *on-line, ready,* or *select,* which controls this). Here are some other things to watch out for:

If you get a message from Word asking if you want to retry, examine the reason for the error. If the printer wasn't on, turn it on and then retry the print job. If the printer ran out of paper, replace it and retry. If the printer jammed, retry if you have a laser, but cancel if you have a dot-matrix. (A laser printer has a better memory than a dot-matrix, and can pick up where it left off.)

If you get something to print, but it looks like the printer is on drugs, you may not have the printer set up for use with Windows. Or if you have more than one printer, you may have chosen the wrong printer for this document. An upcoming section talks about how to choose a printer.

Now, some specifics you can try, depending on the type of printer you have.

If You Have a Laser Printer

Use the right paper and load it correctly. Use special laser paper (I recommend 20-lb. and not a cheaper type of paper). Laser paper has a texture that is easier for the laser printer to grab as it moves through the printer. Do not use stuff that isn't specifically designed for a laser printer; use *laser* labels, *laser* transparencies, etc. Colored paper is okay, but avoid papers with dusty surfaces.

When the paper gets jammed (stuck), remove it. Pop it open and carefully remove the errant page, just as you would with a copier.

My laser printer seems okay, but nothing is coming out. You may need to form-feed (eject) the paper by taking the printer off-line (press the **On-Line** button) and then press the **Form Feed** button. Then press the **On-Line** button again to put the printer back into service. This should get the paper to come out.

Watch out for hot parts—a laser printer is full of them. Most are labeled with warnings, but be safe: try not to touch any part unless absolutely necessary.

Usually laser printers will only eject a page when that page is full. (I wish someone had told me that when I first got my laser!)

If You Have a Dot-Matrix Printer

Use the right paper and load it correctly. Be sure that the continuous-feed paper (if you use it) is not caught on anything, and that the perforation between pages is just barely above the print head when the printer is turned on.

When the paper gets jammed (stuck), remove it. If you have a dot-matrix printer, turn it off. Use the print knob to back the paper out. Avoid the urge to rip the paper out. It'll tear and you'll spend the rest of the day with a pair of tweezers trying to pick out the last remnants.

Everything is printing on one smeary line of ink. Your printer isn't getting the order from the computer to advance the paper before it prints the next line. You can fix this by flipping a small switch called a *DIP switch*. The DIP switch is usually located in some "convenient location," such as the back of your printer, or even inside. Look in your manual for the location of the DIP switches. Each switch has a particular purpose, and the one you're interested in is called "LF after CR" or "Add linefeed" or some such. Turn your printer off, flip the switch, and then turn the printer on and try again.

Everything is coming out double-spaced even though it's single-spaced in Word for Windows. This problem is the opposite of the single smeary line of ink. Only this time, the computer is sending the order to advance the paper, and the printer is adding its own advance. Locate the "LF after CR" or "Add linefeed" DIP switch, turn your printer off, flip the switch, and then try printing again.

Print Manager starts itself when you print a document, and closes itself when it's done printing—though there's an exception to this rule. If you open the Print Manager window (by double-clicking on its minimized icon, or by selecting it from the Task List), and then re-minimize it after the print jobs are completed, Print Manager will remain open and minimized until you close it or exit Windows. Why? Who knows? It's just one of those things.

Printers and the Wonderful World of Windows

All the printing for Word for Windows is actually handled by another Windows program, the Print Manager. When you installed Windows, you told the Print Manager what kind of printer you had. When you print a document in Word for Windows, it simply packages it up and sends it to the Print Manager, and the Print Manager sends it to your printer.

When you're printing a document within Word for Windows, and the **Printing** message disappears from the screen, your print job has been turned over to Print Manager. So if you have any further problems, you need to go there to handle them.

The Print Manager's best feature is that you can pretty much forget about it. Once a printer is set up for Windows, it's set up for *all* Windows-based programs, including Word for Windows. Print Manager also is adept at handling multiple print jobs, so you don't need to wait until a printer is done printing before you start working again or print another document.

Although this book is not about how to use Windows, it's kind of hard to avoid the subject, since you're using a Windows program. Here are some quick steps for cancelling a print job within Print Manager. If you "don't do Windows," refer to Chapter 3 for help in deciphering these instructions.

From within Word for Windows, press **Ctrl+Esc** to bring up the Task List. Select **Print Manager**. While Print Manager still has print jobs waiting to print, its little tiny icon will appear at the bottom of your Windows desktop. So as an alternative to using the Task List, you can open Print Manager from your desktop. Double-click on that icon to open the Print Manager window just as you would any other window.

All the current print jobs will be displayed. If you want to start a print job over because the paper jammed (or for some other reason), just highlight the job you want to cancel and then click on **Delete**.

Default printer The printer that was set up when Windows was installed.

You can do other fancy stuff while you're here—such as reordering the priority of print jobs (just drag the print job to wherever you want it to be in the print queue), or temporarily stopping and resuming the operation of the printer (use the **Pause** and **Resume** buttons).

Minimize the Print Manager window when you're done (click on the **Minimize** button). CAUTION: If you *close* Print Manager at this point, you'll cancel all the jobs waiting to be printed.

Embarrassment of Riches: Choosing from Several Printers

If you're lucky enough to have a choice of printers to use, you should tell Word for Windows *when you start a new document* which printer you'll want to use later when you print. If you don't specify, Word will use the *default printer.*

To change the default printer that's used with Word for Windows, open the File menu and choose the **Print** command, or press **Ctrl+P**. When the dialog box appears, click on Printer, or press **Alt+T**. Click on the printer you wish to make the default, or press **Alt+P** and use the **arrow** keys to highlight one. Click on **Set as Default Printer**, or press **Alt+D**. Choose Close or press **Enter** when you're done. Choose **OK** to print your document, or click on Close. If the printer you want to use is not listed, you will need to install the printer through the Windows Control Panel. Get someone to help you.

The Least You Need to Know

Sometimes getting your document to print can be pretty irritating, but the whole process will go a bit smoother if you remember these things:

- ☛ Before you print your document, you may want to view it first, in either Page Layout or Print Preview mode.

- ☛ Before you print, save your document by clicking on the **Save** button on the **Standard** toolbar.

- ☛ To print one copy of all pages of the document, click on the **Print** button on the **Standard** toolbar.

- ☛ Use the **Print** command on the **File** menu to print selected pages or text within a document.

- ☛ You can also use the **Print** command on the **File** menu to print multiple copies of your document.

- ☛ Use the **Page Setup** command on the **File** menu to change between Portrait and Landscape orientation, for all pages or selected pages of a document.

- ☛ Use the **Envelopes and Labels** command on the **Tools** menu to prepare an envelope for your letter.

- ☛ If you want to cancel a print job or change the priority of a print job, use Print Manager to do it.

- ☛ If you have more than one printer available, select the printer to use with the **File Print** command. After the dialog box opens, click on Printer and select the printer you want to use.

Part II
Document Beauty Makeovers

The irony about using makeup is that most women spend hours trying to look as if they haven't done anything at all. I think of formatting as "makeup" for a document, and in this section I'll show you how to apply it. And believe me, if you spend two hours formatting a document, someone will definitely notice.

Chapter 11

Developing Your Character(s): Changing How Text Looks

In This Chapter

- ☛ Choosing the font (typeface) of text
- ☛ Quick ways to change the size of text
- ☛ Selecting various character formats, such as bold or underline
- ☛ Changing multiple formats at one time
- ☛ Copying character formatting to other text

Character formatting is the process of changing how text looks. For example, through character formatting you can make a word bold or underlined. You can also change the size of text (its *point size*), making it bigger or smaller. And you can change its style by choosing a different *font*.

Character formatting can be used to make titles, headings, and individual words stand out. Use character formatting to emphasize a point, create a mood, and visually organize your documents. (End of commercial; we now return you to our regularly scheduled chapter.)

The font you select determines the mood of your document.

Paragon font

Courier New font

Paradise font

Mystical font

Font   Any set of characters that share the same *typeface* (style or design). Examples are Times Roman and Ariel. Technically, "font" describes the combination of the typeface and the point size of a character, as in *Times Roman 12-point*, but many people use it to describe only a character's style or typeface.

Point size   The type size of a particular character. There are 72 points in an inch.

You can quickly remove all character formatting—such as bold or underline and even font and point size— by selecting the text and pressing **Ctrl+Spacebar**.

You can apply character formatting as you type a word or a heading, or you can go back later and select the text and change its formatting. (I use both methods, depending on my mood.) If you change character formatting as you type, remember to turn it off when you finish typing the text you want to affect. (Think of it as a light switch; if you turn it on, you have to turn it off.) If you go back and select text, only the text you select is changed.

You can also use either the mouse or the keyboard to change character formatting. Again, I use a combination of both, depending on what I'm doing at the time.

If you want the formatting to apply to existing text, you first must select the text. Drag the mouse over the text to select it, or press and hold the **Shift** key as you use the **arrow** keys to highlight the text. Next, choose the formatting you want. More about this in a minute.

If you don't select text first, then the formatting you turn on will apply to the rest of the document until you turn it off. Turn off the text format by selecting it again; you can then continue typing.

Font Memories: Changing the Text Style

The type of font you use helps to set the style of your document: is it fun and light, or crisp and businesslike? One tip if you're new to fonts—don't overdo it (it's very easy, believe me). At most you may want to use only two or three font styles: one or two for different headings, and one for text. Vary the size of text (point size) to create sections in your document, rather than choosing a different font (typeface).

If you have more than one printer, make sure you select the correct printer before you start working; the printer that's selected determines the fonts that Word for Windows makes available to you as you work. Change from printer to printer with the **File Print** command, the Printer option. Back up to the previous chapter for more details.

Remember that you can change the font and point size of text—either before you enter it, or after the fact—by selecting the text and then following these steps:

Some fonts look different on-screen from the way they look when printed. To be sure that you're getting what you want, use the Windows fonts, which are available to all Windows programs (including Word for Windows). You can easily identify these *TrueType* fonts, because they have a little "TT" in front of their names. If you're trying to decide what font to use, use a TrueType font; it will print as you see it on the screen.

Select a font from this box.   Available point sizes for this font

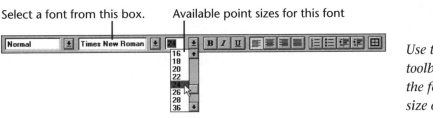

Use the Formatting toolbar to change the font and point size of text.

The steps listed here are pretty much the same for Word 2.0, but keep in mind that the "Formatting toolbar" was called the "Ribbon" in Word 2.0. Keyboard commands are a bit different too. For example, to access the Font box with the keyboard in Word 2.0, press **Ctrl+F**. To access the Point box, press **Ctrl+P**.

When you remove all character formatting by pressing **Ctrl+Spacebar**, your text takes on the characteristics of the Normal style, which is (unless you've changed it) Times Roman 10-point text. You'll learn more about styles in Chapter 14.

If you have a mouse, click on the arrow to the right of the **Font** drop-down list box (on the **Formatting** toolbar) to open it. Select a font by clicking on it. Change the point size in the same way: click on the arrow to the right of the **Point** box, and click on an available point size.

If you want to use your keyboard instead, press **Ctrl+Shift+F** to open the Font box, use the **arrow** keys to highlight a font, and then press **Enter**. Press **Ctrl+Shift+P** to open the **Point** box, and follow the same basic procedure: use the **arrow** keys to highlight a point size, and press **Enter**.

If you're typing text, remember to change the font and point size back to normal later on. Just repeat these steps again to change it back.

What's Wrong with This Picture?

Beth wanted to impress her boss with her department budget report, so she typed the upper report shown on the following page. What's wrong with it?

Answer: If you said, "She's used too many fonts," you're right! Look at the lower report. This one uses only two fonts, one for the headings, one for the text. The size of the second heading is reduced to indicate that it's a subheading.

Department Budget Report

This month, we managed to take more calls, handle more special requests, and yet we didn't use a lot of overtime. I think you'll be pleased with the numbers: (see Attachment.)

As you can see, we did very well at increasing our volume while decreasing our costs. How did we do it? With the training I was able to provide my employees, they responded by handling calls faster and more efficiently. Jane, Pat, and Bill did an especially outstanding job.

How Can We Maintain This Trend?

I propose that we install a new telephone messaging system, such as the Caller 2000. This will allow me to direct the volume of calls to the fastest workers, increasing the chances of our clients reaching a representative. Also, with the Caller 2000, a customized message system will allow the caller to pick and choose from several options, so they reach the department they want with the least amount of hassle.

Department Budget Report

This month, we managed to take more calls, handle more special requests, and yet we didn't use a lot of overtime. I think you'll be pleased with the numbers (See Attachment.)

As you can see, we did very well at increasing our volume while decreasing our costs. How did we do it? With the training I was able to provide my employees, they responded by handling calls faster and more efficiently. Jane, Pat, and Bill did an especially outstanding job.

How Can We Maintain This Trend?

I propose that we install a new telephone messaging system, such as the Caller 2000. This will allow me to direct the volume of calls to the fastest workers, increasing the chances of our clients reaching a representative. Also, with the Caller 2000, a customized message system will allow the caller to pick and choose from several options, so they reach the department they want with the least amount of hassle.

The Incredible Shrinking Text

You can increase or decrease the point size of text to the next available size by pressing these keys:

If the Formatting toolbar is not displayed, use the **View Toolbars** command to display it, or click on the **Standard** toolbar with the *right* mouse button, and select it off the shortcut menu.

To make text one size bigger, press **Ctrl+Shift+>** (greater-than symbol).

To make text one size smaller, press **Ctrl+Shift+<** (less-than symbol).

The amount of change will depend on the font you are using. Some fonts jump several points in size, such as 10, 12, 14, while others may go up one point at a time as in 10, 11, 12. It all depends on the font you're using. You can increase or decrease text by a single point size if you want:

To make text bigger in Word 2.0, press **Ctrl+F2**. To make it smaller, press **Ctrl+Shift+F2**.

To make text one point size bigger, press **Ctrl+]** (right bracket).

To make text one point size smaller, press **Ctrl+[** (left bracket).

Making a Bold Statement (or Italic, Underlined, Etc.)

There are many different kinds of character formatting:

Bold	*Italic*	~~Strikethrough~~
Hidden (not printed)	SMALL CAPS	ALL CAPS
Single (continuous)Underline	Word Underline	Double Underline
Super^script	Sub_script	Dotted Underline

For extra emphasis, you can "combine" any of these formats to create words that are (for example) bold and underlined, or italic double-underlined. Word supports only one kind of underline per character, however, so you can't have such combinations as double-word underline.

Mouseketeers: How to Change Character Formatting

Because there are so many ways to select the character format you want, I thought it would be helpful to include the details in separate sections for keyboard and mouse. First, the mouse ways.

If you want to make something bold, underlined, or italic, just click on the appropriate button on the **Formatting** toolbar. You can make text bold italic (for example) by clicking on both buttons.

Click here for bold.   Click here for underline.

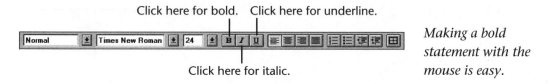

Making a bold statement with the mouse is easy.

Click here for italic.

If you want to make text anything else (such as strikethrough or double underline), you need to access the Font dialog box with the Format Font command. This box also allows you to change the font and point size, among other things. It will be covered in detail later in this chapter.

> ### By the Way . . .
> I normally change text to bold, italic, or single underline with the mouse. If I want to change text to something else, such as strikethrough, I use the keyboard steps shown in the next section because they're more convenient (and fairly easy to remember). I reserve the Font dialog box for times when I want to make multiple changes to the same text, such as changing font, point size, *and* emphasis by making it bold and underlined.

The Format Font command is called the Format Character command in Word 2.0, and some of the keyboard shortcuts are different. For example, to format text in word underline, press **Ctrl+W**. Double underline is accessed by pressing **Ctrl+D**, small caps by pressing **Ctrl+K**, and all caps by pressing **Ctrl+A**. Strikethrough is accessed by pressing **Ctrl+Shift+S**, hidden text by pressing **Ctrl+H**, superscript by pressing **Ctrl+Shift+equals sign**, and subscript by pressing **Ctrl+equals sign**.

Keyboarders: How to Change Character Formatting

In addition to using the keyboard method for certain types of character formatting, I also use it when I'm changing one or two words in a sentence, and don't want to take my fingers off the keyboard. Here are the key combinations for all the character formats:

To Change Characters to	Press
Bold	Ctrl+B
Italic	Ctrl+I
Single Underline	Ctrl+U
Word Underline	Ctrl+Shift+W
Double Underline	Ctrl+Shift+D
Small Caps	Ctrl+Shift+K
All Caps	Ctrl+Shift+A
Hidden	Ctrl+Shift+H
Superscript	Ctrl+Shift+=
Subscript	Ctrl+=

Remember that these key combinations let you select text first and *then* change it, if you want to. If you use this method as you type, remember to press the same keys again to turn that character formatting off. Also, to apply combination character formats (such as bold italic), press **Ctrl+B** and then **Ctrl+I**.

To change capitalization, you can toggle through all caps, all lowercase, initial cap, and initial lowercase by selecting text and pressing **Shift+F3**. I use this when I type a heading too quickly and I've forgotten to capitalize everything.

Put It to Work

Practice Making a Heading

Let's practice what we've learned so far about character formatting. Type something appropriately grand for a heading, such as **The Big Pompous Heading** or **Look, Here's Something You Don't Want to Miss.**

Select the heading quickly by double-clicking in the **selection bar** (our invisible selection buddy that's located to the left of every paragraph).

B Let's start by making it bold. With the heading selected, click on the **Bold** button on the **Formatting** toolbar, or press **Ctrl+B**.

U Next, add single underline to our heading by clicking on the **Underline** button or pressing **Ctrl+U**.

Times New Roman **10** Let's change the font by clicking on the **Formatting** toolbar or pressing **Ctrl+Shift+F**. If you have several choices, try a few of them out for fun. Next, change the point size of the text to something big—click on the **Point Size** list box on the **Formatting** toolbar, or press **Ctrl+Shift+P**. (Normal text is usually 10-point, so try **20** or something even larger.)

Hide and Seek: Using Hidden Text

Hidden text is kind of a neat option, so I thought I'd tell you more about it. To make some text hidden, select it and press **Ctrl+Shift+H**. You can see hidden text displayed on your screen, but it's not printed when you print your document, at least not usually. . . .

You control whether hidden text will be displayed on your screen with the **Options** command on the Tools menu. So if your text just went bye-bye (you can't see it on-screen), click on the **View** tab or press **Ctrl+Tab** until it's selected. Then under Nonprinting Characters, toggle the Hidden Text check box on, and choose **OK**.

Hidden text does not print, even if it's displayed on your screen. You can get hidden text to print if you need it to by once again choosing the Options command on the Tools menu. Click the **Print** tab, or press **Ctrl+Tab** until it is selected. Under Include with Document, turn the Hidden Text option on, and choose **OK**. One warning: *displaying or printing* hidden text can throw off page numbering when you view or print your document, so keep that in mind when you use it.

If you have a favorite font, why not make it the default? Use the **Font** dialog to make your selection, then click on **Default** or press **Alt+D**.

Mix and Match: Selecting Multiple Formats at One Time

Whenever I want to make a lot of changes to some text, I use the Font dialog box. To get to this box, open the Format menu and select Font. If you prefer the keyboard, press **Alt+O**, then **F**.

Use the Font dialog box to select multiple character formats.

This works like any other dialog box: click on items to choose them, or press **Alt** plus the underlined letter to move from place to place; use the **arrow** keys and the **Spacebar** to select items. As you make your selections, the Preview box shows you what your text is going to look like—which is a really nice feature, in my opinion.

You can use the Font box to change the color of your text (the default color is black). Of course, this works best if you have a printer that prints color; it's a nice feature to play around with if you do. You can still use color on-screen, even if you don't have a color printer; this is a good way to display on your screen the editing changes made by someone else.

> ## Put It to Work
> ### Playing with That Heading Again
>
> Select the heading you created earlier, and this time we'll use the Font dialog box to make additional changes.
>
> Select the **F**ormat **F**ont command to make the genie appear. Let's change our underline type to **double underline** by selecting it from the **U**nderline drop-down list box.
>
> Watch the Preview box change to see how your heading will look. Make some additional changes—have fun! If you don't want to keep them, click on **Cancel**; otherwise click on **OK**. The Font box makes it easy to change your mind, but it slows you down when you're making simple changes (like applying bold formatting). Pick the method that's right for you, or use them all (like I do).

When You've Got It Right, Copy It

If you want to repeat the character formatting you just applied, use the **R**epeat Formatting command to apply it to another section of text. Select the text you want to copy the formatting to (or move the insertion point to a place where you want new text with this formatting to appear when you type). Open the Edit menu and select **R**epeat Formatting, or simply press **F4**.

The **R**epeat Formatting command repeats only the last formatting step, so if you used the Formatting toolbar or the keyboard commands to change a word to Ariel font, then bold, the **R**epeat Formatting command will copy only bold formatting onto the next text you select.

If you use the Font dialog box to apply multiple formats in a single step, then the **R**epeat Formatting command *will copy all the formats.*

To copy formatting in Word 2.0, press **F4**, or you can follow these mouse steps: first, move the insertion point to the place *to which* you want to copy the formatting, then point at the text whose formatting you wish to copy, then hold the **Ctrl** and **Shift** keys down as you click.

 You can copy multiple formats from one piece of text to another with the Format Painter button on the **Standard** toolbar. First, select the text you want to copy. Then click on the **Format Painter** button, or press **Ctrl+Shift+C**. Click on a word (or drag over a section of text) to copy the formatting. If you use the keyboard, move the insertion point to a word (or select a section of text), then press **Ctrl+Shift+V**. To copy formatting to multiple sections of text (sorry keyboarders, this requires a mouse) double-click the Format Painter button, then continue to click or drag over text to format it. When you're done, press **Esc**, or click on the **Format Painter** button again.

The Least You Need to Know

All words and no character formatting make a document a pretty dull thing. Yours will sparkle with these tips:

- ☞ You can change character formatting either before you type or after you type (by selecting it).

- ☞ Use the **Formatting** toolbar to change the font and point size quickly.

- ☞ To make text one size bigger, select it and press **Ctrl+Shift+>**. To make it one size smaller, press **Ctrl+Shift+<**. To increase a font's size by a single point, press **Ctrl+]**. To decrease the size by a point, press **Ctrl+[**.

- ☞ **B** **I** **U** If you use a mouse, change text to bold, italic, or single underline by clicking on the appropriate button on the **Formatting** toolbar.

☛ To change text with the keyboard, use the proper key combination—usually **Ctrl** or **Ctrl+Shift** plus some other letter, such as **B** for Bold.

☛ To select multiple formats at once, use the **Format Font** command.

☛ 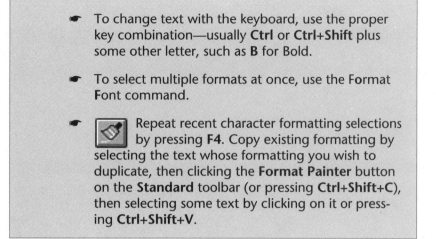 Repeat recent character formatting selections by pressing **F4**. Copy existing formatting by selecting the text whose formatting you wish to duplicate, then clicking the **Format Painter** button on the **Standard** toolbar (or pressing **Ctrl+Shift+C**), then selecting some text by clicking on it or pressing **Ctrl+Shift+V**.

This page unintentionally left blank.

Chapter 12
Beauty and the Paragraph

In This Chapter

- The true meaning of the word "paragraph"
- Aligning paragraphs with the margins
- Changing a paragraph's indents
- Creating a hanging indent
- Changing the spacing before and after paragraphs
- Adjusting the amount of line spacing within paragraphs
- Copying paragraph formatting

You'll want to change the way paragraphs look for many reasons: to create centered headings, indented paragraphs, a right-aligned address, and bulleted or numbered lists. In this chapter, you'll learn how to turn your "beasts" into "beauties."

Webster's Gonna Get a Bit Confused by This

Here is the meaning of the word "paragraph" according to Webster's:

A subdivision of a written composition that consists of one or more sentences, deals with one point, or gives the words of one speaker.

Okay, now forget that definition. In Word for Windows, a *paragraph* is any collection of text or graphics that ends in a carriage return (that is, a pressing of Enter). This includes normal paragraphs, as well as single-line paragraphs, such as chapter titles, section headings, and captions for charts or other figures. When you press **Enter** in Word for Windows, you are marking the end of a paragraph.

You'll know paragraph marks are there when you delete one accidentally and the paragraph takes on the formatting of the paragraph following it. Turning on paragraph marks so you can see them makes this less likely to happen.

If the Formatting toolbar is not displayed, open the **View** menu and select **Toolbars** to display it, or click on the **Standard** toolbar with the *right* mouse button, and select it from the shortcut menu.

So How Can I Tell Where Paragraphs Begin and End?

At the end of each paragraph, Word inserts a *paragraph mark* that is normally invisible, but that you can display if you want to. Why would you want to see these little paragraph "pests" all over your screen? To understand why, you need to know a bit about paragraph formatting.

Just as you can select characters and format them in a particular way, you can format paragraphs as well. For example, you can center a paragraph between the margins, change the indentation for the first line, or change the spacing between paragraphs, among other things. Paragraph formatting is stored in those paragraph marks that you don't see.

Also, when you press **Enter** to create a new paragraph, the formatting of that paragraph continues to the next one. This is kind of like character formatting. For example, if you turned bold on but never turned it off, all subsequent text would be bold. Once you make changes to a paragraph (such as changing its margin settings), those changes are effective forever until you change them again.

¶ So to display these little creatures, click on the **Show/Hide Paragraph Mark** button on the **Formatting** toolbar, or press **Ctrl+Shift+8** (do not press the 8 on the numeric keypad—it won't work).

Show/Hide
Paragraph Mark
button

Microsoft Word - LETBLOCK.DOC

File   Edit   View   Insert   Format   Tools   Table   Window   Help

InsideAddress   Arial   10   B I U

Mr.·Gottfried·S.·Klautchnik↵
Miscellaneous·Other·Bookings,·Inc.·↵ ——————————————Soft returns
Behind·the·Dumpster↵
Suite·B16↵
Las·Vegas,·NV·80015¶ ——————————————

Dear·Gottfried:¶ ——————————————Paragraph marks

This·letter·is·in·regard·to·one·of·the·entertainers·in·your·employ.··Last·21·February,·my·club,·the·
Horace·Palace,·booked·one·of·the·fellows·in·your·line-up,·a·person·whom·your·brochure·listed·as·
The·Amazing·Kreskin.··I·naturally·assumed·that·this·Mr.·Kreskin·of·yours·would·be·something·of·
a·mind-reader,·and·would·thrill·my·regular·audience·with·his·ability·to·recall·the·names·and·
addresses·of·people·he·had·never·met.¶

I·don't·recall·anyone·in·your·employ·having·ever·told·me·that·this·gentleman,·a·Mr.·Elroy·Kreskin·
of·Guymon,·Oklahoma,·had·such·a·way·with·wresting·steers.··This·also·came·as·a·surprise·to·my·
clientele·of·yesterday·evening,·a·Seniors·group·from·the·local·chapter·of·Mensa,·who·were·
somewhat·astounded·when·rather·than·guess·the·contents·of·ladies'·purses,·Elroy·would·juggle·
them·instead.··He·was,·at·last,·able·to·guess·people's·names,·though·only·for·people·who·
promised·in·advance·their·names·began·with·"Y."··"Yvonne?··Yvette?··Yentl?"·he·asked·one·
gentleman.··When·finally·one·of·my·guests·asked·if·he·could·at·least·demonstrate·some·

Page a   Sec 1   1/2   At   Ln   Col   1:03 PM   REC   MRK   EXT   OVR   WPH

Gee, you never know what's out there till you display it.

Some Things You Should Know Before We Go On

Before we get into actual paragraph formatting, I thought you'd like to know that the rules for character formatting apply here as well. You can format paragraphs as you type, or you can select them later and format them.

If you change paragraph formatting as you type (to create a heading, for example), you have to change it back later. (Remember to think of it as a light switch: if you turn it on, you have to turn it off.) If you select already-typed paragraphs, only the selected paragraphs are changed.

TECHNO NERD TEACHES

If you need to move to the next line without creating a new paragraph (as in a list, or an address at the top of a letter), press **Shift+Enter**. This inserts a "soft return" (the opposite of a "hard return," which marks the end of a paragraph).

If you have a mouse, you can check the formatting of a paragraph with a few clicks. First, click on the **Help** button on the **Standard** toolbar, then click on the paragraph you want to check. A box will display, listing the paragraph's formats. These fall into two types. *Direct formatting* is that which you've applied using the techniques in this chapter. You'll learn more about *style formatting* in Chapter 14. To clear the box, press **Esc**.

In addition, you can use either the mouse or the keyboard to change text formatting. Again, I use a combination of both, depending on what I'm doing at the time.

If you want the formatting to apply to specific text, select the text first. Double-click in the **selection bar** in front of a paragraph to select it. Drag the mouse to select additional paragraphs. If you prefer the keyboard, move the insertion point to the beginning of a paragraph, then press and hold the **Shift** key as you press **Ctrl+↓**. Then select the paragraph format. (We'll get to this in a minute.)

If you are using the method of selecting text and then applying the format, you're done. If you're formatting as you type, you'll need to turn off the formatting when you finish typing the text you want to affect. This is done by selecting different formatting. To go back to the original format, reset the formatting to whatever that was (come to think of it, you might want to make a note of that before you change it). Pressing **Ctrl+Shift+N** returns you to the Normal paragraph style.

If you need to remove a paragraph's *manual formatting*, select it and press **Ctrl+Q**. (Manual formatting is formatting that you apply yourself, as opposed to style formatting, which you'll learn about in Chapter 14.) When you press **Ctrl+Q**, you return a paragraph to its default formatting, which is determined by the style that has been assigned to it.

Okay, Everybody A-lign Up!

Paragraph alignment controls how the text in a paragraph is placed between the left and right margins. There are four types of alignment:

Left alignment causes all the text in a paragraph to line up evenly on the left-hand margin. Text along the right-hand margin is "ragged," which means that it doesn't form an even line down the page. This is the default paragraph style.

Right alignment causes all the text in a paragraph to line up evenly along the right-hand margin. Text on the left-hand margin is "ragged." This is the opposite of left alignment. I use this type of alignment to put a date or a return address in the upper right corner of my letters.

Center alignment causes all the text in a paragraph to remain an even distance between the left and right margins. I rarely use this for normal paragraphs, but I use it often for headings.

Justified alignment causes all the text in a paragraph to be evenly spaced out, so that both the left and right margins maintain an even edge. Depending on the size of the words within a single line, this can cause unequal spacing between words. This type of alignment is good for newspaper-style columns.

Changing Alignment

Here's what you do to change a paragraph's alignment. If you have a mouse, click on one of these buttons on the **Formatting** toolbar:

 Left-Aligned Text button

 Right-Aligned Text button

 Centered Text button

Justified Text button

If you prefer to use the keyboard, use one of these key combinations:

Ctrl+L   Left-aligned text

Ctrl+R   Right-aligned text

Ctrl+E   Centered text

Ctrl+J   Justified text

Put It to Work

Playing with Paragraph Alignment

There's nothing better for learning something new than to play with it—work with it until it begins to make sense. So that's what we'll do. First, type in a sample paragraph that has at least two lines of text.

Use the preceding instructions to change its alignment to centered, left, right, and justified. In the next section you'll get a chance to practice indenting paragraphs, and you can come back here and compare what the two options do to a paragraph.

What's Wrong with This Picture?

Mike created two paragraphs like this:

Let's Reach Our Customerrs

I propose that

As Mike was typing, he noticed the mistake in the title (the word "Customers" was misspelled "Customerrs"). From the letter *I*, Mike pressed the Backspace key to back up to the title, and he ended up with this:

Let's Reach Our CustomerrsI propose that

The question is this: what happened to the centering alignment of the title? Why did it become left-aligned?

Answer: When Mike noticed that the title was misspelled, he should have used the cursor to move back to the title. By using the Backspace key, he backed up and deleted the paragraph mark for the title. This deleted its formatting, so that the title took on the formatting of the paragraph following it (the title became left-aligned).

Indents: A Paragraph Margin's First Cousin

I think of *indents* as the first cousins to margins because they are so closely related (as a matter of fact, it's really easy to get the two mixed up). An *indent* is the amount of distance from the page margin to the edge of your paragraph. A *margin* is an invisible boundary that runs down both edges of the page. Normally, a paragraph flows between the margins, but an indent allows you to move the edges of individual paragraphs an extra distance away from (or toward) the margin. You can set these indents:

Margin   Paragraph with a first-line indent

Left-indented paragraph

Right-indented paragraph

Putting a 'dent in a paragraph.

Indent   Paragraph with a hanging indent

First Line   Indents the first line of a paragraph the indicated distance from the left margin. You can even create a *hanging indent.*

Left   Indents all the lines of a paragraph the indicated distance from the left margin.

Right   Indents all the lines of a paragraph the indicated distance from the right margin.

Hanging indent   A paragraph in which the first line of the paragraph hangs closer to the left margin than the rest of the lines in the paragraph.

In Word 2.0, press **Ctrl+N** to indent, and **Ctrl+M** to unindent. To create a hanging indent, press **Ctrl+T**; to remove a hanging indent, **Ctrl+G**.

Putting 'Dents in Your Paragraphs

To change the indents of a paragraph, move the insertion point to the paragraph. If you want to indent several paragraphs at once, select them first.

Once your paragraph(s) are selected, indent a paragraph *one tab stop from the left* by clicking on the **Indent** button on the **Standard** toolbar, or by pressing **Ctrl+M**. Reverse this by clicking on the **Unindent** button on the **Standard** toolbar, or by pressing **Ctrl+Shift+M**. To create a hanging indent, press **Ctrl+T**, and the left indent mark is moved one tab stop to the right. Press **Ctrl+Shift+T**, and the left indent mark is moved back one tab stop to the left.

Changing Indents with the Ruler

You can also change the indention of a paragraph (or paragraphs) with the Ruler. The Ruler is a great way to indent a paragraph more than a single tab stop, or to a point which is an unusual distance from the margin. (You need a mouse to try this one.)

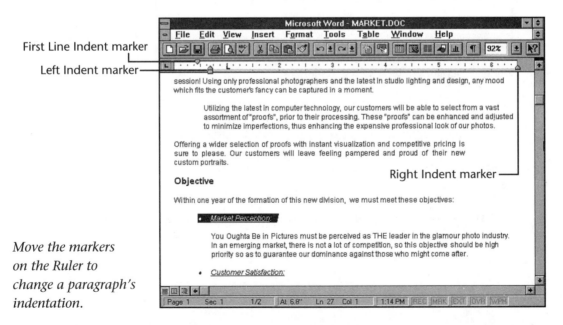

Move the markers on the Ruler to change a paragraph's indentation.

With the mouse, drag the Left, Right, and First Line Indent markers on the Ruler. To create a hanging indent, hold down **Shift** as you drag the First Line Indent marker to the left of the Left Indent marker.

If the Ruler is not displayed, open the **View** menu and select **Ruler** to display it.

If you want to move the left indent inside the left margin (to create a heading that starts inside the margin, for example), press and hold **Shift** as you drag the Left Indent marker.

Put It to Work

Hanging an Indent

Let's practice using the ruler to create a hanging indent, and then just play around. First, type two paragraphs with at least two lines of text. You don't have to get fancy here—you can type garbage if you want, I won't tell.

Now click within the first paragraph to place the insertion point there. Hold down the **Shift** key as you drag the First Line Indent marker to the left of the Left Indent marker, and you've got yourself one beautiful hanging indent!

Notice how the changes you made do not affect the second paragraph, or the margin settings. What you're doing is adjusting the distance *between the margin settings and this paragraph.*

Drag the Right Indent marker and watch what happens. Play with all the indents to create different situations. If you want to try something really cool, create a one-line paragraph and pretend that it is a heading (you can even bold it or increase the point size if you want). Then press and hold the **Shift** key as you drag the Left Indent marker inside the left margin. This is a nice way to dress up reports, because the headings really stand out.

If you want to undo your changes to a paragraph, select the paragraph and press **Ctrl+Q**.

Hanging Around Numbered and Bulleted Lists

A special kind of hanging indent is a *numbered* or *bulleted* list. I've used bulleted lists throughout these chapters to:

- Create snazzy lists like this one.

- Highlight what's coming up.

- Summarize the important points that were covered.

I usually use numbered lists when I want to explain the specific steps for doing something, such as step 1, step 2, and so on. Ready to number or bullet? Here's what to do.

Numbered or bulleted lists A special kind of paragraph with a hanging indent, where the number or bullet is placed to the left of all the other lines in the paragraph.

Click on the appropriate button on the **Formatting** toolbar. Or if you want different bullets or numbering, use the Bullets and Numbering command on the Format menu. You can change the type and size of bullets, the numbering system (letters, Roman numerals, or decimal numbers), and the amount of space between the number or bullet and the rest of the paragraph. If you're using the keyboard, remember to press **Ctrl+Tab** to move between the Bullets and Numbering sections; then use → to select a style, and press **Enter**.

Remember to turn off bulleted or numbered lists when you're through. Pressing Enter to create a new paragraph only continues the list. To turn the list off, click on the appropriate button again, or press **Ctrl+Shift+N** to start a paragraph with the Normal style.

You can interrupt a numbered list by clicking the right mouse button and selecting **Skip Numbering** off the menu. To resume numbering later in your document, click the **Numbering** button on the **Formatting** toolbar.

Spaced-Out Paragraphs

You can adjust the line spacing within paragraphs (for example, making them double-spaced). A double-spaced printout is great for a reader who is also editing; it gives her space to write comments. Double-spacing was big with my high school English teacher—and boy, did she use that space!

> If one paragraph has spacing added *after* it, and the following paragraph has spacing added *before* it, the amount of spacing between the two paragraphs is the *total* of these two amounts.

You can also adjust the number of lines (if any) that precede or follow a paragraph. Start by opening the Format menu and choosing **Paragraph**.

Then, in the **Spacing** section, enter the number of lines to place before or after this paragraph. (One blank line after a paragraph is pretty normal, so why not try that?) If you set up a paragraph so that there is a blank line following it, you don't have to press Enter twice between paragraphs to create a blank line to separate them.

With the **Paragraph** command, you can also adjust the amount of space between lines in a paragraph. Under Line Spacing, select one of these options:

Auto	Lines are adjusted automatically to fit the point size of the font.
Single	Sets single space that Word can adjust as necessary.
1.5 Lines	Sets 1 1/2-line spacing that Word can adjust as necessary.
Double	Sets double-spacing that Word can adjust as necessary.
At Least	Sets a minimum spacing that Word can adjust as necessary.
Exactly	Sets an exact line spacing that Word cannot adjust.
Multiple	Sets multiple line spacing, such as triple line spacing. Select **Multiple**, then enter the number of lines under **At**.

If you're a keyboard user, press **Ctrl+1** for single spacing, **Ctrl+2** for double spacing, and **Ctrl+5** for 1 1/2-line spacing. You can also add one line of space before a paragraph by pressing **Ctrl+O** (the letter, not zero), or delete one line of space before a paragraph by pressing **Ctrl+0** (zero).

> **By the Way . . .**
> You can display the Paragraph dialog box quickly by double-clicking on the **left** or **first-line indent markers** on the left-hand side of the Ruler.

Mind If I Repeat Myself Again?

You can repeat the paragraph formatting with the **Repeat Formatting** command, just as you did with character formatting. Select the paragraph you want to copy the formatting to, or move the insertion point to the place you want new text with this formatting to appear when you type. Then press **F4**.

If you used the Ruler, the Toolbar, or the Formatting toolbar to change the formatting of a paragraph, you should copy the formatting of the paragraph using this method instead: select the paragraph you want to copy the formatting to, or move the insertion point to a place you want new text with this formatting to appear when you type. Move the mouse pointer to the **selection bar** (the invisible area to the left of all paragraphs) for the paragraph whose formatting you want to copy. Then hold down **Ctrl+Shift**, and click the left mouse button.

The Least You Need to Know

Conjure up terrific paragraphs with this bag of tricks:

☞ A paragraph is created when you press **Enter**.

☞ You can display paragraph marks by clicking on the **Show/Hide Paragraph** button on the **Formatting** toolbar.

☞ Double-click in the **selection bar** in front of a paragraph to select it.

☞ Press **Ctrl+Shift+N** (on the numeric keypad with Num Lock off) to return a paragraph to Normal paragraph style. To remove manual formatting, press **Ctrl+Q**.

☞ Use the appropriate buttons on the Ruler to align a paragraph:

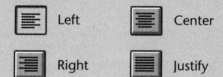

Left   Center

Right   Justify

☞ To change a paragraph's indents, drag the appropriate indent markers.

☞ To create a numbered list, click on this button on the **Standard** toolbar.

☞ To create a bulleted list, click on this button on the **Standard** toolbar.

☞ Change the spacing before, after, and within paragraphs with the **Paragraph** command on the Format menu.

☞ To repeat the last paragraph format, press **F4**.

☞ To copy a paragraph's formatting, select the paragraph you want to copy the formatting to, and then press and hold **Ctrl+Shift**. Click in the **selection bar** to the left of the paragraph whose formatting you wish to copy.

This page unintentionally left blank.

Chapter 13

Now You're Ready for the Big Time: Formatting a Document

In This Chapter

- ☛ Setting margins
- ☛ Adding a header or a footer
- ☛ Creating sections within your document
- ☛ Forcing a page break within a document

At last you're ready for the big time: formatting an entire document, or simply *sections* of it. Formatting a document or a section is not as common as formatting characters or paragraphs—but the stuff you'll learn in this chapter will have a global, worldwide effect.

You're through with minor league stuff; here you get to play with the big boys. Let's start with the kinds of changes that affect an entire document—then I'll show you how to make these same kinds of changes for only part of your document (a *section* of your document).

Section   A part of a document that has different settings from the main document for things such as margins, paper size, headers, footers, columns, and page numbering. A section can be of any length: several pages, several paragraphs, or even a single line (such as a heading).

A Marginal Review

In Chapter 7, you learned how to change margins from the Print Preview window by dragging the margin line to its new location. (Jump back to Chapter 7 if you want a review of that procedure; in this section, I'll show you how to change margins in Page View, without switching to Print Preview.) Remember that when you change margins, you're changing them for the current section only. If you haven't created any sections in your document yet (hold on, you'll learn how to create sections in just a little bit), you'll change the margins for the entire document.

Just drag the margin line.

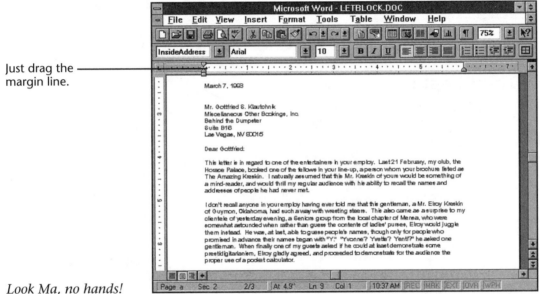

Look Ma, no hands!

To change your document's margins in Page Layout mode, you start by clicking the **Page Layout** button on the horizontal scroll bar. Next, move the mouse pointer to the **Ruler** (if the Ruler is not displayed, select the **View Ruler** command to display it). Position the pointer over the **indent markers**, and it will change to a double-headed arrow. Drag the markers to the desired location, and release the mouse button.

With the keyboard, change margins with the File Page Setup command. To change the left margin, press **Alt+L** then type the correct measurement. Repeat with the right, top, or bottom margins. Press **Enter** when you are through.

Headers Don't Have to Give You a Headache

A *header* is stuff that can be printed at the top of every page in a document, and a *footer* is stuff (such as page numbers, chapter numbers, and so on) that can be printed at the bottom of every page. You don't have to create headers and footers just to add the page number to every page in your document. Instead, you can open the Insert menu and select the Page Numbers command. Under Position, select either **Top of Page** or **Bottom of Page**. Choose the type of Alignment (left, right, centered, inside, or outside the margins) that you want. Normally, page numbers begin on the second page of your document. If you want them to begin on page one, select **S**how number on First Page, and then click on **OK**.

In Word 2.0, the Page Numbers command places page numbers on all pages except page one. So if you want to place page numbers on every page, use headers and footers.

Page Numbers

Position:
Top of Page (Header)

Alignment:
Right

☐ Show Number on First Page

Preview

OK
Cancel
Format...
Help

Now, on page number 42. . . .

If you want to do anything other than just print numbers, such as adding text (for example, The Year in Review) or printing a date, use headers and footers. Headers and footers are pretty easy to create; you simply type text into a little box (called a *pane*), click on a few buttons to add page numbers and such, and you're through.

By the Way . . .

Word weirdness alert: you won't see your headers and footers in Normal view after you create them, so switch to either Print Preview or Page Layout view to see how they'll look when printed.

In Word 2.0, the procedure for creating a header or a footer is slightly different. First, switch to **Normal** view (open the **View** menu and select **Normal**). Then open the **View** menu again and select the **Header/Footer** command. When the dialog box appears, choose **Header** or **Footer**, and then select **OK** to open the box where you type in the header or footer text.

Here's how to enter a header or footer—be warned: you're going to need a mouse for this. Open the View menu and select **Header and Footer**. If needed, click inside the header box to establish the insertion point, and begin typing text. (To enter a footer instead, click the **Switch Between Header and Footer** button.) Press **Tab** one time to center text, and twice to right-align text. Add character formatting, such as bold and italic, by clicking on the appropriate buttons on the **Formatting** toolbar (or by pressing the key combinations you learned in Chapter 11).

To add page numbers, the date, or the time, click on the appropriate button on the **Header and Footer** toolbar. When you're through, click on Close. To edit the header or footer later, switch to **Page Layout** view, then double-click inside the pane.

If you want to get fancy, you can add more than just the date and time to your headers or footers by using fields. Fields are codes which instruct Word to insert current data into the document at a particular place. For

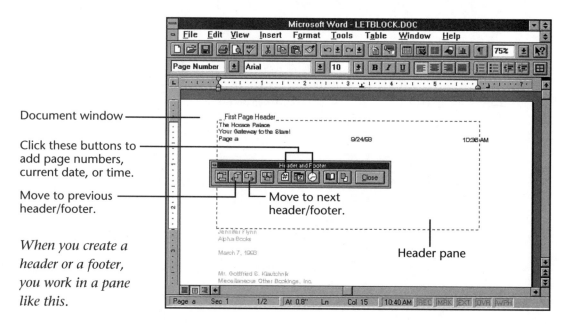

Document window

Click these buttons to add page numbers, current date, or time.

Move to previous header/footer.

Move to next header/footer.

Header pane

When you create a header or a footer, you work in a pane like this.

example, you can insert the author's name, the date the document was last changed, and other information into the header or footer using fields. Position the cursor within the header or footer, then select the Insert Field command. Choose a field from the Field Names list, and click on **OK**.

You can add headers and footers for each section of your document if you want—just repeat these steps for each section. Again, hold on, because you're about to learn how to create sections in your document.

By clicking on the **Page Setup** button on the **Header and Footer** toolbar, you can select special options, such as Different First Page (for a header that's different on the title page, for example) and Different **O**dd and Even Pages (for headers that are different for the left- and right-hand pages). If you want, you can also change the placement of the header or footer in relation to the edge of the page.

Slicing and Dicing Your Document into Sections

Well, finally I can show you how to create sections in your document. But in case you might be asking, "Why bother creating sections?," let me first give you some examples of when I've used sectioning:

☞ To create multiple chapters (for a book or a long report) in one document. Each chapter would have its own headers (such as the chapter title), and you could easily have Word generate a table of contents or an index for the whole document.

☞ For legal documents that require line numbering in some sections but not in others.

☞ To do a company newsletter with various formats. You could create a section just for the front-page heading, so that it reaches from margin to margin on a single line. Underneath, you could change to a three-newspaper-column format for the text of the newsletter.

☞ For business reports printed in portrait orientation (for example, 8 1/2 by 11 inches) with a chart that's printed in landscape orientation (for example, 11 by 8 1/2 inches).

☞ In a small manual, where each section has its own page numbers. The Table of Contents section could use Roman numerals (i, ii, and so on) for page numbers. Each section after the Table of Contents could start with page 1. And since the title page wouldn't need a page number, you could suppress page numbering on just that page.

☞ To include text in two different languages (for example, a human-resources memo). The document could be divided into paired sections—one section for English text and another for Spanish.

Time for a Section Break

Oops! Before I show you how to break your document into little sections, I should tell you this: set the most common document options first. For example, if you want most of the pages to have three newspaper columns, go ahead and set that option before you divide up your document.

Then when you're ready to start slicing and dicing, open the Insert menu and choose the **Break** command. Under **Section Breaks**, choose from these options:

Next Page   The section starts at the top of the next page.

Continuous   The section starts right after the previous section, even if it's in the middle of a page.

Odd Page   The section starts on the next odd-numbered page. In a book like this one, that would be the next right-hand page.

Even Page   The section starts on the next even-numbered page. In a book like this one, that would be the next left-hand page.

Use the **OK** button to close the Section box, and you're done!

So Now That I Have a Section, What Do I Do with It?

Just look at the types of changes you can make that affect a section of a document, rather than the document as a whole:

Margins   You learned how to change the margins of a document from the Print Preview window earlier in this chapter. If you decide to create different sections in your document, you can change the margins within each section separately—you'll learn to do this in a minute.

Sections are marked by a double line in Normal view. Section marks are like paragraph marks; they contain the formatting for that section. So if you delete them, that section reverts to the formatting of the section before it. Just learn to ignore these lines; they won't print, and deleting them causes you to lose your formatting for your section.

Paper size and page orientation   You can choose from lots of paper sizes (such as 8 1/2 by 11 inches and 11 by 14 inches), as you learned in Chapter 10. You can change the paper size by section (although this is pretty rare), or you might want to change page orientation by section (landscape versus portrait).

Headers and footers   A header is stuff that's printed at the top of a page, and a footer is stuff (such as page numbers, chapter numbers, and so on) printed at the bottom. You learned how to create headers and footers for an entire document earlier in this chapter. You can change headers and footers for each section of your document if you want, and you'll learn how in just a moment.

Page numbers   These are usually included as part of a header or footer. You can change the page numbering system from the default of 1, 2, 3 to something else, such as i, ii, iii or A, B, C. You can change the page numbering system within a document by creating sections and using different headers and footers for each section.

Newspaper-style columns   You can create columns in your document that appear like those you'd find in a newspaper or a magazine (for newsletters and such). If you want to vary the number of columns to add interest, you must create a new section. You'll learn how to create newspaper-style columns in Chapter 19.

Breaking a Page Won't Break My Heart

One way to force Word to start another page is to create a section break, and then select the **Next Page** option. But if you just want a page break, and no other changes, starting a new section is a little extreme. Instead, just use a forced page break.

I add a forced page break (called a *hard page break*) when I'm working in a section (like a chapter, for example) and I want to create a subdivision that starts at the top of a page. Maybe you want a supporting chart for a report to appear on a separate page. In any case, you can put a hard page break anywhere in your document by simply pressing **Ctrl+Enter**.

A Marginal Job of Sectioning

Earlier in this chapter, you learned how to use the Print Preview window to change the margins for the entire document or for the current section of the document. If you need to change margins for one or two sections, leave the Print Preview window and follow along with this procedure instead.

First, select the Page Setup command from the File menu. Choose the Margins tab, and enter the margin measurements.

In Word 2.0, the Page Setup command is located on the Format menu. Also, the option Mirror Margins (described here) is called Facing Pages.

Two of these settings may confuse you at first. When you choose Mirror Margins, everything does a quick switcheroo. What used to be the Left margin becomes the Inside margins for the report, and what used to be the Right margin becomes the Outside margins.

The Gutter is added to the Inside margin setting (or the Left margin setting if you don't select Facing Pages). You don't have to create a book to use Gutter; you could use the reserved space for hole punches if you're planning on putting your document in a binder. If you're having a professional printer produce and bind several copies of your document, you might want to leave at least half an inch of gutter space for them to cut the holes.

Mirror margins   An option you can use when creating magazine-like reports: when open, the pages of your report would "face each other."

Gutter   An unused region of space that runs down the inside edges of facing pages of a document, and it's the part of each page that's taken up when a book or a magazine is bound together.

If you want, you can adjust the distance between the top and bottom margins and the header and footer in the **From Edge** area. Finally, in the Apply To box, select the area of the document you want those measurements to apply to. You can select **Whole Document**, **Selected Text**, **This Section**, **Selected Sections**, or **This Point Forward**. When you're done, click on the **OK** button.

A Footnote About Headers and Footers

Earlier in this chapter, you learned how to create headers and footers. If you want different headers and footers for parts of your document, read on:

☛ Create section breaks in your document with the Insert Break command.

☛ Move the insertion point so that it is within the new section, and then use the View Header and Footer command.

☛ The options Different First Page and Different Odd and Even pages refer to pages within a section. For example, the *first page* is not page one in your document, but page one *in that section*.

☛ You can also change the page numbering system within this section to make it different from other sections. For example, the front pages of most books (such as this one) are numbered with small Roman numerals, such as i, ii, and iii.

The Least You Need to Know

I hope that the last three chapters have left you with a feeling of total control: control over text, paragraphs, sections, and your entire document. (Now if I could only gain control over my waistline, I'd be a happy gal.) Here's what you learned in this chapter:

☛ You can change margins, paper size, headers, footers, page numbers, and the number of newspaper columns for individual portions of your document by creating sections.

☛ Create a section break with the **Break** command on the **Insert** menu.

☛ If you need to start a new page but not a new section, use a hard page break. Force a hard page break anywhere in a document by pressing **Ctrl+Enter**.

☛ You can change the margins for several sections at once by using the Page Setup command on the **File** menu.

☛ To create a header or a footer, use the Header and Footer command on the **View** menu.

Chapter 14
Setting Your Own Style

In This Chapter

- ☛ What is a style?
- ☛ How to tell what style a paragraph is using
- ☛ Applying a style to a paragraph
- ☛ Copying a style from paragraph to paragraph
- ☛ Creating your own style
- ☛ Redefining a style
- ☛ Adding a style to a document template

After you've spent a long time getting a sidebar (for special notes), a heading, or a bulleted list just right (with special indentation, character formatting, or unique fonts), the last thing you need is to repeat all those steps the next time you want to add another note, heading, or bulleted list elsewhere in your document. So what do you do?

You create three styles (one to remember each set of formatting selections), and you use those styles to create similar text in other parts of your document. And (surprise, surprise) in this chapter you'll learn how.

If you would rather have Word format your document automatically using preformatted styles, you can skip to the end of this chapter to learn how. Then come back here if you want to override any of the choices Word makes for you.

Getting a Sense of Style

So what exactly is a style? A *style* is a collection of both character and paragraph formatting that defines a particular element *within a document*. For example, you can create a style for each different heading level within your document. You can create *paragraph styles* (which define such things as alignment and indentation, as well as font and character formatting for a paragraph) and *character styles (which define font and character formatting for a section of text)*. Word lists paragraph styles in bold within the Style list; character formats are listed in regular text. Just remember that character styles are applied to the entire word within which the insertion point is located, or to text you have selected. Paragraph styles are applied to the paragraph within which the insertion point is located, or to groups of selected paragraphs.

Character style

Paragraph styles

Style area

Create styles for different elements in your document.

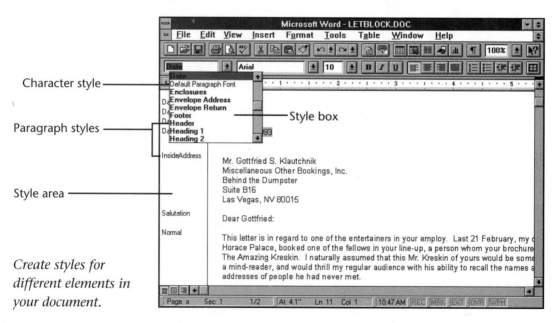

Now don't get too depressed; you don't have to create a style for every little thing. If a paragraph is unique, don't bother to create a style. But remember that styles save you the hassle of having to make the same character and paragraph formatting changes over and over again as you create your document.

Sorry, Word 2.0 users—you can't create character styles. Now don't put on a pouty face; paragraph styles exist, and they work as described here.

Up until now, every paragraph you've typed has started its life in the Normal style: Times New Roman 10-point font, in a left-aligned paragraph. All other styles are based on the Normal style, so if you hate Times New Roman font, modify the Normal style to use some other font before you create any new styles.

By the Way . . .

Ready to be confused? Don't read this unless you're really interested in how Normal style works.

When you make a change to your Normal style, whether or not the change affects another style in that document depends on what non-Normal attributes the other style has. For example, suppose you had a style called *Title* that was centered, specified a 24-point size, and used the same font as Normal style (Times New Roman). If you changed the Normal style from 10-point to 12-point, you *would not affect* the Title style because its 24-point style is non-Normal—it overrides the Normal point size. If you changed Normal style to Palatino font, the font for the Title *would change*, because its font (Times New Roman) is based on the Normal font (which would now be Palatino).

When you create a style, formats that you change will no longer be affected by subsequent changes to the Normal style. Formats that you leave at Normal's default *will change* if you change the Normal style.

When you change the Normal style (its font for example,) you're changing the starting point for all the other styles you create *in that document.* If you want to change the Normal style for all documents, there is a way to do that, and you'll learn how at the end of this chapter. Before making any changes to the Normal style, be sure that's really what you want to do.

Style Area   An area that can be made to appear at the far left side of the screen, and which displays the style for every paragraph in a document.

How Can I Tell What Style Is Applied to a Paragraph?

When the insertion point is placed in a paragraph, the style you are currently using appears in the Style box on the Formatting toolbar. If a character style has been applied to a word, its style will appear in the Style box when the insertion point is placed *within the word.* So you don't strain your neck looking up at the Style box all the time, you may want to show the paragraph styles next to each paragraph in your document. To do this, turn on the *Style Area.*

First, open the Tools menu and choose the Options command. With the keyboard, press **Alt+T**, then **O**. Select **View** by clicking on it or pressing **Ctrl+Tab**, and then change the Style Area Width to some positive number, such as **.5** (half an inch). With the keyboard, press **Alt+Y**, and use the **arrow** keys to change the measurement. Choose **OK** or press **Enter** when you're done.

The Style Area does more than save you neck strain—it saves you time selecting paragraphs and modifying styles. With the Style Area displayed, you can select a paragraph by clicking once on the paragraph's style name. If you double-click instead, you'll display the Style dialog box, where you can make changes to the style, assign a shortcut key for applying a style, or simply verify the formats that make up the style. Now that's stylin'!

Selecting a Style to Use

Let's start with simple things first. Suppose you wanted to section off text by preceding it with a heading. Well, you're in luck: Word has quite a few styles (including several heading styles) already defined for you. Once a style has been created, all you need to do is apply one of the styles to a paragraph and make modifications if necessary.

Here's how to apply a sense of style. First, place the insertion point where you want the style applied. This can be an existing paragraph, or some place within the document where you want the style to start. Select several paragraphs if you want to format multiple paragraphs at one time.

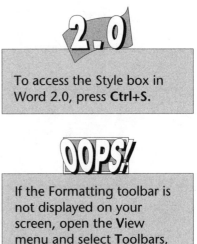

To access the Style box in Word 2.0, press **Ctrl+S.**

Next, click on the **down arrow** next to the Style box on the Formatting toolbar. Select an existing style. If a style you want to use isn't listed, press **Shift**, then click on the arrow next to the Style box. A box will appear, displaying all of Word's built-in styles (normally Word lists only a few common styles, and those you create in the Style box). If you want to use the keyboard, press **Ctrl+Shift+S**

If the Formatting toolbar is not displayed on your screen, open the **View** menu and select Toolbars, then choose **Formatting.**

to access the Style box, use the **arrow** keys to highlight a style, and then press **Enter**. To create a heading based on one of the existing styles, select **Heading 1**, **2**, or **3**.

If you've assigned a shortcut key to a style, you can apply a style to a paragraph by pressing the shortcut key combination. (You'll learn how to assign shortcut keys later on in this chapter.)

Repeating the Same Ol' Style

 To repeat a style you've applied to one paragraph for another paragraph in your document, select the same style again from the **Formatting** toolbar. You can also copy styles from one paragraph to the other with the Format Painter. To copy a paragraph's style to single paragraph, select it, click on the **Format Painter** button, then click the paragraph to which you wish to copy formatting.

To copy styles in Word 2.0, select the paragraph whose styles you wish to copy. Move the mouse pointer to the **selection bar** in front of the paragraph you want to copy to, and (while holding down **Ctrl** and **Shift**) click the mouse button. If this doesn't work for you, you may not have received an update to your program. Call Microsoft support and ask them for the update to Word 2.0.

To copy formatting to several paragraphs, select them, and then *double-click* the **Format Painter** button. After that, simply click inside as many paragraphs as you wish. Press **Esc** to end the multiple formatting.

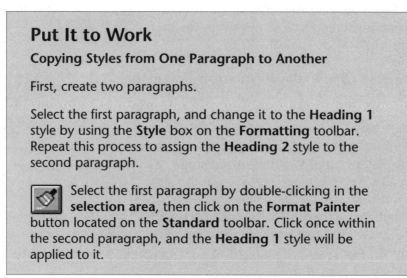

Put It to Work

Copying Styles from One Paragraph to Another

First, create two paragraphs.

Select the first paragraph, and change it to the **Heading 1** style by using the **Style** box on the **Formatting** toolbar. Repeat this process to assign the **Heading 2** style to the second paragraph.

Select the first paragraph by double-clicking in the **selection area**, then click on the **Format Painter** button located on the **Standard** toolbar. Click once within the second paragraph, and the **Heading 1** style will be applied to it.

Creating Your Own Style

Let's create a style for the sidebar paragraph I mentioned earlier. Suppose you were going to use the sidebar paragraph for special instructions to the reader, and you'd like to add indentation, italicized text, and a different font to set it off from the rest of the document.

The easiest way to create a style is to format a paragraph first, and then use its formatting to define a style. So start by typing a paragraph that we can use as a sample. Then follow along with me to create your first style.

First, change the indentation of the sample paragraph to right-aligned by clicking on the **Right-Align** button on the **Formatting** toolbar. Then select the text for the paragraph by double-clicking in the **selection bar**.

Next, make the text italic by clicking on the **Italic** button on the **Formatting** toolbar. Finally, select a font from the **Font** box on the **Formatting** toolbar.

When you have the paragraph looking the way you want it, define a style based on it. With the paragraph selected, move to the Style box by clicking on it, or by pressing **Ctrl+Shift+S**. Type a name (such as **Sidebar**) in the **Style** box on the **Formatting** toolbar, and press **Enter**. A style name can contain up to 24 characters, including spaces.

Redefining an Existing Style

If you want to change the font (or some other characteristic) of an existing style, it's pretty easy to do. Keep in mind that any changes you make to the Normal style affect *all other styles in this document*. So as a rule, you'll want to keep changes to the Normal style to a minimum, though changes to other styles are okay. Here's what you do.

Pick a paragraph that has the style you want to change. If you want to change the Sidebar style, for example, select a paragraph with that style. Go ahead and make any changes you want to the paragraph. Then select the paragraph again so that it's highlighted.

TECHNO NERD TEACHES

When you create a style, it's available for that document only. If you want to make a style available for more documents (or if you want to make the changes to the Normal style affect more than one document), you must add that style to a template (which you'll learn how to do later in this chapter). A *template* defines the working environment for a document, such as its margin settings, page orientation, and so on. The template also controls which menu commands are available, and what tools appear on the toolbars.

As you learned in Chapter 6, Word for Windows comes with additional templates you can use to create specialized documents, or you can create your own. To see which template you are using, choose the **Templates...** command on the **File** menu. If it says **NORMAL** under Document Template, then you're using the default template. You'll learn more about templates in Chapter 17.

Select the style from the **Style** box on the **Formatting** toolbar and press **Enter**. Word will ask you if you want to redefine the style. Click on **OK**. If you decide not to change the style, click on **Cancel**.

By the Way . . .

You'll probably want to include a single blank line after most paragraph styles. This reduces keying time by providing a blank line between paragraphs for you. To add a line after a paragraph style, select a paragraph with that style (like maybe our Sidebar style). Next, open the Format menu and select the Paragraph command. With the keyboard, press **Alt+O** and then **P**. Under Spacing After, click once on the **up arrow**, or press the **Up arrow** key on the keyboard. The number of points then displayed depends on the current font. Click on **OK** or press **Enter**.

If you changed a style accidentally and you didn't mean to, don't worry—just change it back! Follow these instructions to change the style back to what it was, or click on the **Undo** button (keyboarders: just press **Ctrl+Z**).

What's Wrong with This Picture?

Mary decided that it would be good to create a style for a heading that she was planning to use several times within her document. She formatted the first heading as Palatino, 12-point, centered alignment.

After applying this same style to several headings within her document, she decided that she really liked the look of the Arial font. Because she wanted to use it throughout her document, she changed the Normal style to Arial. All of her paragraphs did not change to Arial. What did she do wrong?

Answer: If you guessed that some of her styles (such as the heading style she created) had been assigned a specific font, you're right. By assigning a font to a style (such as assigning the Palatino font to the heading style), she *overrode* the Normal style in the font category. So any further changes to the Normal style's font are ignored.

Adding a Shortcut Key to a Style

If you want to add a shortcut key to a style, open the Format menu and select Style. From the Styles list, choose the style you want to change. Click on **Modify** or press **Alt+M.** Click on Shortcut Key, then press the keys you want to use for the shortcut key (for example, you could use Alt+S for the Sidebar style). To see whether some other command is already using this shortcut sequence, look under **Currently Assigned To**. If the sequence is already assigned, you should probably pick another letter, or use the Ctrl or Shift keys instead of Alt. You can also combine keys for an unlikely sequence, such as Alt+Shift+S. Click on Assign or press **Alt+A.** Click on **Close** or press **Enter.** Click on **OK** or press **Esc.** Finally, click on Apply or press **Enter.** Whew! Were there enough dialog boxes or what?

To use the shortcut key, either select text you want to change, or move to a place in your document where you want to begin using the style. Next, press the shortcut key sequence (for example, **Alt+S**).

You can also change a style through the Format Style command, but it's not terribly easy. If you want to do it anyway, open the Format menu and select Style. From the **Style Name** list, choose the style you want to change. Click on **Modify** or press **Alt+M.** Then click on Format or press **Alt+F.** Select the part of the style you want to modify (such as paragraph), and press **Enter.** Follow the instructions in Chapter 12 for changing that option. Click on **OK** to return to the Modify Style dialog box, click on **OK** again to return to the Style dialog box, then click on **Apply** to apply the change to the style.

Saving Styles to Use in Other Documents

When you buy a VCR, chances are good that the remote that you use with your TV won't work with the VCR. After playing juggle-the-remotes for several years, I finally bought one of those universal remote things that works with both my TV and my VCR. Creating a style is like using the remote that comes with your TV: having the style is great, but you can only use it on that one document, unless . . .

Template A template defines the working environment for a document, such as its margin settings, page orientation, and so on. A template also stores styles for you to reuse in every document you base on that template.

Unless of course, you save your style to a *template*. Word has many templates already customized for creating common documents, such as memos, reports, and sales proposals. Word also has one central template called *NORMAL.DOT*, which is the template that all new documents are based on (unless you select some other template when you start a new document). So before you save your styles to a template, you'll want to see which template you're currently using by selecting the Templates... command on the File menu. Adding styles to the NORMAL template makes those styles available to all documents; adding styles to another template makes those styles available to only the documents you create using that template.

Whew! If I haven't lost you, and you're still interested in adding a style to the current template, here's how. (If you want to create your own template based on the styles you've created, rather than change an existing template, jump to Chapter 17.)

Start by opening the Format menu and selecting **Style**. Click on **Organizer** or press **Alt+O**. You'll see the styles in your current document displayed in the list on the left-hand side of the dialog box. The template you'll copy styles to is listed on the right-hand side of the dialog. First, select the template to which you wish to add styles by selecting a template from the Styles Available In drop-down list, or by pressing **Alt+B** and using the **arrow** keys to select a template. Remember that if you don't change the template listed on the right-hand side of the dialog box, you'll be adding styles to NORMAL.DOT, which makes them available for all *new* documents. From the list on the left, select the style you want to add to the template, and click on Copy or press **Alt+C**. Select additional styles and repeat the copy process if you want. When you're through, click on **Close** or press **Enter**.

When you exit Word for Windows, it will ask you whether you want to save the global glossary and command changes. Translation: it's asking you if you want to save the changes you've made to your templates, among other things. Click on the **Yes** button to save the changes. If you decide not to save your changes, click on the No button; the styles you tried to add to the current template will still be available when you use the document.

Putting Styles on Automatic

With *AutoFormat*, Word analyzes each paragraph within your document to determine its purpose (for example, is this paragraph a heading, part of a list, a quote, or regular text?), and then applies an appropriate style from the current template. If styles have been applied to some paragraphs within the document, those paragraphs are ignored, and the original styles are preserved (you can override this, of course, and have Word reformat your document completely). After AutoFormat is through making its "best guess" as to how to format your document, you get a chance to review each change—and either accept or reject it.

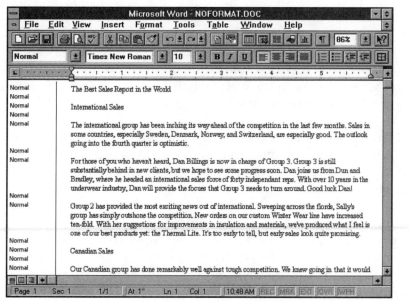

Our document before AutoFormat applies its style.

Once styles are applied, you can use the directions given earlier in this chapter to change aspects of the style that you don't like. For example, if Word assigns the Heading 1 style to several of your headings, you may not like the font or point size. By changing the style, you will automatically change all the Heading 1 headings throughout your document. It just couldn't be easier! So kick off your shoes and relax as you follow these simple steps:

Select your AutoFormat options first. For example, you may wish to have Word override your assigned styles (if you have any of them). To select your options, open the Tools menu and select Options. With the keyboard, press **Alt+T** and then **O**. Click on the **AutoFormat** tab (or press **Ctrl+Tab** to select it). To choose an option, click on it, or press **Alt** plus its underlined letter.

Open the Format menu and select AutoFormat. With the keyboard, press **Alt+O**, then **A**.

The AutoFormat dialog box will appear. Click on **OK** or press **Enter**. Pull up a chair; AutoFormat will format your document while you wait.

Reject or accept all the changes, or review each revision. To accept all the changes without reviewing them, click on **Accept** or press **Alt+A**. To reject all the changes, click on **Reject All** or press **Alt+R**. (If you really hate what Word has done, you may find something better in the **Style Gallery**— you'll visit this style museum in the next section.) To review each revision, click on Review Changes or press **Alt+C**.

If you decide to review all changes, click Find or press **Alt+F** to locate the first change. Word marks its changes in blue (for additions) and red (for deletions). If these marks annoy you, click on Hide Marks (or press **Alt+M**) to turn them off.

When Word highlights a change, decide what you want to do. If you want to accept the change, click on Find or press **Alt+F**. To reject the change, click on **Reject** or press **Alt+R**. To save time while reviewing, click Find Next after Reject (or press **Alt+N**), and Word will automatically take you to the next change any time you reject a change. Return to a previous change by clicking on Find or pressing **Alt+I**. If you reject something and change your mind, click Undo Last, or press **Alt+U**.

When you're done, click **Close** or press **Enter**. You'll return to the AutoFormat dialog box. Click on Accept or press **Enter**, and you're through!

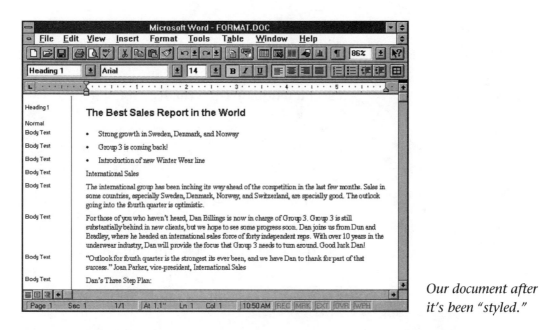

Our document after it's been "styled."

A Tour of the Style Gallery Museum

After a document has styles applied to it (either the good old-fashioned way—by hand—or with AutoFormat), you can change its overall look by selecting a different template through the *Style Gallery*.

The Style Gallery lets you review how your document will look with a different template's styles applied to it. Go from a formal look to a contemporary one with the click of a few buttons. Here's what you do:

Even if you didn't select any styles yourself, your document already has styles applied to it. When you type text into a document, the Normal style is applied to each paragraph. AutoFormat overrides the Normal style automatically.

Make sure your document has some style. Either add the styles by hand (see how-to's earlier in this chapter), or have AutoFormat do it for you.

Open the Format menu and select Style Gallery. With the keyboard, press **Alt+O** and then **G**.

Select a template from the list. You'll see a preview of your document formatted with the styles from that template. If you would rather see an example document, click Example or press **Alt+E**. To see a list of the template's styles, click Style Samples or press **Alt+S**.

When you're through, click on **OK** or press **Enter**. The Style Gallery will change templates, and apply the chosen template's styles to your document.

The Least You Need to Know

The reason for creating styles is to save time in formatting paragraphs. This list will save you time in creating them:

- You can tell what style is applied to each paragraph by displaying the Style Area (select the **Options** command on the **Tools** menu). Choose the **View** tab and then change the Style Area Width setting.

- With the Style Area displayed, you can select a paragraph by clicking on the style name. If you double-click on a style name, the Style dialog box will be displayed.

- **Normal**   To apply a style to a paragraph, select it from the Style box on the **Formatting** toolbar.

- To copy a paragraph's style to another paragraph, select the paragraph whose style you want to copy, click on the **Format Painter** button, then click within the paragraph to which you want to copy the style.

☛ To create a style, format a paragraph and then select it. Type a name for the style in the **Style** box on the **Formatting** toolbar, and press **Enter**.

☛ To make changes to a style, change a paragraph with that style, and then select it. Make sure that the style name is correctly displayed in the Style box on the Formatting toolbar, then press **Enter**. Click on **OK** to confirm that you want to make changes to the style.

☛ To save a style to the current template, open the Format menu and select **Style**. Click on **Organizer** or press **Alt+O.** Under **In...**, select the style you want to add to the template, and click **C**opy or press **Alt+C**. Click on **Close** or press **Enter** to close the dialog box.

This page unintentionally left blank.

Chapter 15

Picking Up the Tab for the Whole Table

In This Chapter

- ☞ When to use tabs, and when to use a table
- ☞ Setting tabs and adding tab leaders
- ☞ Creating tables and adding text to them
- ☞ Adding rows and columns to a table
- ☞ Creating a table heading

What is there to say about tabs or tables? Tabs and tables aren't nearly as interesting or as important a subject as global warming, the economy, Amy Fisher, or the clear version of Pepsi. I'm glad I don't have to write a whole book on tabs or tables (and I bet you're glad you don't have to read one). Oh, well, let's get on with it: to paraphrase the Latin poets of old, who never concerned themselves with tabs, tables, skin cancer, or Madonna's next album—"Carpe Diem!" Or more to the point, "Carpe Tabum!"

Picking Up the Tab

The Tab key in a word processor is like the Tab key on a typewriter. When you press it, the cursor jumps to the next tab stop (but it does not pass Go or collect $200). Tabs are great for creating short lists like this one:

Department	Department Number
Accounting	100
Sales	200
Marketing	210
Client Services	300

If you need more than three columns, or more than just a few rows, you should probably create a table. A *table* makes it easier for you to enter large amounts of information, adjust column widths, and add borders and shading. You'll learn how to make tables later in this chapter.

Treatise on Tab Types

There are four different types of tabs, each one perfect for some suitable occasion:

Left-aligned   This type of tab aligns characters on the left (the default tab type is left-aligned). For example:

Jane	Salesperson
Scott	Client Service Representative
Beth	Corporate Trainer

Right-aligned   This type of tab aligns characters on the right. For example:

Description:

Syntax:

Example:

Decimal   This type of tab is great when working with numbers. It aligns numbers by the decimal point:

100.21

10.927

3515.65

.5586

Center   This type of tab is great for centering headings above your columns of data:

Stock	Buy/Sell
TM Technologies	Buy this one!
GSA	Sell right away!
American Paper	Buy this one soon!
Paramount Comm.	Buy lots of this!

Follow the Leader

Normally the space between tabbed columns is empty, like all the examples I've shown you so far. As an option, you can have Word fill the space with a *leader*. A leader is often used in a Table of Contents:

Leader   Dots or dashes that fill the spaces between tab positions in a columnar list.

Introduction 1

Sales Analysis 5

Market Share 11

Fiscal Plan 13

The idea behind a leader is that it "leads the eye" across the page to the next item in the list. In this example, the leaders help you see that the Sales Analysis starts on page 5 of the report. There are different types of leaders: dotted, dashed, and solid.

Take Me to Your Ruler: Setting Tab Stops

The easiest way to set tabs is with the Ruler. Here's what you do. First, select the paragraph(s) whose tabs you wish to set. You can also pre-set tabs before you type if you want. Click on the **Tab Alignment** button on the **Ruler** to select the type of tab you want. Then click on the **Ruler** to set the tab. Tab marks show on the Ruler, in a shape that matches the type of alignment you chose.

Tab Alignment button ———

Tab marks ———

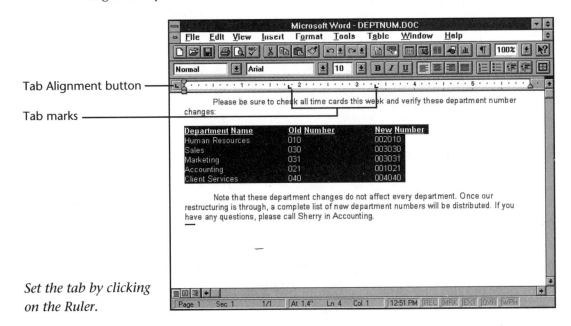

Set the tab by clicking on the Ruler.

Click the Tab Alignment button until you see the type of alignment you want:

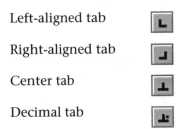

Left-aligned tab

Right-aligned tab

Center tab

Decimal tab

If you want to add a leader, double-click on a tab mark on the Ruler, and you'll see the Tabs dialog box. Click on the leader of your choice, and then click on **OK**. You can also use the Tabs dialog box to set precise tab locations. Again, either double-click on an existing tab, or open the Format menu and select **Tabs**.

If the Ruler is not displayed, open the **View** menu and select **Ruler**.

Under **Tab Stop Position**, type a number to add a new tab. To delete an existing tab, select it, and click on the Clear button or press **Alt+E**. You can clear all the tabs by clicking on Clear All or pressing **Alt+A**. To add a tab leader, press **Alt** plus the underlined number. When you're done, click on **OK** or press **Enter**.

Put It to Work

Creating a Sales List

Let's practice what you've learned about tabs by creating a small sales list. Type this information, and then we'll come back and set the tabs (make sure you press **Tab** between each sales item and its price):

Widgets	$11.22
Whatsits	$212.34
Whosits	$7.99

Now, select the list by dragging over it. Click on the **Decimal Tab** button, and then click on the **Ruler** to set the tab.

Great! Now let's add a leader just for fun. Double-click on the tab to display the Tabs dialog box. Choose the number three leader, and click on **OK**.

Getting Rid of a Tab

If you need to remove a tab, the easiest way is to just drag the tab off the Ruler with the mouse.

If you want to make this more difficult, do it with the keyboard. Open the Format menu and select Tabs by pressing **Alt+O** and then **T**. Under **Tab Stop Position**, select a tab to delete, and press **Alt+E**. You can clear all the tabs by pressing **Alt+A**.

What's Wrong with This Picture?

Look at this and tell me what, if anything, is wrong with this picture:

Salesperson	Territory	April Miles	April Expenses
John	North Canton	1230.5	1422.32
Georgia	Eastwood	933.12	533.76
Tom	South Canton	1221.6	1387.66
Laurie	Kints Cove	1330.56	433.89

Answer: If you said, "A lot!" you're right. First of all, leaders are not appropriate in this situation, but even if they were, leaders should not be used in column headings (the headings get confused with the data that way). Also, decimal tabs (and not left-aligned tabs) should have been used with the two numerical columns.

Setting a Table

A table makes it easy for you to keep food off your lap. In Word, it makes entering and organizing large amounts of information easier than if you use tabs. Tables are made up of *rows* (the horizontal axis) and *columns* (the vertical axis). The intersection of a row and a column is called a *cell*. If that sounds like the definition of a spreadsheet, you're right—tables are very much like simple spreadsheets.

By the Way . . .

You can use a table for more than just tabular data; tables are great for creating side-by-side text (such as résumés) and/or graphics.

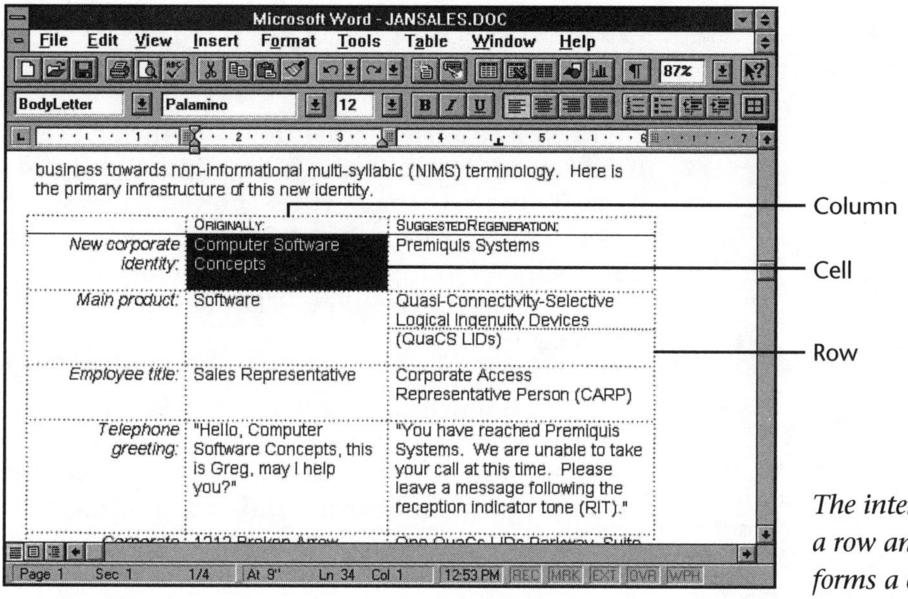

The following screenshot shows Microsoft Word with a table. Labels point to **Column**, **Cell**, and **Row**.

The intersection of a row and a column forms a cell.

Get the knives and forks ready: here's how you "set" a table into your document. Start out by placing the insertion point where you want to set the table.

Click on the **Table** button on the **Standard** toolbar, and then drag over the grid to select the number of rows and columns. An empty table—with the number of rows and columns you specified—will appear at the insertion point. With the keyboard, open the Table Insert Table command by pressing **Alt+T** and then **I**. Press **Alt+C** to move to Enter Number of Columns, and then type the number of columns you desire. Move to Number of **Rows** by pressing **Tab**.

If you want to create a table and you'd like Word to format it for you, skip to the end of this chapter to learn about the Table Wizard. Then come back here to learn how to enter data into the table and make changes to it.

The gridlines that you see help you enter data into the cells, but they don't print. If they bother you, remove them from your screen by opening the Table menu and selecting Gridlines. When a check mark appears beside this command, gridlines are displayed. By selecting the command when a check mark is displayed, you toggle the Gridlines command off.

If you use **Shift+Tab** to back up to a cell, you select the contents of the entire cell, and by typing, you'll replace it completely. If you don't want to do that, use the mouse to click on the cell instead (this procedure does not select the cell's entire contents). For you keyboarders out there, follow these steps: press **Shift+Tab** to move back to a previous cell, and before you start typing, use the **arrow** keys to move the cursor to the exact location within the cell where you want to add your new information.

Instead of typing data, you can copy information from a spreadsheet program (such as Microsoft Excel) into Word, which creates a table automatically. Use the old "cut and paste" method, with the **Cut**, **Copy**, and **Paste** commands on the **Edit** menu of each program.

The Three T's: Typing Text in a Table

Enter text into a table by starting with the first cell. (If necessary, click in it to move the insertion point there.) To move to the next cell, press **Tab**. Press **Shift+Tab** to move to a previous cell. When you get to the end of a row, pressing **Tab** will move you to the first cell in the next row. Alternatively, you can click on a cell to move there.

Here are some tips for entering data into a table:

- ☞ If you want to type several paragraphs in the cell, press **Enter** at the end of each paragraph (just as you would at any other time). The height of the table will grow to accommodate the amount of text you enter.

- ☞ If you want to insert a tab in a cell (for example, you've typed several paragraphs in a cell, and you want to indent them), press **Ctrl+Tab**. Just remember this: In a table, Tab moves you from cell to cell, and Ctrl+Tab moves you to the next tab stop. (Weird, I know.)

- ☞ If you want to change the width of a column, move the pointer to the column's right edge (the pointer will change to two vertical lines). Drag the column's edge to any location to make the column bigger or smaller.

Selecting the Cells You Want to Change

You can select entire rows or columns in order to format them in one step. For example, you can select a row of column headings and format them as bold so they stand out. To select a cell or a row, just click to the left of it. To select a column, click at the top of it. To select an entire table, open the Table menu and choose Select Table or press **Alt+5** (on the numeric keypad, with **Num Lock** off).

To select a single cell, simply press **Tab** or **Shift+Tab** to move to that cell. If you're already at the cell, you can press **Shift+End** to select the entire contents of the current cell.

Why do you have to add borders when they're already there? Well, the "borders" you're seeing are the *gridlines* that help you enter text into a table. Remember that gridlines don't print; to have borders, you must add them.

Formatting Cells

B After selecting the cell or cells that you want to format, follow the normal steps to apply character formatting. For example, if you want to make the selected cells bold, click on the **Bold** button on the **Formatting** toolbar. If you want to change the font, select a new one from the **Font** box on the **Formatting** toolbar. If you want to change the alignment, press the appropriate button on the **Formatting** toolbar. See Chapters 11 and 12 for more tips on changing formatting.

You can access the table commands (such as inserting rows, columns, Table AutoFormat, etc.) by placing the insertion point within a table and clicking the *right* mouse button.

Adding *borders* (dark lines around cells) is an especially effective type of formatting with tables—as is shading (adding a bit of gray to darken a particular cell and call attention to it). See Chapter 20 for help with borders and shading.

Changing Your Mind: Copying, Moving, and Deleting Cells

You can copy or move the contents of cells by selecting cells and then clicking on the appropriate button:

Copy   Copies a cell

   Cut/Paste   Moves a cell

If you want to delete the contents of a cell, select the cell and press **Delete**.

When you copy or move a cell's contents to another cell, anything currently in the cell you're copying (or moving) to is wiped out (replaced).

You can move a cell's contents very quickly by selecting the cell and dragging it to its new location. To copy a cell, hold down the **Ctrl** key as you drag (if you don't press Ctrl, you'll move the cell's contents). I find it easier to grab a cell if I position the pointer in the *middle of the cell* I want to copy or move, and *then drag*. When you move or copy a cell's contents like this, the mouse pointer changes to a small grey square. Look for this "flag" when you move or copy cells to let you know that "you've got 'em."

Put It to Work

Creating and Formatting a Practice Table

 Click on the **Table** button on the **Standard** toolbar. Create a table that's three columns wide and four rows high. Type this information, remembering to press **Tab** to move from cell to cell:

Item	Regular Price	Sale Price
Widgets	12.00	11.20
Whatsits	9.75	8.15
Whosises	11.20	9.85

Select the first row of the table by clicking to the left of the row. Then click on the **Center Alignment** button on the **Formatting** toolbar to center the headings in their cells. Select the **Item** column and center it as well, by clicking on the **Center Alignment** button again.

Select row one again, and click on the **Italic** button to make the headings stand out:

Item	Regular Price	Sale Price
Widgets	12.00	11.20
Whatsits	9.75	8.15
Whosises	11.20	9.85

Now let's get those numbers lined up. Drag over the first column of numbers to select them. If necessary, click on the **Tab Alignment** button on the **Ruler** to change to decimal alignment. Then click on the **Ruler** to place the decimal tab. Repeat this process for the second column of numbers.

Item	Regular Price	Sale Price
Widgets	12.00	11.20
Whatsits	9.75	8.15
Whosises	11.20	9.85

Making Your Table Bigger

Want a bigger table? Just add more rows or columns.

To add a single row, you can simply move to the last cell in the table and press **Tab**. To add more than one row, start by selecting some of the rows *above* where you want to add additional rows. For example, to add two rows, select two rows. Then open the Table menu and select the Insert Rows command. New rows are added above the rows you selected.

To add more columns, select the column to the right of where you want to add the additional column. If you want to add more than one column, select several columns. Open the

Why *don't* you need to insert a tab (by pressing Ctrl+Tab) in front of the numbers so you can use the Decimal Tab button later to align them? How can the Decimal Tab button align something that doesn't have tabs in front of it? Who knows—it's just another Word weirdness. Use Ctrl+Tab to insert tabs when you want to align *text*, not numbers. (I found this out the hard way, and I thought I'd pass it along.)

Table menu and select the Insert Columns command. New columns are added to the left of the columns you selected.

Put It to Work

Adding a Table Heading

To insert a row at the top of the table you created earlier in this chapter, select the first row of the table, open the **Table** menu, and select **Insert Rows**.

Now we're going to merge the three cells in this row to form a single cell that we can use as a table heading. Select the new row, and open the **Table** menu. Select the **Merge Cells** command.

Type this heading:

April Sales Campaign

Use the **Bold** button on the **Formatting** toolbar to bold the heading, and your table looks like this:

April Sales Campaign		
Item	*Regular Price*	*Sale Price*
Widgets	12.00	11.20
Whatsits	9.75	8.15
Whosises	11.20	9.85

Spaced Out

Is everything all scrunched up? You can add more space between rows in a table to make them easier to read. Just select the rows you want to affect, and then open the Table menu by clicking on it (or by pressing **Alt+A**). Choose Cell Height and Width by clicking on it or pressing **W**. Under Height of Row *x*, select either **At least** or **Exactly**. Then enter the number of lines you want to add as space in the **At** box, and select **OK** or press **Enter**.

Remember that you can also add borders and shading to cells to emphasize important information. As a suggestion, you can add shading to every other row to make it easier to read across your table instead of adding space. You'll learn how to add borders and shading in Chapter 20.

Let Word Set Your Table for You

If you don't want to fuss too much over a table (and who can blame you?), why not let Word do the work for you? Just use the Table Wizard, and if you still want to customize the table, go back to any of the prior sections for a quick how-to.

Why was the title automatically centered? Because the title row retained the formatting of the row above which it was inserted (and that row featured *centered* column headings).

Here's how to rub the genie's lamp:

Open the Table menu and select the Insert table command. With the keyboard, press **Alt+A**, then **I**.

Select Wizard. With the keyboard, press **Alt+Z**.

Select a style. With the keyboard, press **Alt** plus the underlined number of your choice. Click on Next or press **Alt+N**.

Follow the instructions on the screen, and move onto the next screen when you're through. To use the keyboard, simply press **Alt** plus the underlined letter of your choice. To move to the next screen, click on Next or press **Alt+N**. When you get to the end, click on Finish or press **Alt+F**. Word will take you to the Table AutoFormat dialog box.

Table AutoFormat		
Formats:	Preview	OK

Formats:
Simple 3
Classic 1
Classic 2
Classic 3
Classic 4
Colorful 1
Colorful 2
Colorful 3
Columns 1
Columns 2

Preview:

	Jan	Feb	Mar	Total
East	7	7	5	19
West	6	4	7	17
South	8	7	9	24
Total	21	18	21	60

OK
Cancel
Help

Formats to Apply
☒ Borders   ☒ Font   ☒ AutoFit
☒ Shading   ☐ Color

Apply Special Formats To
☒ Heading Rows   ☐ Last Row
☒ First Column   ☐ Last Column

Let Word do the work!

Table AutoFormat allows you to select a sample format for your table. This makes it easy to add a finished look to your table without a lot of fuss. Of course, for that custom look, you can make border and shading selections yourself—see Chapter 20 for more info.

To format your table automatically, select a format from the Formats list. You'll see a preview so you can decide whether you like your choice. You can fine-tune your selection by selecting or deselecting items under **Formats to Apply** and **Apply Special Formats to.** When you're satisfied, click on **OK** or press **Enter.**

By the Way . . .

By selecting the Table AutoFormat command on the Table menu, you can format (or reformat) your table automatically at any time. So don't feel like you're stuck if you decide you don't like the table style you've chosen.

The Least You Need to Know

I'll put my cards on the table—here's what I feel were the most important points of the chapter:

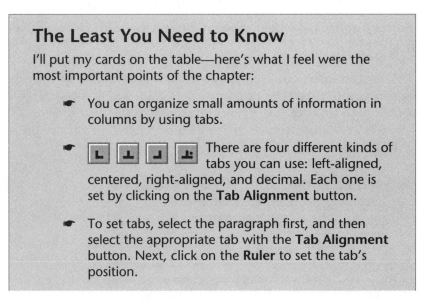

- ☞ You can organize small amounts of information in columns by using tabs.

- ☞ There are four different kinds of tabs you can use: left-aligned, centered, right-aligned, and decimal. Each one is set by clicking on the **Tab Alignment** button.

- ☞ To set tabs, select the paragraph first, and then select the appropriate tab with the **Tab Alignment** button. Next, click on the **Ruler** to set the tab's position.

☛ You can add a tab leader, which puts dots or dashes in the empty space normally taken up by a tab. Double-click on a tab stop on the Ruler, and a box will appear that enables you to select a leader character.

☛ 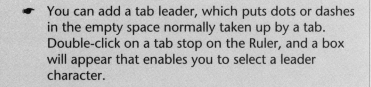 Tables are better to use than tabs if you have large amounts of data to organize. To create a table, click on the **Table** button on the **Standard** toolbar, and drag over the grid to select the number of columns and rows.

☛ Enter data into the various cells in a table by pressing **Tab**, and use **Shift+Tab** to move from cell to cell.

☛ To change the width of a column, drag the column's right edge to its new location.

☛ If you need to move a cell's contents, select the cell's contents by clicking in the middle of the cell. Then drag the cell to its new location. To copy a cell, hold down the **Ctrl** key as you drag.

☛ To add more rows or columns, select the area where you want the new row or column placed, then choose either the Insert **C**olumns or Insert **R**ows command from the **T**able menu.

☛ To add a heading to a table, merge cells across the width of a table by using the **M**erge Cells command on the Table menu.

☛ You can add more space between the rows of a table by using the Cell Height and **W**idth command on the **T**able menu.

☛ You can access the table commands through a shortcut menu, which is available when you place the insertion point within a table and click on the *right* mouse button.

This page unintentionally left blank.

Chapter 16

Getting It Right: Checking Your Document for Errors

In This Chapter

- Checking your document for spelling errors
- Looking up an alternative for a word
- Finding grammatical errors
- Searching and replacing words within a document

I am not the world's best speller. Poor Miss Dingerham, she tried so hard, but I just never got it: "I before E . . . except in the 2,000 other words where it's E before I." Thank goodness for spell checkers, grammar checkers, and all those nifty programs built into Word that help me focus on what I'm trying to say, rather than how I'm saying it.

Spelling Bee

When Word checks a document for spelling errors, it searches for mistakes everywhere (it reminds me of ol' Miss Dingerham). Word checks headers, footers, footnotes, and annotations (but not hidden text). Spell checking a document is simple—just click on the **Spelling** button on the **Standard** toolbar. For you keyboard users out there, just press **F7** to start spell checking. Word immediately starts checking for spelling errors. Also, if you've repeated a word accidentally, or mis-capitalized it, Word will tell you so.

If you want Word to spell-check your document from the beginning instead of looping around, move to the top of the document by pressing **Ctrl+Home**. Then start spell-checking by clicking on the **Spelling** button on the **Standard** toolbar, or by using the Spelling command on the **Tools** menu.

When Word checks your document for spelling errors, it begins its search at the insertion point. (You remember the insertion point: it's that blinking vertical line that marks your place in your document.) If you start spell-checking from the *middle* of a document, at some time a message box will appear asking whether you want to spell-check the beginning part of the document. Just choose Yes to continue.

You can quickly check a single paragraph or section of your document by selecting it first, and then clicking on the **Spelling** button on the **Standard** toolbar or pressing **F7**. Only the highlighted text will be checked.

By the Way . . .

You can customize the way Word spell-checks your document with the **Tools Options** command. For example, Word can be instructed to ignore the capitalization of words that are all uppercase, or to ignore words with text and numbers. Click on the **Spelling** tab, or press **Ctrl+Tab** until it's highlighted. To select an option, click on it (or press **Alt** plus the underlined letter).

If you want to spell-check a single word (or a selection of text), make sure the text is selected, and then press **F7** or click on the **Spelling** button. After it's done checking the word or the selection, Word will ask you if you want to spell-check the rest of the document. Click on **Yes**, and the spell check will continue.

What to Do If Word Finds a Mistake

If Word finds a misspelled or repeated word, a box with more buttons than an airplane cockpit appears, giving you lots of options.

Spelling: English [US]	

Not in Dictionary: focues

Change To: focus
Suggestions:
focus
focuses
focused
fauces

Add Words To: CUSTOM.DIC

[Ignore] [Ignore All]
[Change] [Change All]
[Add] [Suggest]

[AutoCorrect] [Options...] [Undo Last] [Cancel] [Help]

All these buttons in this dialog box, and they still forgot one: Panic.

Correct the spelling of the word. If you agree with the suggestion in the Change To box, just click on the Change button. If you want, you can type your own correction, or select an alternative from the Suggestions list box. If you want to correct this word throughout the document, click on Change All instead.

Ignore the correction. If you want to skip just this occurrence of the unrecognized word, click on the Ignore button. To skip all occurrences of the unrecognized word, click on the Ignore All button.

Add this word to the dictionary. That way, it won't be considered misspelled ever again. Just click on the Add button. Choose this option for specialized words that you use in your job, such as "cardiopulmonary," "electrolyte," "anthropomorphic," "Nanotechnology," or "Standard toolbar."

Add this misspelling to the AutoCorrect library. If you add a misspelling to AutoCorrect, and later you type the word in the same incorrect way, Word will correct it for you automatically. Forget what AutoCorrect is? Just flip back to Chapter 6 and I'll reintroduce you.

Delete the repeated word. If a word is repeated twice and it shouldn't be, click on the Delete button. (You won't see this button unless Word encounters a repeated word.)

Undo a previous correction. You can undo any of the last five corrections in your document by clicking on Undo Last. This is great for people like me, who love to click on the Change button, only to realize that the last word was spelled correctly in the first place.

You continue this process until the spell check is finished.

Handling the Informant

I was going to use the title "Using the Thesaurus" for this section. But then I decided to see what synonyms the Thesaurus would use to spice up my title. "Handling the Informant" is what it came up with. I guess that shows one of my reservations about using a thesaurus: it can make your writing sound stilted and fake. I mean, how often does someone say, "Our sales for the fourth quarter were consequential" instead of simply, "Our sales for the fourth quarter were great."

To use the Thesaurus, just follow these *consequential* (or great, important, considerable, critical) steps. First, select the word you want to look up, or move the insertion point to the word. Then open the Tools menu and select the Thesaurus command, or press **Shift+F7**. A box "full of meaning" will appear. The word you selected in the document appears under **Looked Up**.

You can select from the alternative meanings listed in the Thesaurus box.

Thesaurus: English (US)
Looked Up: competition	**Replace with Synonym:** rivalry	**Replace**
Meanings: rivalry [noun] / athletic event [noun]	rivalry / opposition / vying / contention / striving / marketing / free market condition / trial / strife	**Look Up** / **Cancel** / **Previous** / **Help**

In the Thesaurus dialog box, you can select from several options:

- ☞ If the word you selected is not found, enter an alternate word and click on Look Up.

- ☞ Choose from the synonyms listed in the Replace with Synonym/ Antonym/Related Word list box.

- ☞ To change the synonyms listed, choose from general variations of the selected word that appear in the Meanings box. If the **Related Words** or **Antonyms** options are listed under Meanings, select either one of them to display additional choices.

- ☞ Look up additional meanings for the word displayed in the Replace with Synonym/Antonym/Related Word box by clicking on Look Up.

☛ Decide whether to replace the selected word. Click on the **Replace** button to substitute the selected word with the word displayed in the Replace with Synonym/Antonym/Related Word box, or click on **Cancel**.

I Doesn't Need No Grammar Checker!

The **Grammar** command checks your document for problems of a grammatical nature, and suggests ways to improve your writing and clarify your meaning. As an added bonus, while Word is checking your grammar, it also checks for spelling errors.

To check the grammar in your document, open the **Tools** menu and choose **Grammar**. If Word finds something questionable, you see a box offering some suggestions.

The **Grammar** command works just like the spelling checker; it starts checking your document at the insertion point. If you want to start checking the grammar at the beginning of your document, press **Ctrl+Home**. Then use the **Grammar** command on the Tools menu.

Grammar: English (US)

Sentence:
Dan joins us from Dun and Bradley, where he headed an international sales force of forty independant reps.

Ignore
Next Sentence

Suggestions:
The word an does not agree with sales.

Consider ____ instead of ____

Change
Ignore Rule
Cancel

Explain...   Options...   Undo Last   Help

May I make a suggestion?

From here, you have these options:

☛ *Accept a suggestion* by selecting one of those listed in the Suggestions box and clicking on Change.

☛ *Get more information about what's wrong* by clicking on the Explain button.

☛ *Make your own correction* by clicking inside the document window and changing your text. To check the grammar in the rest of the document, click on Next Sentence.

☞ *Bypass the suggestion* by clicking on the **I**gnore button. You can bypass the entire sentence by clicking on the Next Sentence button instead. You can tell Word to ignore this "grammatical faux pas" for the rest of the document by clicking on Ignore **R**ule.

Is the **G**rammar command being too picky? Or not picky enough? By clicking on the **O**ptions button, you can choose from predefined grammar styles, including Business or Casual Writing, if you want.

At the end of the grammar check, Word displays something it calls Readability Statistics: the total number of words, the percent of sentences that use *passive voice*, and the *readability index*. You can choose not to display this information by clearing the Show **R**eadability Statistics After Proofing check box (in the **G**rammar options). For an average reader, look for a Flesch Reading Ease of about 65, a Flesch-Kincaid Grade Level of about 7 or 8, a Coleman-Liau Grade level of about 13, and a Bromuth Grade level of about 10. Numbers above these indicate some rather difficult material. (Translation: "Instead of two sleeping pills, try reading this.") Lower numbers than these indicate easier material. (Translation: "This text makes a perfect accompaniment to cereal.")

What's Wrong with This Picture?

After spell-checking her document, Joan found this mistake:

For the poor performance of our product, their seems to be no excuse.

What's wrong with this picture?

Answer: If you said that everything in the sentence is spelled correctly, you are right. Spelling is not what is wrong here; diction (a part of grammar) is. Where Joan used the "their," she should have used "there." Would the Grammar command catch such a mistake? Try it and see.

Indiana Fulton and the Hunt for the Great Lost Word

Suppose you just finished a big report, only to find out that your client's real name is *Pets Are Us Incorporated*, not *Bill's Pet Shop*. You can use Word's

Find and Replace feature to replace all occurrences of the incorrect name right before the meeting with the Top Dog. You can also search for a word without replacing it; this is helpful when locating the correct section within a document.

The Hunt Is On!

To find a word or a phrase in your document, open the Edit menu and select the Find command, or press **Ctrl+F**. Type the word (or phrase) you're looking for in the Find What text box. There are some handy options you can choose from:

- ☞ If you want to locate only the word you typed, and not words that include it as a part (for example, you want to find "search" but not "searching"), use the Find **W**hole Words Only check box.

- ☞ If you want to match upper- or lowercase (for example, "Word" but not "word"), then use the Match Case check box.

- ☞ If you want to search backward through the document, open the Search list and select the **U**p option.

- ☞ If you want to search for a word with particular formatting, click on **F**ormat or press **Alt+O**, select Font, Paragraph, Language, or Style, and make the selections you want.

- ☞ To search for a special mark, such as a page break or a tab, click on Special or press **Alt+E**, then select an item from the list.

Passive voice   A type of sentence that states what *is done* by (or to) the subject, rather than what the subject *does*. For example, compare "the race was won by Mary Ann" (passive voice) to the same phrase in *active voice*: "Mary Ann won the race." Passive voice can make your sentence vague and confusing. Four out of five English teachers recommend using active voice. (But forget the teachers—use it anyway. It works.)

Readability index   A way of measuring the educational level a reader would need in order to understand your text easily. The grammar checker makes this estimate by counting the average number of words per sentence, and the average number of characters per word. (A good average is about 17 words per sentence.)

When you have selected all the options you want, click on Find Next. Word begins the search from the current location in the document, but you can continue the search at the beginning by clicking on Yes when the message appears.

Word will look for the first occurrence of the selected word. If you want it to continue looking, click on the Find Next button. To return to your document, click on **Cancel**. To continue the search (search for the same text or formatting) at a later time or in another document, press **Shift+F4**.

The Great Switcheroo: Finding a Word and Replacing It with Something Else

To search for a word or phrase and replace it with other text, start by opening the Edit menu and selecting the Replace command (or by pressing **Ctrl+H**). Type the word (or phrase) you're looking for in the Find What text box, and type the word (or phrase) you want to replace it with in the Replace With box. Here are some handy options you can choose from:

- ☞ If you want to locate only the word you typed, and not words that include it as a part (for example, you want to find "search" but not "searching"), use the Find **W**hole Words Only check box.

- ☞ If you want to match upper- or lowercase (for example "Word" but not "word"), use the Match Case check box.

- ☞ If you want to search backward through the document, open the Search list and select the **Up** option.

- ☞ If you want to search for a word with particular formatting, click on Format (or press **Alt+O**), select Font, Paragraph, Language, or Style, and make the selections you want.

- ☞ To search for a special mark, such as a page break or a tab, click on Special or **press Alt+E**, then select an item from the list.

When you're ready to start, click on either Find Next (confirm changes before replacing) or Replace All (do not confirm). Word will look for the first occurrence of the selected word. If you chose Find Next, confirm the replacement by clicking on Replace, or continue searching by clicking on Find Next.

Getting Fancy with Find

Using advanced criteria, you can specify some pretty complex search patterns. First, from within the **Search or Replace** dialog boxes, select Use Pattern Matching, or press **Alt+M**. Then click on Special and select one from the list, or enter your search pattern in the Find What text box. Here's a list of patterns and what they can do:

Pattern	What It Searches for	Sample	What It Finds
?	Any single character	b?t	but, bat, bit
*	Multiple adjacent characters	b*t	but, bat, boat, etc.
[*list*]	Any character in the *list*	b[a,i]	bat, bit, not but
[*range*]	Any character within *range*	[b-g]at	bat, cat, eat, fat
[!*c*]	Not character *c*	b[!i]t	bat, but, not bit
c[*n*]	*n* occurrences of character *c*	10[4]	10000
c[*n*,]	*n* and lower occurrences of character *c*	10[4]	10, 100, 1000, 10000
c[*n*,*m*]	*n-m* occurrences of character *c*	10[2,4]	100, 1000, 10000
c[@]	Any occurrences of character *c*	10[@]	10, 100, etc.
<(*char*)	*char* found at beginning of word	<ed	education, Ed, editorial, etc.
>(*char*)	*char* found at end of word	>ed	worked, loaded, etc.

The Least You Need to Know

Let's see if I can help you "find" the important points in this chapter:

- To spell-check a document, click on the **Spelling** button on the **Standard** toolbar, or press **F7**.

- To check the spelling of a single word or selection, select the text and press **F7**.

- To look up an alternative for a word, select it, and then open the **Tools** menu and choose the **Thesaurus** command.

- To check your document for grammatical errors, open the **Tools** menu and choose **Grammar**.

- To search for words in a document, use the **Find** command on the **Edit** menu or press **Ctrl+F**.

- To replace words in a document, use the **Replace** command on the **Edit** menu or press **Ctrl+E**.

Part III
Other Stuff You Paid For But Never Learned How to Use

Yes, I am one of the millions of Americans who own one of those new handi-cams (that's a video camera that was left in the dryer too long). Anyway, it comes "full-featured," which is a nice way of saying that there are entirely too many buttons on it. I've had the camera for a year and I only know what the ON button is for.

Maybe you've been using Word like I use my handi-cam: just point and shoot—never mind the fine-tuning. There's nothing wrong with that; I've got a shelf full of videos to prove it. But when you're ready to know what "all those other buttons are for," come back and read this section.

Chapter 17
Templates: Creating "Paint by Number" Documents

In This Chapter

- What is a template?
- How to use a template
- Changing your document's template
- Using Word's custom templates
- Creating your own templates

The one thing that most of us don't have in excess is time. But if you want to send a business letter, you have to

- Open a new document.
- Set the page margins, paper size, and orientation.
- Create headers and footers (such as a company logo or a page number).
- Enter the addresses and the salutation.

But with *templates*, most of this groundwork would already be done for you. I guess that's why I like them: templates help fill the emptiness so I don't have to start each document from scratch. Like a paint-by-number kit that provides a rough outline, a template acts as a pattern for your document.

SPEAK LIKE A GEEK

Template Defines the environment for a document, such as margin settings, page orientation, and so on. Word for Windows comes with additional templates, which you can use to create specialized documents (if you are using one of these templates, your screen may look different from the ones shown in this book).

In Word 2.0, AutoText was called the Glossary, but its purpose was much the same—a depository for pet phrases and graphics you use over and over in many documents.

To Template or Not to Template

Even with that great intro, you're probably thinking: "*I* don't need no stinkin' templates." Okay, templates are a potentially boring topic, so I can understand your reluctance to learn more about them. But hang in there; templates, although not as interesting as Amy Fisher or the Elvis stamp controversy, can still do some pretty fantastic things.

The purpose behind templates is based on a simple idea: although you may do a lot of work in Word, you probably create *only a few* distinct types of documents: memos, business letters, reports, and proposals. So when you use a template, most of the up-front formatting work is already done, and you're ready to type the text for *the current* memo, letter, report, or proposal.

A template can be constructed for each type of document, with margin settings, paper size, and other information already selected. In addition, you can save some *boilerplate text* in the template, such as a return address, a greeting, and a salutation, to save time in creating documents of that type. A template can also store the styles you've defined, as well as AutoText entries you've saved.

For example, a template for business correspondence might have "holes" in it for the recipient's address, the salutation ("Dear John:"), and the closing ("Most respectfully yours"). A template for personal correspondence would have similar "holes" for the address and the salutation ("Dear *whomever :*") and might even have some boilerplate text: "You are the most important person in my life, *whomever*, and I feel that while I profess my love for you, we must sit down soon and work out property distribution arrangements. . . ." (The previous sentence was suggested by my *ex*-fiancé.)

But templates are more than just a stencil for a document that you "fill" with text. Your choice of templates affects which commands are available on the menus, and which tools are displayed on the toolbars.

Boilerplate text   Generic text (such as a standard greeting or a return address) that's saved as part of a template so it does not have to be retyped into every document that uses that template.

Generic Is Not Always Better

Once, in order to save some money, my sister tried some generic pasta. Well, needless to say, she soon discovered that the pasta tasted about as good as the box it came in. Not that it was all that bad, it just wasn't all that great either.

Word comes with its own generic: the Normal template. Unless you switch templates when you start a new document, your document is based on the Normal template. But keep in mind that because it's generic, the Normal template doesn't come with anything special to help you get work done on a specific document. Word comes with many other templates, each designed for a specific purpose, such as reports, newsletters, and so on. It pays to get to know them.

Selecting a Template for Your Document

Suppose you wanted to use one of the Word templates to produce a particular style of letter or for a particular type of business document. Here's what you do to select one of the Word templates when you start a new document.

First, open the File menu and select New. Under Template, select the template you want to use. Then click on the **OK** button. Later, when you have created your own templates, you can follow these same steps to use your templates for creating documents.

If you've already opened a document, and you want to change the template it's based on, open the File menu and choose Templates. Click on Attach or press **Alt+A** and select the template you'd like to use. When you're done, click on **OK** or press **Enter** to return to the Templates dialog box. Click on **OK** or press **Enter** again to attach the selected template.

> ### By the Way . . .
>
> If you want to know what a template will look like *before you choose it*, just open the **F**ormat menu and select Style **G**allery (with the keyboard, press **Alt+O** and then **G**). You may remember Style Gallery from the chapter on styles—Chapter 14. Anyway, once the Style Gallery dialog box is open, simply select a template from the **T**emplate list. Then click on **E**xample or press **Alt+E**. Once you've found a template you like, follow these instructions to create a new document based on that template.

If you want to make this real easy, use one of the Word Wizards, which walk you through the creation of a perfect customized document. For example, instead of using the template Letter1, use the Letter Wizard. You can review the instructions on using wizards by returning to Chapter 8.

After you select one of these templates for a new document, you'll see areas whose text you'll need to replace. For example, in the letter templates, you'll see a place for your recipient's address. Move the insertion point to the area you need to replace, press **Insert**, and you're in Overtype mode (you'll see **OVR** on the Status bar). Simply type the real information over the sample text.

Creating Your Own Templates

You can create your own template based on an existing document by opening that document, and then following along with this procedure.

First, delete any text you don't want to reuse in other documents. Verify that the document settings, such as margins, columns, and page orientation, are set the way you want to save them. Create common text elements, such as headers, footers, or headings. You may also want to create the styles you'll want to use when designing a document based on this template. Once your template is ready, save it.

To save your template, open the File menu and choose the Save As command. Enter a name for the template, using a name that describes the template's purpose, such as SALESRPT. Under Save File as Type, select **Document Template**.

Put It to Work

Using a Template to Create a Document

So that you can understand the extent to which templates simplify the task of creating a document, let's walk through the process of creating a document based on one of Word's templates, Letter1.

First, open the **File** menu and select **New**. With the keyboard, press **Ctrl+F**, then **N**. In the Template box, select **Letter1**. If you're using a keyboard, press **Alt+T**, then use the **arrow** keys to select **Letter1**. You'll see sample text marking the areas you need to complete. Move the insertion point to **Company Name** and press **Insert**. You are now in Overtype mode. Enter your company's name (press **Delete** to delete extra characters). Press the **Right arrow** key to move to the next line, the **company address**. Enter the address and delete any excess characters. Press the **Right arrow** key to move to the next line. Continue the process of entering information until the sample letter is complete.

 When you're through, click on the **Save** button on the **Standard** toolbar, or press **Ctrl+S**. Enter a filename like **COLETTER** and press **Enter**.

The Least You Need to Know

Here's a paint-by-number guide for using templates:

- ☞ To see which template you are using, choose the Templates command on the File menu.

- ☞ When you create a new document, select the template you want to use in the Template list box.

- ☞ To change the template your document is using, open the File menu and select the Templates command. Click on Attach or press **Alt+A**, then select the template you'd like to use.

- ☞ If you use one of Word's custom templates, look for special commands, such as Instructions on the Format menu.

- ☞ You can create a template based on a document by opening the File menu and choosing the Save As command. Enter the name for the template, then select **Document Template** under Save File as **Type**.

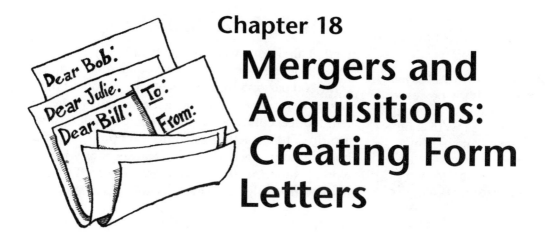

Chapter 18

Mergers and Acquisitions: Creating Form Letters

In This Chapter

- ☞ The magical world of merging
- ☞ Creating a data source
- ☞ Writing your dummy letter
- ☞ Merging to create form letters
- ☞ Creating matching envelopes or mailing labels

About six months ago, I was reading one of the magazines I subscribe to when I spotted an ad with my name in it. The ad read, "If you've been thinking of buying a computer, Jennifer Flynn, now is the time." I must have stared at that for at least a few minutes. I mean, how did they get my name there?

Then it hit me—it was just another variation of the old form letter. You would've thought that I was over the thrill of seeing my name in a *personalized* letter. I mean, who really believes that "you may have already won!"?

But there's no denying that form letters and mailing labels are two of the best reasons for typing your letters on a computer, so let's see how this computer magic is done.

Look Before You Merge

First of all, let me warn you that this very boring topic produces some real cool results: for example, print 200 personalized letters when you only type *one.* So before you continue, get a caffeine equivalent (coffee, cola, chocolate, or a large mallet), some aspirin, a ton of letterhead, and then prop this book up someplace where you can see it as you work. Believe me, this is not a process you'll want to *memorize.* All set? Okay, let's go!

In order to create form letters or mailing labels in Word, you need two files:

☛ Your *main document* file contains the generic text and formatting (such as margin settings, paper size, and the like) that you want to appear in every copy of the final document.

☛ Your *data source* contains the variable information (such as the individual names and addresses).

The process of taking the names and addresses from the data source and mixing them into the main document to create multiple form letters (or mailing labels) is called *merging.*

Still awake? Well, you're almost past the worst of the boring background stuff. Just one more section to go before you get to do something.

That's One for the Record

The data source contains the stuff that changes with each form letter or each mailing label. For example, if you wanted to send a letter to each of your customers, the data source (or *data document,* if you prefer) would contain each customer's name, address, and maybe even a customer number.

In your customer data source, each individual client would represent a *data record.* A data record is a collection of the related information about that specific client: name, address, phone number, and client account number. Each client would have a corresponding record in the data source.

The individual pieces that make up a data record are called *fields*. For example, the client's name would be one field, while the address would be another. Each field has its own name—for example, the client name field could be called NAME, and the account number field could be called ACCOUNT (clever, eh?). The names for each field are stored in the *header record*, which is usually just the first line in the data source.

After you create a data source, you'll enter the field names into your dummy letter, so Word will know where to place the real information from each record. For example, you'll enter a field called **First Name** in your dummy letter, and Word will replace it with real data, such as the name **George**.

Giving Birth to a Data Source

Before you create your data source, think about how you are going to use the individual fields. In a typical business letter, for example, you usually include the client's full name and address:

Mr. George Blabberton
Chief Cook and Bottle Washer
Universal Foods, Incorporated
210 W. 86th Street
Piggstown, Vt. 31209

But in the greeting, you can get more friendly:

Dear George,

However, if you create a NAME field which contains the client's entire name, you'll be stuck with a greeting like this:

Dear Mr. George Blabberton,

It's just a guess, but I think that with this greeting, even Mr. George Blabberton would be able to figure out he'd just received a form letter. So instead, break the client's name into several parts: Mr_Ms_Mrs, Firstname, and Lastname.

Something else to think about: will you want to sort the data source's records in any particular order before creating your form letters or mailing labels? Even though it may make sense to have one field for a client's entire address, you can't sort by town or ZIP code unless each of these is its own field. (You can't sort on something that's *part* of a field.) In this case, you will want to create separate fields for the parts of an address: Address, City, State, and ZIP.

Creating a Dummy Letter

Well, I've given you enough to think about; let's get down to business! As step one in the process of creating form letters, we'll create a dummy letter. After we create our data source, we'll go back into the dummy letter and place the field names.

First, open the Tools menu and select Mail Merge. With the keyboard, press **Alt+T**, then **R**. Under Main Document, click on **Create** or press **Alt+C**. Select Form Letters or press **Alt+L**.

Mail Merge Helper

The main document and data source are ready to merge. Choose the Merge button to complete the merge.

Cancel
Help

1 Main Document:

Create ▼   Edit ▼

Merge Type: Form Letters
Main Document: H:\PROJECTS\WWI\DOCS\PHONEY.DOC

2 Data Source:

Get Data ▼   Edit ▼

Data: H:\...\DOCS\TEST.DOC

3 Merge the Data with the Document:

Merge...   Query Options...

Options in Effect:
Suppress Blank Lines in Addresses
Merge to New Document

Your merge forms control center.

Now, if you have opened a document you want to use as the basis for your form letter (or if you have an empty document open), click on Active or press **Alt+A**. If you have a document open which you want to keep, but not use as a form letter, click on New Main Document or press **Alt+N**.

That's it for now. We'll create our data source next, and return to finish the form letter later on.

With Word 2.0, you enter data into a table, rather than a dialog box as shown here. First, you need to enter the fields for your data file, clicking on **Add** as you enter each field. When you're done, click on **OK**, enter a **filename**, click on **OK** again, and Word creates a table into which you enter your data.

At Last! Creating the Data Source

To create a data source, just follow these steps. (If you want some hands-on practice rather than some generic steps, skip ahead to the "Put It to Work" exercise. When you're ready to create your own real data source, come back to this section.)

With Word 2.0, click the **New** button on the Toolbar to create a new document. Open the **File** menu and select Print **Merge**. Click on Attach **Data** File and on **C**reate Data File.

Under **Data Source**, click Get Data or press **Alt+G**. Select Create Data Source or press **Alt+C**.

Now you're ready to select the field names for your data source. Word has thoughtfully filled the data source with common fields, but you may not want to use them all, and/or you may have some new ones of your own. Here's what to do:

Remove fields you don't want to use. Select a field from the Field Names in Header Row list, and click on Remove Field Name or press **Alt+R**.

Add new fields. Type a field name (anything with up to 40 characters with no spaces—use an underscore to substitute for a space if you want to use one) in the Field Name box, then click on Add Field Name or press **Alt+A**.

Change the order of the fields. In order to make data entry as smooth as possible, you might want to change the order of the fields to match the records you'll be typing from. Select a field in the Field Names in Header Row list, then click on the **up** or **down arrow** to move it.

When you're satisfied, click on **OK** or press **Enter**. Enter a name for your data source (different from the name you'll use for your dummy letter). If you were creating a client address data source, you could call it something clever like ADDRESS or CLIENTS, but just remember that file names are limited to eight characters. Click on **OK** or press **Enter** again. A message will appear, telling you that you haven't entered any information into the data source (duh). Click on Edit Data Source or press **Alt+D**.

Put It to Work

Creating a Sample Data source

Let's create a small data source as practice. Open the **Tools** menu and select Mail Merge. Click on **Create** and select Form Letters. Click on **Active Window**. Now we can create the data source. Under **Data Source**, click on **Get Data**. Select **Create Data Source**.

First, we'll remove the fields we don't want. Select each of these fields from the Field Names in Header Row list, and click on **Remove Field Name** to remove each one:

Title
Country
HomePhone
WorkPhone

Now we'll add a field to replace "Title" (which I found to be a bit vague). Under Field Name, type **Mr_Ms_Mrs** and click on Add Field Name. (Actually, we could have left "Title" because that's what it's for, but I had to have you add something!) Let's move the Mr_Ms_Mrs field to where it needs to be—select it, and click on the **up arrow** until it's the first field in the list.

We're done adding and removing fields, so click on **OK**. Enter **TEST** as a name for your data source, and click on **OK**. Click on Edit **D**ata Source. Congrats! Your data source is created, and waiting for you to enter some data (which you'll do as soon as you learn how).

Filling In the Blanks

Entering information into the data source is fairly simple:

- ☞ It's okay if the data is bigger than one of the text boxes; it won't affect how that data appears in your document.

- ☞ Press **Tab** to move to the next field, or **Shift+Tab** to move backward. If you get down to the bottom of the dialog box, and there are still more fields to enter, that's okay—just press **Tab** and you'll move on to the next field.

- ☞ If a field does not apply for a particular record (for example, you don't know a client's title), leave it blank by pressing **Tab** to bypass it.

Entering data into your data table is similar to the instructions listed here— press **Tab** to move from field to field, and **Shift+Tab** to move backward. You don't need to click on anything to move to the next record; just press **Tab**! When you're done, click on the **Save** button on the Toolbar to save your data file.

- ☞ When you're through entering the data for a single record, click on Add New or press **Alt+A**.

- ☞ When you're through entering data, click on the **OK** button to save the data source.

Put It to Work

Entering Our Sample Data Source's Variable Information

Starting with the first field of our test data source, enter these client records. If a field doesn't apply, press **Tab** to move to the next field. When you're through adding a record, click on **Add New** or press **Alt+A** to move on to the next record.

Mr_Ms_Mrs	FirstName	LastName	Job Title	Company
Ms.	Jolene	Smitt	Comptroller	Bobco
Mr.	John	Axe		PI
Mr.	Scott	Cooper	Field Manager	Electric Allied Limited

Address 1	Address 2	City	State	Postal Code
12 North St.		Olmo	OK	73521
One Fire Pl.	Suite #312	Guston	NJ	07401
5218 N. 118th		Spud	ID	83318

When you are finished adding records, click on **OK**. You'll be taken to the dummy letter, which we'll enter in a moment.

Completing the Dummy Letter

Now we get to have fun. First, let me tell you the steps for creating a form letter, and then we'll do one together.

| Insert Merge Field | We left off just after entering data into the data source. After clicking on **OK**, we were placed in the dummy form letter document. So here's where we start entering the form letter's text. It's fairly easy; just type! When you get to the place where you need to insert a field from the data source (for example, you get to a place where you want to insert a first name), click on the **Insert Merge Field** button on the **Mail Merge** toolbar. Choose the field you want to insert. In your document, you'll see something like <<**FirstName**>>, which represents the inserted field.

Keep entering text and inserting field codes until the letter is done. When you're done with your form letter, save it by clicking on the **Save** button on the **Standard** toolbar.

By the Way . . .

Remember to add spaces between field codes when necessary. When I was setting up the sample that you're about to do, I got in a hurry and forgot to insert a space between the field codes for the first and last names. When I merged the data source with my dummy letter, I got names like:

Ms.JoleneSmitt

So check your form letter carefully **before** you perform the actual merge (and have hundreds of them to correct).

Put It to Work

Creating Our Form Letter

Let's create a simple form letter for practice:

Start by inserting the client address fields: click on the **Insert Merge Field** button on the **Mail Merge** toolbar, and insert the **Mr_Ms_Mrs** field. Press the **Spacebar**, insert the **FirstName** field, press the **Spacebar** again, and insert the **LastName** field. Press **Enter**.

Insert the **Title** field and press **Enter**. Insert the rest of the address fields, each on its own line (except for the City, State, and Postal Code fields).

Now press **Enter** four times to insert some space between the address and the greeting. Type **Dearest**, press the **Spacebar**, and insert the **FirstName** field. Add a **comma** and then press **Enter** twice.

continues

continued

Type the body of your letter:

You may have already won 1 million dollars! To obtain a complete list of winners, send $100 in small unmarked bills to me. Thank you and come again.

Click on the **Save** button on the **Standard** toolbar and save your form letter. Call it PHONEY or something equally clever.

With Word 2.0, click on the **New** button on the **Toolbar** to create a new document for your dummy letter. Enter text, then click on the Insert Merge **Field** button when you want to insert a data field. When you're through, save your letter by clicking on the **Save** button on the Toolbar.

The Fat Lady Sings: Merging the Data Source with the Dummy Letter

Finally! Congratulations on making it to our final act: merging the data source with the dummy letter to create form letters. This part is really easy, as you'll soon see.

You have two choices at this point. All you've got to do is to click on the appropriate button on the **Mail Merge** bar.

☛ You can merge the data source and dummy letter to create one big file that you can print later (each form letter will appear in the file on its own page).

☛ You can merge the data source and dummy letter together and print the form letters *now*.

If you've closed your document and reopened it, you may need to reopen your data source as well. Click on the **Open Data Source** button on the **Mail Merge** toolbar, and select your data source file.

If you want to specify a range of records for your merge, click on the **Mail Merge** button on the **Mail Merge** toolbar, and enter your range. You can also specify that blank lines are inserted whenever a record does not contain a field—for example, if a record did not contain any data in the FirstName field, you could specify that a blank line be inserted instead. This is the exact opposite of what normally happens; when you do the "Put It to Work" that follows, you'll see that records without a second address line do not have a blank line inserted—instead, everything just moves up a line in the address.

You have the same two options in Word 2.0—you can create a large merged file to print later, or you can print now. The Merge to Document button depicts pages merging into a file. The Merge to Printer button depicts those same pages merging to a printer. They are both located on the Print Merge bar.

Put It to Work

Merging Our Sample Files

If you want, turn on your printer. Then click on the **Merge to Printer** button on the **Mail Merge** toolbar, and print your form letters. It's as simple as that!

Final Steps: Creating Envelopes and Mailing Labels

The process of creating envelopes and mailing labels from your data source is remarkably similar to the one you used to create your form letter. This will seems a bit like déjà vu, but here goes:

To create envelopes, you'll need a new, blank document. Start by opening the Tools menu and selecting Mail Merge. With the keyboard, press **Alt+T**, then **G**. Under **Main Document**, click on Create or press **Alt+C**. Select Envelopes or press **Alt+E**. Click on New Main Document or press **Alt+N**.

Font Any set of characters which share the same *typeface* (style or design). Fonts convey the mood and style of a document. Technically, font describes the combination of the *typeface* and the *point size* of a character, as in Times Roman 12-point, but in common usage it describes only a character's style or typeface.

Now, attach your data source. From the **Mail Merge Helper**, click on Get Data or press **Alt+G**. Select Open Data Source or press **Alt+O**. Select the data source from the list. When you're done, click on **OK**.

Now it's time to prepare the document for printing envelopes. Click on **Set Up Main Document**, or press **Alt+S**. If you read Chapter 10, this will seem like double déjà vu: select the envelope size from the Envelope Size box. To change sizes, click on the **down arrow** to open the list box, or press **Alt+S**. Select an envelope size by clicking on it (or highlighting it with the **arrow** keys and pressing **Enter**). If you want, you can change the *font* for both the delivery and the return address. Click on the appropriate option, or press **Alt+F** for the delivery address, and **Alt+O** for the return address.

Finally, If you need to verify the feed options (the method used to insert the envelope into the printer), click on the Printing Options tab or press **Ctrl+Tab**. Select an appropriate option, and click on **OK** or press **Enter**.

Move to the Sample Envelope Address area by clicking in it or pressing **Alt+P**. Click on Insert Merge Field or press **Alt+S** to select a field from the data source. (For example, your first field might be MR_MS_MRS.) Repeat for each field in the address, pressing **Enter** at the end of each line. Remember to use the **Spacebar** to insert spaces between fields, and to add commas and other punctuation where necessary. When you're done, click on **OK**. You'll return to the Mail Merge Helper. Click on **Close**.

You'll see a sample envelope. Your return address will displayed automatically if it's been entered with the Tools Options User Info command. If not, just type one in. (If a return address is present, but you don't want to print one, just delete it.) The recipient's address is enclosed in a frame, so you can move it if you want. Just click on it and drag.

You can print it now, or you can print it later. If you want to print the envelopes now, click on the **Merge to Printer** button located on the **Mail Merge** toolbar. Click on the **Merge to New Document** button to print the envelopes later, by saving them within a document file.

Look Fo-o-r the Mai-ai-ling La-bel

Creating mailing labels is very similar to creating envelopes, so I won't bore you with all the details. Here's a brief run-down of all the steps—if you need help with some step, refer to the envelope section (just under the "Final Steps" heading earlier in this chapter) for details.

Open the Tools menu and select Mail Merge.

Select Create, then choose Mailing Labels.

Click on New Main Document.

Click on Get Data, then Open Data Source. Select your data source file from the list, and click on **OK**.

Click on Set Up Main Document. If necessary, select your printer by clicking on it, or by pressing either **Alt+M** (for a dot-matrix printer), or **Alt+L** (for a laser). Select the type of labels you use under Label Products— with the keyboard, press **Alt+P**. Select the appropriate Product Number by clicking on it or pressing **Alt+N**. When you're through, click on **OK**.

 Click on either the Merge to Printer or Merge to New Document button, located on the **Mail Merge** toolbar.

The Least You Need to Know

Congratulations! You have won several million dollars' worth of wonderful tips on merging files:

- ☛ A *record* is a collection of related information about a single person or thing, such as a client. The individual pieces that make up a record are called *fields*.

- ☛ To create a dummy letter, open the **Tools** menu and select Mail Merge. With the keyboard, press **Alt+T**, then **G**. Under Main Document, click on **Create** or press **Alt+C**. Select Form Letters or press **Alt+L**. Click on Active or press **Alt+A**.

continues

continued

☞ To create a data source from the Mail Merge Helper, click on **G**et Data or press **Alt+G**. Select **C**reate Data Source or press **Alt+C**. Select the field names you want. To remove a field, select it and click on Remove Field Name or press **Alt+R**. To add new fields, type a field name in the **F**ield Name box, then click on **A**dd Field Name or press **Alt+A**. To change the order of the fields, select one and click on the **up** or **down arrow**. When you're done, click on **OK** and enter a name for the data file. Click on **OK** again.

☞ To enter data into the data source, click on Edit **D**ata Source or press **Alt+D**. Enter data into the table by pressing **Tab** to move from field to field. When you're through entering data, click on the **OK** button to save the data source.

☞ | Insert Merge Field | To create a form letter, type the text of the letter. When you need to insert a field into the letter, click on the **Insert Merge Field** button, and select the field name from the list box.

☞ To merge the data source with the form letter, click on either the **Merge to Printer** or the **Merge to New Document** button on the **Mail Merge** bar.

☞ To create matching envelopes or mailing labels, use the Tools Mail Merge command. Click on **C**reate, and select the appropriate option. Click on **N**ew Main Document. Click on **G**et Data and select your data source file. Click on **S**et Up Main Document, and either enter a sample address, or select your label options. Click on either the **Merge to Printer** or **Merge to New Document** button on the **Mail Merge** toolbar.

Chapter 19
Extra! Extra! Read All About Columns!

In This Chapter

- ☛ The difference between a table and a column
- ☛ How to add newspaper-style columns to a document
- ☛ Deciding which view mode to use when working with columns
- ☛ Adding vertical lines between columns
- ☛ Keeping text and graphics together

I'll let you in on a little secret: *columns* are not just for newsletters anymore. This may shock those of you who thought you would just skip this chapter because you don't write the company newsletter, but columns are found in some of the better documents the world over. For example, you might add interest to a report by splitting the document into two columns—a skinny one on the left for short summaries of major points, and a fatter one on the right for your actual report. And what better way to format an index than to use two columns?

Newspaper-style columns   Similar to the style of column found in newspapers. Text in these columns flows between invisible boundaries, down one part of the page. At the end of the page, the text continues at the top of the first column on the next page.

A different type of column is the *parallel column*, which is just a fancy way of saying "table." With a table, you read *across* (instead of down) several columns of text and numbers. If you want to "set a table" into your document instead of creating newspaper-style columns, see Chapter 15.

Sorry, but you cannot create columns of uneven width in Word 2.0.

This Just In: What You Should Know About Using Columns

Newspaper-style columns are like those you find in your hometown newspaper. Columns can be "interrupted" by graphics (pictures or charts) that illustrate the story being told. (You'll learn how to insert graphics and other objects into a document in Chapter 20.)

When you start a new document, you are typing text into a *single column* that stretches the width of the margins. At any point in your document, you can change the number of columns by creating a *section*.

When you add columns to a document, the width of the columns is adjusted automatically so they fit equally between the margins. For instance, if you add three columns, the width of your paper is divided into three equal parts. You can elect to create column widths that are uneven (to achieve an interesting effect) if you want.

Reading the Fine Print: Viewing Column Layout

Each viewing mode displays columns a little differently, with each mode offering its own advantages. For example, in Normal view, you can enter text faster than in other views, but your document will look like it's on drugs. Although you may have four columns set up, Normal view will display the text in one long column running along the left side of the page. To switch to Normal view, open the **View** menu and choose the **Normal** command, or click on the **Normal View** button on the horizontal scroll bar.

Switch to Page Layout view to see how your columns will really look when printed. Use this view to make final adjustments to text and column widths. To switch to Page Layout view, open the View menu and choose the **Page Layout** command, or click on the **Page Layout** button on the horizontal scroll bar.

In Page Layout view, columns appear as they will when printed.

In Normal view, columns appear as one long column.

Columns appear differently in different views.

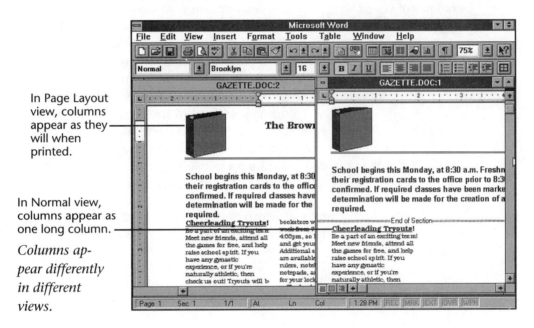

Within either Normal or Page Layout view, you can zoom in (to get a closer look at text) or zoom out (to get an overview of the page layout). Simply open the View menu and select the Zoom command, or choose a zoom mode from the **Zoom** drop-down list box (located on the **Standard** toolbar).

Gossip Column: How to Insert Columns into Your Document

Here's Miss Mayflower (our gossip columnist) with the latest on inserting columns into

Section A part of a document that has different settings from the main document for things such as the number of columns, as well as margins, paper size, headers, footers, and page numbering. A section can be of any length: from several pages to several paragraphs—or even a single line (such as a masthead for your newsletter.)

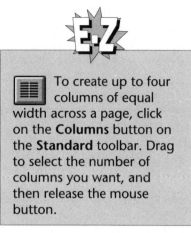

To create up to four columns of equal width across a page, click on the **Columns** button on the **Standard** toolbar. Drag to select the number of columns you want, and then release the mouse button.

your document. (Stay tuned for an update on a recent Elvis spotting.) First, move to the *section* in the document where you'd like to change the number of columns.

To create columns, open the Format menu and select Columns. With the keyboard, press **Alt+O** and then C. Select any of the preset column patterns by clicking on them, or by pressing **Alt** plus the underlined letter. As an alternative, you can enter the number of columns you want in the Number of Columns text box. If you need to create a section break so you don't affect earlier text, select the number of columns you want, and then choose **This Point Forward** in the Apply To list box. You'll see a preview of your choices.

To create columns of unequal width, deselect the Equal Column Width checkbox by clicking on it or pressing **Alt+E**. Enter the width and spacing desired for each column.

Click on **OK**.

Miss Mayflower Discusses How to Enter Text

Miss Mayflower says that if you want to enter text in a column, you just type. When you reach the bottom of a page, text will flow into the next column automatically. If you want to force a paragraph to start at the top of the next column before you reach the bottom of a page, you can insert a *column break*.

For example, perhaps you have a heading that you want to start at the top of the next column. To insert a column break, just place the insertion point where you want to start a new column (on the first letter of the column heading, for example) and press **Ctrl+Shift+Enter**.

What's Wrong with This Picture?

Irene wanted her two-page report to have two columns on the first page and three columns on the second. After creating two columns and typing the text for page one, Irene changed to three-column format on page two. When she had completed her report, she went back to look at page one and saw to her horror that it had mysteriously changed to three columns. What should she do?

Answer: Irene must have used the Columns button on the Standard toolbar when she switched from two- to three-column format. The Columns button changes the number of columns for the current section, but does not create a section break. Irene should have used the Columns command on the Format menu instead, because it can create section breaks. What Irene should do now is use the Insert Break command to insert a section break.

Making Columns Fatter

You can change the width of columns with the horizontal ruler. If your columns are of equal width, changing one changes them all. To change the width of a column, just drag the column marker on the horizontal ruler to wherever you'd like.

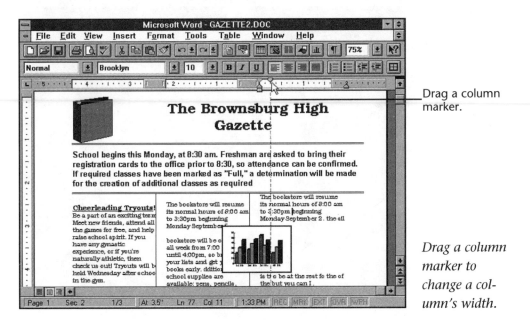

Drag a column marker.

Drag a column marker to change a column's width.

To change the width of columns with the keyboard, open the Format menu by pressing **Alt+O**, then select the Columns command by pressing **C**. Press **Alt+I** to move to Width, and enter a new measurement. If column widths are even, the other columns will adjust automatically. If you're using uneven columns, use the **Tab** key to change the width of other columns. By pressing **Alt+S**, you can change the spacing between columns.

Pinstriping Your Columns

You can add a vertical line (I think of it as a pinstripe) between columns, but when you do, don't be surprised if it doesn't show up. The vertical lines will appear only on the Page Layout and Print Preview screens. So go there to see how your columns will look.

Okay, here's what you do to pinstripe your columns. First, move to the section where you want to add lines. Open the Format menu and select Columns. Then click in the Line Between check box, or press **Alt+B**. Using the Apply To box, select how much of the document you want to affect.

Vertical lines added between columns —

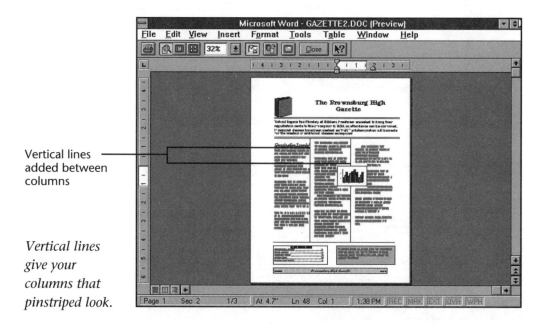

Vertical lines give your columns that pinstriped look.

By the Way . . .

The vertical-lines option will place lines between all the columns in that section. There is no way, for example, to place a line between two columns in a three-column section using this option. If you're desperate, you can create a line with the Drawing toolbar and place it between just two of the columns on a page if you want. (You'll learn more about Drawing in Chapter 21.) One thing you should keep in mind: Word for Windows is a great word processor, but only a fair-to-middlin' desktop publisher. If you really want to create great brochures, newsletters, etc., without a lot of fuss, you might want to look at a real desktop publishing program, such as Ventura Publisher, Microsoft Publisher, or PageMaker.

If you insist on trying to be creative in Word, you can add interest (as I did) to a newsletter by placing borders or shading (or both) around paragraphs. I'll be glad to show you how to do that, as soon as I get done with this chapter on columns and what they can or can't do in Word for Windows. Actually, I think you'll like borders and shading (if you can hang on until the next chapter). They're pretty cool, and they actually make creating columns in Word for Windows a lot of fun.

The Great Balancing Act

At the end of your document, you might want to *balance* (make even) the text in your columns. For example, if you're using two columns, and on the last page of your document the left column is full and the right one contains one paragraph, you might want to redistribute the text between the two columns so they end at the same point on the page (that way they look even or balanced).

This is easy to do—simply insert a section break at the end of the document. First, open the Insert menu and select **Break**. Under **Section Breaks**, choose **Continuous**, and then click on **OK**.

Keeping It All Together

When you insert a picture or graphic into your newsletter or brochure (something you will learn to do in Chapter 20), you may want to position that picture in a particular spot. For example, you may want the picture of your company's president to always stay in the upper right-hand corner of the front page, regardless of the surrounding text changes (either adding or deleting) you make. Or you may want the chart you've imported to stay with the paragraph that explains it. In either case, here's what you do:

First, import the graphic, following the instructions in Chapter 20. I know that not including the instructions here sounds like cheating, but there are just too many choices to cover them all in this chapter. Just keep your thumb here, read the first few pages of Chapter 20, and come back. I'll wait.

Frame   A small box in which you place text or graphics so you can maneuver them easily within your document.

Select the graphic by clicking on it. If you did not use a *frame* to import the graphic, you'll need one, so add one now by opening the Insert menu and selecting Frame. (You'll learn more about frames in Chapter 20.) With the keyboard, press **Alt+I** then **F**.

Open the Format menu and select Frame. With the keyboard, press **Alt+O** and then **M**. To force the graphic to stay with a particular paragraph, click on Move with Text or press **Alt+M**. To force the graphic to remain in the same spot on a page, regardless of what happens to the surrounding text, click on Lock Anchor or press **Alt+K**. Click on **OK** or press **Enter**. (You'll learn more about the Format Frame dialog box in— yes, you guessed it—Chapter 20.)

The Least You Need to Know

Probably the very least you need to know is that Word for Windows is *not* a desktop publishing program. What you can do with Word and columns is limited, but with a lot of patience, you can turn out a fairly respectable newsletter. Just remember these things:

- ☛ In newspaper-style columns, text flows from one column to the next when it reaches the bottom of a page. In a table, text is read across.

- ☛ To vary the number of columns within a document, create a new section by opening the Format menu and selecting **C**olumns. Type the number of columns you'd like, and select **This Point Forward** in the **A**pply To list box. Click on **OK** when you're through.

- ☛ Columns within a section are of equal width. To create columns of uneven width, use the Format **C**olumns command, and deselect the **E**qual Column Width checkbox.

- ☛ Use Normal mode to enter text into a column—it's faster. Use Page Layout mode to see how your columns will look when printed.

- ☛ To force text to start at the top of the next column, insert a column break by pressing **Ctrl+Shift+Enter**.

- ☛ You can add vertical lines between all the columns in a section by opening the Format menu and selecting **C**olumns. Click in the Line **B**etween check box, and use the **A**pply To list box to select how much of the document you want to have vertical lines.

- ☛ To force a graphic to stay in a particular spot on a page, insert a frame around it, and then choose the Format Frame command. Select Loc**k** Anchor. To allow the graphic to move in order to stay near a particular paragraph, select **M**ove with Text.

This page unintentionally left blank.

Part IV
Why I Always Stick Around for the Credits

You've seen them: those people who are still in their seats after the movie is over and the credits are rolling. You'll be halfway home while they're still waiting for the movie to end. Well, I'm one of those people—because when I watch the credits, I find out all sorts of interesting things I wouldn't have otherwise: like who the "best boy" is and where the movie was made. This section is like movie credits; it's full of all those interesting things I wanted to tell you about Word, but ran out of room for earlier.

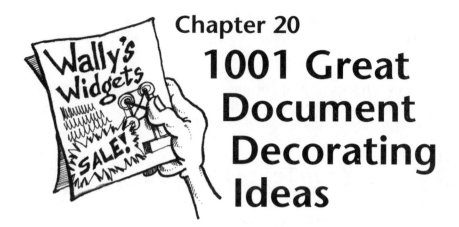

Chapter 20
1001 Great Document Decorating Ideas

In This Chapter

- ☛ Adding borders and shading
- ☛ Importing graphics, text, charts, tables, and other objects
- ☛ Resizing a graphic
- ☛ Placing a frame around text or a graphic
- ☛ Moving or resizing a frame
- ☛ Controlling how text flows around a frame

My mother always told me "a house is not a home until you decorate it." The same is true about documents; adding a chart here or a picture there really "dresses things up."

Of course, you should avoid "over-decorating" your document. If you dress your document up with too much shading or too many borders and frames, your reader won't be able to spot your point through all that glitter.

On the other hand, you shouldn't choose just one technique (such as shading) and use it everywhere in your document. I once baby-sat for a lady who loved owls, and had them all over her house: little owls, big owls, owl wallpaper, owl salt-and-pepper shakers, and even owl toilet paper. (I'll never know where she found that!) I couldn't help but think I was being watched—but whooo? Whoooo?

To avoid the owlish look in your documents, vary your decorating with several techniques (shading, borders, text frames, and graphics) to avoid overloading your reader with one type of formatting.

You can't add shading to the *background* of a graphic. To do that, you need to access the program that was used to create the graphic, and change it there.

Your Text Is Surrounded!

Borders and shading are two of my favorite ways to emphasize important text. *Borders* are lines placed on any (or all) of the four sides of a text paragraph, the cells in a table, or a graphic (a picture or a chart). *Shading* is a box of gray (or color, if you use a color printer) that forms a background for the text or cells in a table.

Use a box border to frame text or charts.

Shading can highlight important information.

Use a border to create sections in your document.

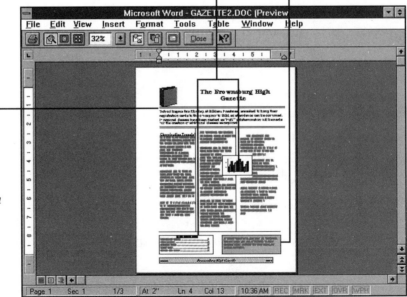

You can do a lot with a little when you use borders and shading to emphasize the important parts of your documents.

Across the Border

Placing a border around text or a graphic is fairly easy: first, select the text or graphic item to which you want to apply a border. You can select text or cells by dragging over them, or a graphic (a picture or a chart) by clicking on it.

After making your selection, open the Format menu and select **Borders and Shading**. On the left-hand side of the dialog box, you'll see a make-believe page with two paragraphs. The selections you make will be represented here as a sample. If you want to add a box (a border around all four sides) or a shadow, or if you want to remove a border, click on that option under **Presets**. With the keyboard, press **Alt** plus the underlined letter of the preset option you desire. After choosing a border option, select the type of line style you'd like to use. With the keyboard, press **Alt+Y**, and then use the **arrow** keys to high-light a selection. For example, under **Presets**, click on Box and select a thick line, and you'll see a thick box border placed around the sample paragraphs. If you like what you see, click on **OK**. If not, try another line type.

To save time, you can add borders or shading to par-ticular styles within your documents, instead of formatting each paragraph. To do so, open the **Format** menu and select the **Style** command. Under **Styles**, select the style you want to add borders or shading to. Click on **Modify**, and then click on **Format**. Select **Border** from the list. At this point, you can follow the steps in either of these two sections to add borders or shading to the style.

If placing a border around all four sides of your text makes you feel "boxed in," you can add a border on only one, two, or three sides. First, click on Box, and select the line style you'd like to use. Then deselect the appropriate sides by clicking on them in the Border area. For example, to remove a border that runs underneath the selected text, click on the **bottom** border line on the sample. You'll notice that when you do this, that the arrows marking both ends of that border disappear. The arrows indicate which borders have lines. You can even click between the para-graphs to add a border between them. When you're through making your selections, click on **OK**.

Removing selected borders without a mouse can be done, but not easily. First, press **Alt+R** to move to the Border area. Use the **arrow** keys to highlight the side you want to remove, then press **Alt+O**. Repeat this process until you've removed all the borders you no longer want.

By the Way . . .

If, later on, you want to remove a border completely, select the same text or graphic, open the Format menu, and select Borders and Shading. Click on **None**, and then click on **OK**.

Sporting Some Cool Shades

You can add shading behind any text, or within any cell in a table. If the paragraph you select is indented, the shading will begin at the indents. For cells in a table, the shading simply fills the cell. Here's what you do.

If you want to apply borders and shading to a lot of areas within your document, use the **Borders** toolbar. To display the toolbar, open the **View** menu and select **Toolbars**, or click the *right* mouse button while pointing to a displayed toolbar, and select **Borders** from the list.

Select the text or the cells you want to apply shading to. Then open the Format menu, and select **Borders and Shading** (there's that dialog box again). Click on the Shading tab or press **Ctrl+Tab**.

Use the Shading box to select the percentage of gray that you want. If your letters are small, choose a lighter percentage, say 10%. If your letters are larger, choose a higher percentage. I usually start with 20%. The result is really determined by the type of printer you have, and how well it handles shading, so experiment until you get the results you want. Use a font with clean, crisp lettering, such as Arial, or apply bold formatting for better results.

> **By the Way . . .**
>
> If you have a color printer, you can mix the Foreground and Background colors to create interesting shades.

Okay, that's it. Click on the **OK** button to return to the Border Paragraph box, and then click on **OK** again.

You Oughta Be in Pictures!

They say that nothing says it better than a picture (except maybe some *words*). Anyway, if you want to dress up your document with a graphic (*nerd word* for picture) or a chart, you've got several options:

> **Spreadsheet**   A computer program that organizes information in columns and rows, and performs calculations. If you want to balance a checkbook or last year's budget, use a spreadsheet program. Common spreadsheets include Lotus 1-2-3, Microsoft Excel, and Quattro Pro.

- ☛ You can create your own picture in Microsoft Draw, a drawing program that comes with Word for Windows.

- ☛ You can create a picture in some other program, such as PC Paintbrush, DrawPerfect, or CorelDRAW!.

- ☛ You can take it easy, and simply buy and import some artwork (called *clip art*) drawn by someone else. Word for Windows comes with a limited selection of clip art, but there are thousands of other clip-art disks you can buy from various sources. Ask your computer dealer to help you find a nice selection.

- ☛ You can create a chart using Microsoft Graph (another program that comes with Word for Windows), or import one from your *spreadsheet* program.

Welcome to the Import Business

When you bring a graphic into your document, you *import* it. (Bet you didn't know you'd be getting into the import business.) When you import a graphic, it pretty much stays where it was placed within the document. You can move it around a little by cutting and pasting as you would text, but if you want complete control over where the graphic appears on the page, import the graphic into a *frame*. For example, if you want to place your graphic in a margin or between columns, you're going to need a frame.

Frame A small box in which you place text or graphics so you can maneuver them easily within your document.

Importing Without Frames

You'll learn more about frames in a minute, but first let's learn the easy import method—importing without a frame.

First, move the insertion point to the spot where you'd like to place the graphic. Then open the Insert menu and select **Picture**. With the keyboard, press **Alt+I** and then **P**. As you may have guessed, a dialog box appears.

From this dialog box, select a graphic to import. Click on the graphic file you want in the File **Name** box. If you'd like to see what you're getting, make sure that the Preview Picture checkbox is selected. If you want to link your picture to the program you used to create it, use the Link to File check box. (More on this in a moment.) When you're ready, click on **OK**.

By the Way . . .

If you want to use one of the Word clip-art drawings, change to the **\WINWORD6\CLIPART** directory. There you'll find a rather nice selection of predrawn art you can use (free of charge!) to dress up your documents.

Just a Trim, Please

If your graphic is the size of a small elephant, you can adjust its size (this is called *scaling* a graphic), or cut parts away or trim (this is called *cropping*).

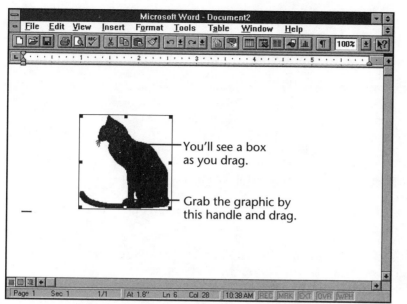

You'll see a box as you drag.

Grab the graphic by this handle and drag.

When you want to scale or crop a graphic, you grab it by one of its handles.

To scale a graphic, select it by clicking on it, and then drag one of the corner handles until the graphic is the size you want. (As you drag, you'll see a ghostly outline—but don't let that spook you!) If you drag the graphic by a side handle, you'll get a kind of "squashed" look, which may not be what you want, so it's best to use one of the corner handles.

To crop (trim) a graphic, select it by clicking on it. Press and hold the **Shift** key as you drag a handle to shrink the frame around the area of the graphic you want to keep.

If you mess up, and want to restore the graphic to its original size and shape, open the Format menu and select the Picture command. Click on Reset and then **OK** to restore the graphic.

Put It to Work

Getting into the Import Business

Let's import a Word clip-art picture and practice resizing and cropping. Open the Insert menu and select **Picture**. If necessary, change to the **\WINWORD6\CLIPART** directory by clicking on it. Select **EASTER.WMF** from the File **Name** list, then click on **OK** or press **Enter**.

Click on the graphic to select it. Click on one of the corner handles, and drag until the picture is almost twice its original size. Release the mouse button, and the picture is resized to fit the outline.

Let's crop a flower. Press **Shift** and click on the **lower left** corner of the picture. Holding the **Shift** key down, drag towards the upper right corner, until just the flower shows. Release, and the picture is cropped with just the flower left.

Linking an object Creating a connection between an imported object (such as a graphic) and its original application, so that any changes you make to the original object can be updated into your document.

The Ins and Outs of Linking and Embedding

When you import a graphic, you can *link* it to the original application you used to create it. That way, if you were to go back to that application and change the original graphic in some way, you could update the imported graphic and avoid having to import it again.

If you chose the *linking* option when you imported the graphic, and you've made some changes to your original document that you want to update in your imported graphic, open the Edit menu and select Links. Select the name of the graphic file, and then click on Update Now. The graphic in your document is updated to reflect the changes you made to it.

Okay, So What's Embedding?

You have an alternative to linking a graphic (or other object)—and that's *embedding*. The difference between linking and embedding is where the actual object is stored. When you import a graphic and link it to its original application, the graphic is *not* stored as part of the document. Instead a link (or connection, if you prefer) is maintained between your document and the program that created the graphic. Because the graphic is not actually part of your document, when you open that other program and make changes to the graphic, those changes are not reflected within your document until you update it. The link helps your document find the changed graphic and update the linked version of it.

Embedding an object
Creating a connection between an object and the application that created it, so that if changes are needed, you can access that application (by double-clicking on the object).

With embedding, on the other hand, a graphic *is* stored as part of the document. Just as in linking, however, there is a special connection between the document and the program that created the graphic. But this time the connection takes a different form. When you want to make changes to an embedded graphic, you don't go to the program that created it, but to your document. Double-click on the graphic, and you'll be escorted to the original program, where you'll work within its program window to make your changes. Finish making your changes and exit the graphics program, and you're whisked back to your document—where the graphic already reflects your changes. Unlike a linked object, an embedded object is updated immediately as soon as any changes are made. That's because you're not making changes to an object that's stored somewhere else, but to the one that's stored within the document.

To embed a graphic into your document, start with the graphics program. Select the graphic, open the Edit menu, and choose Copy. Switch to Word for Windows, open its Edit menu, and choose Paste Special. In the box that opens, make sure that the **Data Type** has been correctly identified (it will probably say either **Picture** or **Bitmap**), and then click on **Paste** and **OK**. Your graphic is embedded into the document. Remember that when you want to make changes to it, just double-click on the graphic.

Get Ready for the Great Frame-Up

Normally, you can't just plunk down a graphic in the middle of a column of text and expect the text to avoid the graphic like some party crasher. If you want to place a graphic in the middle of a column or two (or three) of text, and you want your text to wrap around it neatly (without leaving gaping holes to the left or right), you should create a *frame* first. Text wraps easily around a frame. You can then place the graphic within the frame, which will shield the graphic from the text, and the text will never know it's there.

If you've created a graphic in another application and saved it, you don't have to reopen that other application in order to embed the object. Simply open the **Insert** menu and select **Object**. With the keyboard, press **Alt+I** and then **O**. Click on **Create from File**, or press **Ctrl+Tab**. Select your graphic file from the list, then click on **OK**.

You also use a frame to gain better control of where a graphic is placed in your document. For example, if you want to place your graphic in a margin (or alongside a particular paragraph), you use a frame. If your document is going to be professionally printed, you can use frames as "placeholders" for pictures and other artwork that will be inserted at the print shop. You can use frames to position other objects, such as tables, charts, or even text (a quote, for example, or a summary of an important point).

By the Way . . .

When you work with frames, you should use Page Layout view, because you'll be able to see exactly where a graphic is located within your document.

Which Came First, the Graphic or the Frame?

You can insert a graphic (or other object, such as a table, chart, or text) into your document, and then place a frame *around* it—or you can insert an empty frame into your document, and import a graphic (or other object) *into* it. Which is better? Here are some tips:

☞ If the graphic, table, or text is already in your document, don't sweat it now. If you want to position the object in the margins or between columns, just place a frame around it.

☞ If you want to retain the original size of the graphic, table, or chart, import it first, and then frame it.

☞ If you want to make sure that the imported graphic, table, or chart is a particular size, create a frame in the size you need, and then import the object.

Getting the Frame Straight

Well, you've hung in this far, so I guess you're ready for the nitty-gritty on inserting frames into a document.

First, switch to Page Layout mode. (Open the View menu and select **Page Layout**, or click on the **Page Layout** button on the **horizontal** scroll bar.) Then, either select an item you want to frame, or move the insertion point to the spot where you'd like to place a frame. (To select a graphic, simply click on it.)

Next, click on the **Frame** button on the **Drawing** toolbar. If the Drawing toolbar is not currently displayed, open the Insert menu and select Frame instead. With the keyboard, press **Alt+I**, then **F**. If you're framing a selected item, the frame will appear in your document. If you're creating an empty frame, you've got one more step. When you click on the **Frame** button, the mouse pointer changes to tiny cross-hairs. Move the cross-hair pointer to where you want to locate the upper left corner of the frame-to-be. Click and drag towards the imaginary lower right corner of the frame-to-be. When you've got the size you want, release the mouse button, and you've got yourself a brand-new baby frame!

If you want to import a graphic into the frame, make sure that the frame is still selected, and then open the Insert menu and select Picture. Choose the graphic file you want to import, and click on **OK**. The graphic is resized to fit the frame.

By the Way . . .

When you create a frame, it's invisible (it doesn't print). If you like the look of a frame around your graphic, or if you're using the frame as a place holder for your printer to insert a graphic, add a border with the Format Borders and Shading command. (Turn back a few pages if you need help with borders.) Also, if you are going to place text in the frame, don't worry. All the rules for formatting, alignment, and indentation are the same as before; just treat the text like any other text in your document. The difference is that because the text has a frame around it, you can move that text anywhere you want.

Frame Maintenance

Okay, you've got a frame, but what can you do with it? Well, to *resize* a frame, select it by clicking on it, and drag a corner handle until the frame is the size you want.

To *move* a frame, click on it to select it. Move the mouse pointer over the frame until you see it change into an arrow pointing north, south, east, and west. Drag the frame to its new location, and then let go of the mouse button. When you move a frame, whatever's in it moves too.

If you want to place your frame in an exact spot relative to some point of reference, open the Format menu and select Frame. You can align your frame horizontally (somewhere between the left and right edges of the paper) or vertically (somewhere between the top and bottom edges of the paper).

Under Horizontal, there are three reference points you can choose from: Margin, Page, or Column. For example, to position the frame so that it is centered between the left and right margins, move to the **Horizontal** area and select **Margin** under Relative To. With the keyboard, press **Alt+L** and use the **arrow** keys to select a reference point. Once you've chosen a reference, choose a Position relative to that reference. For example, once you've chosen **Margin** as your reference point, you can position the frame so that it is centered, left, right, inside, or outside of the margins. With the keyboard, press **Alt+S** and use the **arrow** keys to choose a position.

Under Vertical, there are two reference points: Margin and Page. Follow the same steps as you would under Horizontal: select a reference (Margin or Page), and a position relative to that reference (top, center, bottom). For example, if you selected **Margin** and **Bottom**, the frame would be placed at the bottom of the page, just inside the bottom margin.

Actually, there is a third reference point under Vertical, and that's Paragraph. When you select **Paragraph**, your frame will move with the paragraph immediately following it in Normal view. If you enter a number under Position, the frame will *move the specified distance down* from the paragraph it is anchored to. If you want the frame to remain in the same spot on the page, click Lock Anchor or press **Alt+K**.

Keep That Text A-Flowin'

When you first insert a frame, it's set up so that the text in your document will flow (*wrap*) around the edges of the frame. If you want to be sure your text does not appear next to the frame (only above or below it), you can change this arrangement.

First, make sure you are in Page Layout view. Select the frame by clicking on it, and open the Format menu. Choose the Frame command. In the Text Wrapping area, click on **None**, and then **OK**.

If you want text to flow around a frame, and you want to adjust the space between the text and the frame, follow these same instructions, and then (under **Horizontal** or **Vertical**) enter a measurement in the Distance from Text box.

What's Wrong with This Picture?

Mike imported a picture of a wine glass into a document, and to make it show up better, he decided to add a border around it and add some shading. Mike used the Format Borders and Shading command to make his selections. When he got back to his document, the border was there, but the background behind the wine glass was still white. What happened to his shading?

Answer: Mike forgot that you can't add shading to the background of a graphic. You only can place shading behind text, or within the cells of a table.

How Do I Import Text?

If you want to open an existing document that was created in another program (such as WordPerfect), click on the **Open** button on the **Standard** toolbar, and select your file. Select a file type from the List Files of Type drop-down list box, by clicking on the **down** arrow and then picking a type. If your file type is not listed, select **All Files**, and then click on **OK**. Word will offer a guess as to which file converter it should use to open the file. Change to another file format if necessary, or click on **OK**.

If you want to copy just part of a document that was created in another Windows program, open that document and select your text. Open the Edit menu and select Copy. Switch to Word for Windows, open its Edit menu, and select Paste. (The text may lose some formatting in the process.)

You cannot copy and paste part of a document created in a non-Windows program. You must open the entire file and let Word convert it.

How Do I Import a Chart or Other Object?

Some charts, such as those created by Microsoft Graph, Lotus 1-2-3 for Windows, and Microsoft Excel, can be imported through the Edit menu. Just switch to the other program, select the chart or other object you want to import, open the Edit menu, and select Copy.

Now switch back to Word, move the insertion point to the place where you want the chart, and open the Edit menu. If you want to link your chart to the application you used to create it, select Paste **S**pecial and click on the Paste Link button in the box that appears. If you want to embed the chart, click on the Paste button instead. Remember, *linking* means that the graphic is not stored in your document, but that the graphic and the program that created the document are linked so that if changes are made to the original graphic, they are reflected within your document. *Embedding* means that the graphic is stored within your document, but you can access the creating program from within your document, and still make changes.

By the Way . . .

You can create and embed certain objects (such as a Microsoft Excel chart) without leaving Word for Windows. Open the Insert menu and select the Object command. If your program is listed, click on it, and you'll be escorted to that program so you can create your "object." Exit that program, and the object will be embedded into your document automatically. As usual, you can double-click on an embedded object to make changes to it. If your program is not among those listed, you'll have to use the Edit Copy and Edit Paste Special commands (as explained in the preceding paragraphs).

The Least You Need to Know

You're traveling into another frame of mind, a graphic dimension of linking and embedding. At the signpost up ahead, your next stop . . . the Document Zone! Submitted for your approval are these tips on graphics, borders, and shading:

- ☛ To place a border around text or a graphic, select it, and then open the Format menu and choose Borders and Shading. Select a border option and click on OK.

- ☛ To add shading to text or cells in a table, select what you want, and then open the Format menu and choose Borders and Shading. Click on the Shading tab. Select the percentage of gray (using the Shading box), and select a foreground and background color if you want. Click on OK when you're through.

- ☛ To import a graphic, move the insertion point to the spot where you would like to place the graphic. Open the Insert menu and select Picture. Select a graphic to import; if you want to create a link to the original application, click on Link to File and then OK.

continues

continued

☞ To scale a graphic, select it and drag one of the corner handles. To crop a graphic, press the **Shift** key as you drag; this shrinks the area around the part of the graphic you want to keep.

☞ 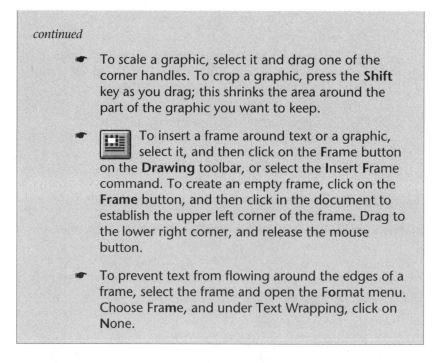 To insert a frame around text or a graphic, select it, and then click on the Frame button on the **Drawing** toolbar, or select the Insert **Frame** command. To create an empty frame, click on the **Frame** button, and then click in the document to establish the upper left corner of the frame. Drag to the lower right corner, and release the mouse button.

☞ To prevent text from flowing around the edges of a frame, select the frame and open the Format menu. Choose **Frame**, and under Text Wrapping, click on **None**.

Chapter 21

What I Was Going to Tell You, When I Ran Out of Room

In This Chapter

- Turning text upside down and every which way with cool special effects
- Creating simple artwork to enhance your documents
- Creating a graph for a document
- Adding a caption or callouts to a figure, table, or chart
- Adding a drop capital to a paragraph
- Letting others add comments to your work
- Creating your own hidden reminders
- Customizing a distribution list
- Entering special characters

This chapter is a hodgepodge of some neat things that Word can do. Use this as a springboard for ideas—or a really good excuse to avoid opening the Word manual.

Cool Things You Can Do with Text

Word for Windows contains a program called MS WordArt that allows you to do neat things with text, such as

Colorize text. (Ted Turner, watch out!)

Turn it upside down.

Gets you nowhere fast.

Put a shadow behind the text. (Scary!)

Run it around in circles.

Slant it up or down.

Bend it around.   Let your text take shape.

So how do you create all this loveliness? Well, first, move to the place in your document where you'd like to add some special text. Open the Insert menu and select Object, and one of those dialog boxes will open. Select **Microsoft WordArt 2.0** and click on **OK.**

If WordArt doesn't update the display to reflect your choices, click on **Update Display**, or press **Alt+U**.

If you want, change the font and point size, then type your text. Choose any combination of WordArt effects. When you're through, you just click in the document.

If you want to move the text to a particular spot within your document, add a frame by clicking on the **Frame** button. Then drag the text wherever you want.

Let Yourself Draw!

Word for Windows comes with a Drawing toolbar you can use to create simple objects (such as circles, rectangles, etc.). To add interest and pizzazz to your documents, you can fill these objects with color or patterns, and place them behind text or in the margins.

To display the **Drawing** toolbar, click on the **Drawing** button on the **Standard** toolbar. With the keyboard, open the View menu by pressing **Alt+V**; select the Toolbars command by pressing **T**. Display the Drawing toolbar by pressing **Alt+T** and using the **arrow** keys to select it from the list. Press **Enter** to close the dialog box.

Create a decorative logo.

Bring attention to notes.

Point to important information.

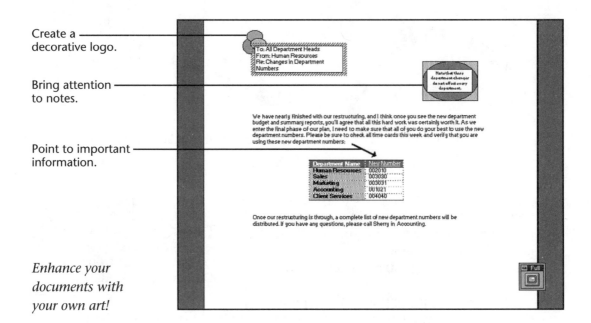

Enhance your documents with your own art!

There is a lot you can do with the Drawing toolbar—too much to show you in a quick lesson—but we'll be using the Drawing toolbar throughout this chapter, so you'll be pretty familiar with it by the time we finish. Here's some stuff to get you started:

To create a perfect square or circle, hold the **Shift** key down as you drag.

Polygon A multi-sided object which is not a square or a rectangle. Polygons include stars, hexagons, octagons, and open free-form shapes.

To use a tool, click on it.

To draw something, click on the appropriate tool. Then move to the drawing area, and click to establish the upper left corner of the object. Drag downward to the right; the object will form as you drag. Release the mouse button to create the object.

To use the Polygon tool, click on it. Move to the drawing area, and click to establish the first point. Move to the second point and click. Move to the third point and click, etc. Double-click to form an open polygon, or click on the first point to join the ends and form a closed polygon.

When you draw something, its outline is determined by the Line tool. Normally, whatever you draw will have a thin black border. To make the border thicker or to eliminate it entirely, click on the **Line Style** tool and select an option. You can even do this after an object is created—simply click on the object to select it, then click on the **Line Style** tool to change its border. You can change the color of the border with the **Line Color** tool.

When you draw something, its color is determined by the Fill Color tool. Normally, whatever you draw will be white with a black border. To change the interior color from white to something else, use the **Fill Color** tool. If you've already drawn the object, simply select it, and then use the **Fill Color** tool to change its color.

To select an object, click on it. To select multiple objects at once, click on the **Select Drawing Objects** tool, and drag over the selected objects to "rope 'em in."

To place an object over another one, just drag it on top. If there's more than one object in a stack, use the **Bring to Front** tool to bring an object to the top (that is, the foreground).

To place an object *under* another one, click on the **Send to Back** tool.

To place an object under text, click on the **Text to Front** tool. To place an object over text, drag it on top or click on the **Text to Back** tool.

Drawing in Word 2.0 is a bit different. There is no Drawing toolbar, so you'll have to use the menus to simulate the commands discussed here. To change the fill or line colors, use the appropriate bars at the bottom of the Draw window. When you are through drawing, open the **File** menu and select **Exit and Return**. If asked, update your document by clicking on **Yes**.

Put It to Work

Drawing Our Own Conclusions

Let's create a few objects for practice. Click on the **Rectangle** tool and drag to create a rectangle. To create a square, repeat the process, but hold down the **Shift** key as you drag.

Let's change the color of the square. Click to select it, then click on the **Fill Color** tool. Select a bright green.

Make the border of the square thicker by clicking on the **Line Style** tool. Change the color of the border to **blue** by clicking on the **Line Color** tool.

Place the square over the rectangle, then click on **Send to Back**. Click on **Send to Front** to reverse the process.

Graphing Your Ideas

Word for Windows includes a simple tool to create graphs—called (cleverly enough) Microsoft Graph. If you already use Lotus 1-2-3 or Microsoft Excel, you can import your data from those *spreadsheets* instead of using WordGraph. See Chapter 20 for help.

 To create a graph, first move to the place in the document where you want to insert a graph. Then start Microsoft Graph by clicking on the **Graph** button on the **Standard** toolbar. You'll see some fake data already entered; this makes it easier to figure out how to enter your own data.

Column   Cell   Click here to turn off column.

	1st Qtr	2nd Qtr	3rd Qtr	4th Qtr			
East	20.4	27.4	90	20.4			
West	30.6	38.6	34.6	31.6			
North	45.9	46.9	45	43.9			

Microsoft Graph - Graph in XBFIG02.DOC

File   Edit   DataSeries   Gallery   Chart   Format   Window   Help

XBFIG02.DOC - Datasheet

XBFIG02.DOC - Chart

— Datasheet window

— Row/Series

— Graph window

Enter data into the Datasheet window, and it's graphed automatically in the Chart window.

Row titles   These titles represent each *series*. A series is a collection of related data—for example, the travel expenses for one year for a single salesperson. Additional salespeople are represented by additional rows; each row is considered a series.

Column titles   These titles represent a single point in time, such as January or February, or 1992 or 1993.

Cell   Here's where the values go.

There are a lot more terms I could throw at you, but the only thing that will make any sense is simply creating your first graph. So let's get to it.

SPEAK LIKE A GEEK

Spreadsheet   A computer program which organizes information in columns and rows, and performs calculations. If you want to balance a checkbook or last year's budget, use a spreadsheet program. Common spreadsheets include Lotus 1-2-3, Microsoft Excel, and Quattro Pro.

To turn off a row or a column so that it does not affect the graph, double-click on the button at the front of that row or column.

Oh, Boy, a Sample Chart!

Suppose you wanted to graph the travel expenses for your sales department for each month of the first quarter. The points in time are entered across the top of the datasheet as *column titles*. Begin with the cell that says **1st Qtr**, and type **January, February, March**. To enter these, type over the existing column headings, using **Tab** to move from cell to cell. To erase the last cell, 4th Qtr, press **Tab** to move to that cell, and then press **Backspace**. You'll see a box—just ignore it and press **Enter**.

The names of the series are entered along the left-hand side of the datasheet as row titles. You don't have to have more than one series. (After all, we have only *one* World Series, so why spoil a good thing?) For example, if you were graphing the total travel expenses by month for the entire sales department, you'd have only one series (row) called **Sales Department**, and you'd enter the data for each month in a separate column. If you want to break the total expenses down by salesperson (as we do in our sample graph), you'll need a row (or series) for each salesperson. Move to the first cell in the second row and type **John**. Press the **Down arrow** key and type **Jane**. Press the **Down arrow** key again, and type **Ted**. Enter the amounts you see here. Delete the numbers in the last column by selecting those cells and pressing **Backspace** or **Delete**, then pressing **Enter**. You can eliminate the entire column in one stroke by double-clicking on the gray button at the top of that column.

What You Want Is What You Get

Microsoft Graph graphs your data automatically as a column chart, but you can use other chart types instead. Here's what each chart type might be best suited for:

Column   Compares values at a given point in time.

Bar   Like a sideways column chart; use this just like a column chart to compare values at a given point in time.

Line   Emphasizes trends and changing values over time.

Area   Like a filled-in line chart; use this just like a line chart to emphasize changing values.

Pie   Use this to show the relationship between parts of a whole.

If you don't want a *legend* in your chart (that little box that explains what each series stands for), simply click on it and press **Delete**. If you don't like where the legend was placed, click on it to select it, and then drag it wherever you'd like.

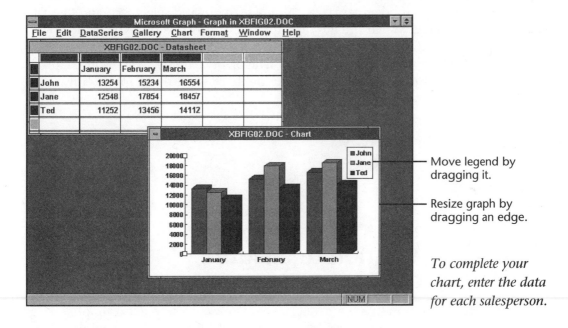

Move legend by dragging it.

Resize graph by dragging an edge.

To complete your chart, enter the data for each salesperson.

I used a 3-D column for my sample chart, but you may prefer something else. To change the chart type, open the Gallery menu, and choose the chart type you want. You'll see varieties of the chart type you chose; just select one of the available varieties and click on **OK**.

> **By the Way . . .**
>
> After your graph is complete, you can resize it by dragging the edge of the graph window. You can also resize a graph after it is inserted into your Word document.

Copying Your Great-Looking Chart into a Word Document

Well, you're almost done. Now all you have to do is copy the completed chart into your document. Open the File menu and select Exit and Return to Document. When the message appears, asking whether you want to update your chart, click on Yes or press **Alt+Y.** Your chart will be embedded at the point in your document where you activated Microsoft Graph. Because it's an *embedded object*, just double-click on the graph to edit it.

> **By the Way . . .**
>
> In your document, you can add a border around the chart by using the Format Borders and Shading command.

Adding a Caption to a Figure, Table, or Chart

Adding a caption to a figure (a graphic) allows you to make a simple statement that summarizes your point. In addition, you can compile a list of items with captions: tables, figures, etc. You can also create a *cross-reference* which refers to a captioned item—for example, "Figure 10.1 on page 42 shows the difference in sales during the first and second quarter." Even if the figure is later moved or renumbered, both the cross-reference and the table can be easily updated.

By the Way . . .

I've been adding *captions* throughout this book whenever I include a picture. Captions help summarize your point, so the reader knows what to look at in the figure, table, or chart.

Adding a caption to a figure, table, or chart is relatively easy. Start by clicking on the object to select it. Open the Insert menu and select Caption. With the keyboard, press **Alt+I**, then **I** again. Select the type of label you want from the Label list; keyboarders: press **Alt+L** and use the **arrow** keys to select it. You'll see a label such as "Figure 1" appear in the Caption text box. If you want to add something, just type it after the label. Press **Enter** or click on **OK** when you're done.

To add a caption to a figure in Word 2.0, simply click on it, press **Enter**, and then type your caption.

Microsoft Word - CAPTION.DOC

File Edit View Insert Format Tools Table Window Help

March
February
January

0 20,000 40,000 60,000 80,000 100,000

Figure 1: The sales figures for our Midwest division.

Page 1   Sec 1   1/1   At 3.2"   Ln 3   Col 54   10:40 AM

Caption

Adding a caption to a chart or other object is easy.

Using the Numbering button, you can change the numbering system to include chapter numbers—or create your own label (for example if you want to call them "Pictures" instead of "Figures")—with the New Label button. You can even create automatic captions when you insert certain items into your document—such as tables, pictures, etc. Just click on AutoCaption or press **Alt+A**. Click on an item to select it for automatic captioning.

Calling All Callouts

To add a note of explanation to a figure or a graph, add *callouts* with the Drawing toolbar. (If you skipped the lesson on the Drawing toolbar earlier in this chapter, sneak a peek at it now.) To display the Drawing toolbar, click on the **Drawing** button on the **Standard** toolbar. With the keyboard, open the View menu by pressing **Alt+V**; select the Toolbars command by pressing **T**. Display the **Drawing** toolbar by pressing **Alt+T** and using the **arrow** keys to select it from the list. Press **Enter** to close the dialog box.

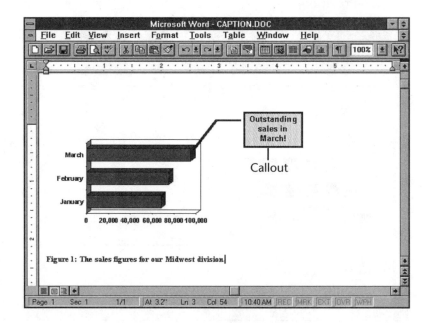

Better than a Post-it.

Click on the **Callout** tool, then move to the document area. Click at the point where you want the callout line to begin, then drag to create the callout. Enter your text, and click within the document when you're done.

To add a border or change the callout style, click on the **Format Callout** tool and select your options. To change the angle of the callout, click on the text box and drag it. To change the size of the text box, click on a corner of the box and drag it to its new size.

You can change the color of the callout line and the text box border with the **Line Color** tool.

Instant Epic: Creating Drop Caps

Medieval bibles often featured *drop caps*, the first letter of a verse which was ornately designed, and which was always two or three times larger than the other letters. Normally the top of a drop cap lines up with the first line of the paragraph, with the text of the paragraph flowing along the right side and bottom of the drop-cap frame. In Word, you can design your drop cap this way, or place your drop cap in the left margin instead.

To create a drop cap, move to the paragraph where you want to place it, then open the Format menu, and select **Drop Cap**. With the keyboard, press **Alt+O** and then **D**. Oh joy! Another dialog box!

Drop cap   A *drop cap* (or "dropped capital," as Word calls it) is used to set off the first letter in a paragraph. The letter is enlarged, and set into (or next to) the text of the paragraph at its upper left-hand corner.

To create a drop cap in Word 2.0, use Word Art to create a simple letter which uses a large point size and is center-aligned. Frame the letter and resize it. Then place it into the paragraph so that the top of the frame aligns with the top of the paragraph, and you're set!

You can drop-cap an entire word if you want, by selecting it before you choose **Drop Cap.** If you select a paragraph instead, you can create a margin note.

From here, change the font and point size if you want, and then click on either Dropped or In Margin. If you want, change the number of Lines to Drop by clicking on it, or by pressing **Alt+L.** This determines the size of the drop-capped letter. You can even change the distance between the drop-cap and the paragraph text—just click on Distance from Text, or press **Alt+T.** Then choose **OK** or press **Enter.** Switch to **Page Layout** view to see the drop cap in your paragraph.

Annotations: An Easy Way for Others to Comment on Your Work

Have you ever sent a copy of a report around for comments and gotten back a bunch of scribbled notes that are difficult to decipher? Well, you can use *annotations* instead. Annotations provide a way for reviewers to add their comments to the document without actually changing it. Annotations are formatted as hidden text so they won't print.

Reviewer's initials ———

Annotations pane ———

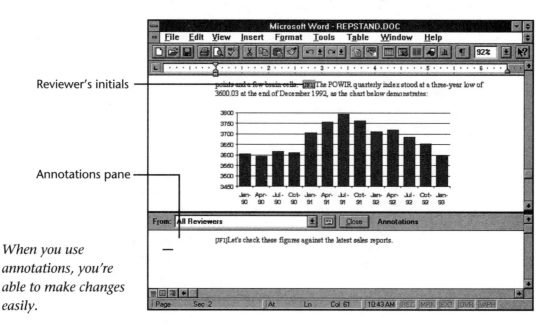

When you use annotations, you're able to make changes easily.

What the Critics Say . . .

A reviewer adds a comment to your file by opening it and selecting the text on which she would like to comment. Next, she opens the Insert menu and selects the **Annotation** command. The reviewer's initials are inserted into the document, and she types her comments into the *Annotation pane* (a window that opens at the bottom of the screen). After she finishes entering comments, she clicks on the Close button. Your reviewer can add comments without using a mouse by pressing **Alt+Ctrl+A**.

> ### By the Way . . .
>
> If the initials are not set correctly on your reviewer's system, have her open the **Tools** menu and select **Options**. Have her click on **User Info**, or press **Ctrl+Tab** until it's selected. Correct the user initials as necessary, and click on **OK**.

To see comments in the file when you get it back, open the View menu and select Annotations. The Annotation pane will open, and if the reviewer selected a particular section of text prior to annotating it, that passage will be highlighted. If you want to see only the comments from a particular reviewer, select that person from the reviewer's list by clicking on it (or by pressing **Alt+R**). When you're done reading the comments, click on the Close button.

You can also view annotations by first displaying hidden codes, then double-clicking on the annotation code. To display hidden codes, click on the **Show/Hide Paragraph Marks** button on the **Standard** toolbar.

To locate the next annotation, scroll through your document, or open the Edit menu and select Go To. In the Go to What box, click on the annotation, or press **Alt+W** and select it from the list. Click on Next or press **Alt+T**. To move to a previous annotation, click on Previous or press **Alt+P**.

You can copy the changes from the Annotation pane into your document by using the **Copy** and **Paste** buttons on the **Standard** toolbar. To delete an annotation, select it and press **Delete**.

If you want to print your document and the annotations, open the File menu and select Print, or press **Ctrl+P**. Click on the Options button, and under **Include with Document**, use the Annotations check box. If you want to print the annotations only, open the File menu and select Print. Select Annotations in the Print What list, and click on the **OK** button.

If hidden text is displayed, it affects page numbering, so keep that in mind before you print your document.

Making Notes to Yourself

Why should your critics have all the fun with annotations? You can add private notes to your document, such as "Remember to update these figures" or "Ask Tom about the new sales report." Using hidden text, these notes will be displayed on-screen but won't print (unless of course you *want to* print them).

To add a secret note, press **Ctrl+Shift+H** and type your note. When you're done, press **Ctrl+Shift+H** again. To display hidden text, open the Tools menu and select Options. Click on **View** (or press **Ctrl+Tab**) to select it. Turn on the Hidden Text option by clicking on it, or by pressing **Alt+I** and selecting **OK**.

If you want to print your notes with your document, open the File menu and select Print, or press **Ctrl+P**. Click on the Options button, and under **Include with Document**, select Hidden Text.

Read All About It: Creating Your Own Distribution List

If you create documents that need to be routed through several people, you can create a distribution list with boxes that the reader can check off to indicate that she has read the document.

```
                    Microsoft Word - XBFIG07.DOC
  File  Edit  View  Insert  Format  Tools  Table  Window  Help
```

Distribution list

❑   Joe

❑   Maxine ————————————————————— Create these check
                                   boxes using the
❑   William   Drawing toolbar.

❑   Jennifer

❑   Eileen
                                   Create your own
                                   check boxes to use
                                   in your Word
                                   documents.

```
Page 1   Sec 1      1/1    At 1"    Ln 1   Col 1    10:45 AM  REC  MRK  EXT  OVR  WPH
```

As you learned earlier, Word for Windows comes with a drawing toolbar, and you'll be using it to create your check boxes. If you need a quick review, refer to the section on the Drawing toolbar earlier in this chapter.

100% Since we're going to be working on a fairly small object, let's increase the view by clicking on the **Zoom** button on the **Standard** toolbar, and selecting **200%**. With the keyboard, open the View menu and select Zoom (press **Alt+V**, then **Z**). Choose **200% Size** (press **Alt+2**).

Now click on the **Rectangle** tool, and move the mouse pointer to the drawing area. Press the **Shift** key, and hold it as you click and drag to create the square for the check box.

If you want to create a "shadow" as in the sample, click on your square to select it. Click on the **Copy** button on the **Standard** toolbar, then click on **Paste**.

TECHNO NERD TEACHES

Holding the **Shift** key as you drag helps you to create a perfectly square (or round, as the case may be) object.

If necessary, select the new square by clicking on it, then click on the **Fill Color** button on the **Drawing** toolbar and select **black**.

 Now you have a white square and a black square. We'll place the black square behind the white square to create a "shadow." Here's what you do: click on the **black square** to select it. Drag the black square so that its top right-hand corner is just below and to the right of the top of the white square (use the picture as a guide). If you have trouble moving the two squares precisely, press **Ctrl** and use the **arrow** keys to move the black square one pixel at a time. We still have one problem: it appears that the black square is on top of the white square. No problem: just use the **Send to Back** tool on the **Drawing** toolbar.

Group the two objects together by holding the **Shift** key down as you select each box. Next, click on the **Group** tool on the **Drawing** toolbar.

Select the check box. You can resize it by dragging a corner handle. You can create several copies of the check box by clicking on the **Copy** button, and then on the **Paste** button.

By the Way . . .

 If you want to keep your check box for posterity (and to use in other documents), select it by clicking on it. Click on the **AutoText** button on the **Standard** toolbar, or press **Alt+E** to open the **Edit** menu and then press **X** to select AutoText. Enter a short name for the check box, such as **CHKBX**, and click on Add or press **Ctrl+A**.

When Regular Text
Just Isn't Enough

What do you do if you want to enter a date, but you want that date to change whenever you update your document? Well, you use *intelligent fields.* Here are some examples of fields you can insert into your document:

- ☛ Current date and time.

- ☛ Name of person who made the last change to this document.

- ☛ Current page number and total number of pages in document.

- ☛ Total number of words and characters in document.

- ☛ Revision number of document.

- ☛ Date the document was last printed.

Intelligent field An intelligent field is text within a document (such as the current date) that is updated automatically as changes are made.

So how do you get this marvelous feature to work? First, open the Insert menu and select the Field command. (With the keyboard, press **Alt+I**, then **E**.) In the dialog box that's displayed, scroll through the Field Names list until you see the field that you're looking for. (Keyboarders: press **Alt+N** and use the **arrow** keys to select a field.)

You can narrow the list of fields by selecting from the list of Categories. With the keyboard, press **Alt+C**, then use the **arrow** keys to select a category.

Some fields have options. For example, the Date field allows you to select the date format. After selecting your field, click on **Options** or press **Alt+O**. Click on an option to select it, or press **Alt** plus the underlined letter. Press **Enter** or click on **OK** to insert the field into your document.

Entering Characters That Aren't on Your Keyboard

Sometimes you may need to enter a character into your document that isn't on your keyboard, such as the cents sign (¢), a trademark (™), the Japanese yen symbol (¥), a tilde (~), or an umlaut (¨). Word makes it super easy to insert strange characters into your document when you need to (or just for fun). Just open the Insert menu and select the Symbol command. With the keyboard, press **Alt+I**, then **S**.

Font A font is any set of characters of the same *typeface* (design) and *type size* (measured in points). For example, Times Roman 12-point is a font; Times Roman is the typeface, and 12-point is the size. (There are 72 points in an inch.)

In the dialog box that appears, click on any symbol; then click on Insert or press **Alt+I** to insert it into your document. If you want to insert additional symbols, click on them and repeat the process. To close the dialog box, press **Esc** or click on **Close**.

If you want to browse, open the Font drop-down list box, and select a different font. You'll probably find some very interesting fonts, such as MusicalSymbols and Greek Math Symbols.

If you use this particular symbol a lot, assign a shortcut key to it: click on Shortcut Key or press **Alt+K**. Press some obscure key sequence (such as Ctrl+Shift+Y for yen), and make sure that it's not currently assigned to anything important. Then click Assign or press **Enter**.

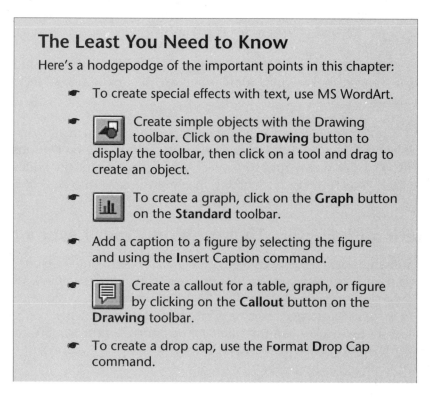

The Least You Need to Know

Here's a hodgepodge of the important points in this chapter:

- ☞ To create special effects with text, use MS WordArt.

- ☞ Create simple objects with the Drawing toolbar. Click on the **Drawing** button to display the toolbar, then click on a tool and drag to create an object.

- ☞ To create a graph, click on the **Graph** button on the **Standard** toolbar.

- ☞ Add a caption to a figure by selecting the figure and using the **Insert Caption** command.

- ☞ Create a callout for a table, graph, or figure by clicking on the **Callout** button on the **Drawing** toolbar.

- ☞ To create a drop cap, use the Format **Drop Cap** command.

☛ Use the Insert Annotation command to insert comments into someone else's work. Use the View Annotations command to view comments added to your work.

☛ To create hidden text, press **Ctrl+Shift+H**, type the text, and press **Ctrl+Shift+H** again.

☛ To create your own check boxes for a distribution list, click on the **Drawing** button on the **Standard** toolbar.

☛ To add a date or other intelligent field to your document, open the Insert menu and select the Field command.

☛ To insert a special character into your document, use the **S**ymbol command on the **I**nsert menu.

This page unintentionally left blank.

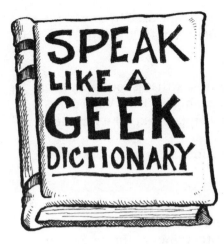

Speak Like a Geek: The Complete Archive

The computer world is like an exclusive club, complete with its own language. If you want to be accepted, you need to learn the lingo (the secret handshake will come later). The following mini-glossary will help you get started.

accelerator keys   (1) The one thing you don't want to be pressing when you see a cop. (2) Sometimes called *shortcut keys*, these are used to activate a command without opening the menu. Usually a function key or a *key combination* (such as Alt+F12), accelerator keys are displayed next to the menu command. To use an accelerator key, hold down the first key while you press the second key.

active document   The document you are currently working in. The active document contains the insertion point, and if more than one document window is being displayed on-screen, the active document's title bar appears darker than the other title bars.

alignment   Controls how the text in a paragraph is placed between the left and right margins. For example, you might have left-aligned or centered text.

application   (1) The placement of shampoo on the head. (2) Also known as a *program*, a set of instructions that enables a computer to perform a specific task, such as word processing or data management.

ASCII file   A file containing characters that can be used by any program on any computer. Sometimes called a *text file* or an *ASCII text file*. (ASCII is pronounced "ASK-key.")

boilerplate text   Generic text within a template that is reused by every document created from that template. For example, "Dear Valued Customer" and "Sincerely Yours" qualify as boilerplate text for a form letter.

border   A line placed on any (or all) of the four sides of a block of text, a graphic, a chart, or a table.

bulleted list   Similar to a numbered list. A bulleted list is a series of paragraphs with hanging indents, where the bullet (usually a dot or a check mark) is placed to the left of all the other lines in the paragraph. A bulleted list is often used to display a list of items or to summarize important points.

cell   (1) The opposite of "Buy!" (2) The box formed by the intersection of a row and a column in a Word table. The same term is used when describing the intersection of a row and a column in a spreadsheet. A cell may contain text, a numeric value, or a formula.

click   After you have moved the mouse pointer over an object or icon, a single press and release of the mouse button.

clip art   A collection of prepackaged artwork, whose individual pieces can be placed within a document.

Clipboard   (1) A wooden or plastic rectangle to which you can affix important notes so you can lose them for a week after the wooden or plastic rectangle accidentally falls behind your filing cabinet. (2) A temporary storage area that holds text and graphics. The Cut and Copy commands put text or graphics on the Clipboard, erasing the Clipboard's previous contents. The Paste command copies Clipboard data to a document.

columns   A vertical section of a table. See also *newspaper-style columns*.

command   An order that tells the computer what to do. In *command-driven* programs, you have to press a specific key or type the command to execute it. With *menu-driven* programs, you select the command from a menu.

computer   (1) A hole on my desk I throw money into. (2) Any machine that accepts input (from a user), processes the input, and produces output in some form.

Control-menu box   A special button located in the upper left corner of a window, containing a special menu that can be used to move, size, and close a window with the keyboard.

crash   (1) A sound you don't want to hear when you're moving your computer. (2) Failure of a system or program. Usually, you will realize that your system crashed when the display or keyboard locks up. The term *crash* also refers to a *disk crash* or *head crash*, which occurs when the read/write head in the disk drive falls on the disk. This would be like dropping a phonograph needle on a record. A disk crash can destroy any data stored where the read/write head fell on the disk.

cropping   The process of cutting away part of an imported graphic.

cursor   A vertical line that appears to the right of characters as you type. A cursor acts like the tip of your pencil; anything you type appears at the cursor. (See also *insertion point*.)

data   (1) That guy on *Star Trek: The Next Generation*. (2) A computer term for information. You enter facts and figures (data) into a computer, which then processes it and displays it in an organized manner. In common usage, *data* and *information* are used interchangeably.

data source   A special document file that contains the variable information that is later merged with a main document to produce individual form letters or mailing labels.

database   A type of computer program used for storing, organizing, and retrieving information. Popular database programs include Microsoft Access, dBASE, Paradox, and Q&A.

desktop publishing (DTP)   A program that allows you to combine text and graphics on the same page, and manipulate the text and the graphics on-screen. Desktop publishing programs are commonly used to create newsletters, brochures, flyers, résumés, and business cards.

dialog box   (1) Geek name for a telephone. (2) A special window or box that appears when the program requires additional information before executing a command.

directory   Because large hard disks can store thousands of files, you often need to store related files in separate directories on the disk. Think of your disk as a filing cabinet, and think of each directory as a drawer in the filing cabinet. By keeping files in separate directories, you can locate and work with related files more easily.

disk   A round, flat, magnetic storage unit. See *floppy disks* and *hard disk*.

disk drive   (1) A street in Silicon Valley. (2) A device that writes and reads data on a magnetic disk. Think of a disk drive as being like a cassette recorder/player. Just as the cassette player can record sounds on a magnetic cassette tape and play back those sounds, a disk drive can record data on a magnetic disk and play back that data.

document   Any work you create using an application program and save in a file on disk. Although the term *document* traditionally refers to work created in a word processing program (such as a letter or a chapter of a book), *document* is now used rather loosely to refer to any work, including spreadsheets and databases.

document window   A window which frames the controls and information for the document file you're working on. You can have multiple document windows open at one time.

DOS (disk operating system)   DOS, which rhymes with "boss," is an essential program that provides the instructions necessary for the computer's parts (keyboard, disk drive, central processing unit, display screen, printer, and so on) to function as a unit.

DOS prompt   An on-screen prompt that indicates DOS is ready to accept a command. It looks something like C> or C:\>.

double-click   After you move the mouse pointer over an object or icon, pressing and releasing the mouse button twice in quick succession.

drag   (1) Losing a winning lottery ticket. (2) To drag the mouse, first move the mouse pointer to the starting position. Now press and hold the left mouse button. Move the mouse pointer to the ending position, and then release the mouse button.

drop cap   An option used to set off the first letter in a paragraph. The letter is enlarged and set into the text of the paragraph, at its upper left-hand corner. Word calls this letter a *dropped capital*.

edit   To make changes to existing information within a document. Editing in a word processor usually involves spell-checking, grammar checking, and making formatting changes until the document is judged to be complete.

embedded object   An object that maintains a connection to the application that created it, so that if changes are needed, you can access that application by double-clicking on the object. An embedded object is stored within your Word document.

end mark   A way of marking the end of the document; as you enter text, this mark will move down.

exit   Technical name for stopping or quitting a program such as Word for Windows.

extension   In DOS, each file you create has a unique name. The name consists of two parts: a filename and an extension. The filename can be up to eight characters. The extension (which is optional) can be up to three characters. The extension normally denotes the file type.

field   (1) What someone is always out standing in. (2) One part of a data file *record*. A field contains a single piece of information (for example, a telephone number, ZIP code, or a person's last name). A field is also a code inserted into a document which is updated when the document is opened, such as the Date field.

file   (1) What every prisoner wants to find in a birthday cake. (2) DOS stores information in files. Anything can be placed in a file: a memo, a budget report, or even a graphics image (like a picture of a boat or a computer). Each document you create in Word for Windows is stored in its own file. Files always have a filename to identify them.

fixed disk drive   A disk drive that has a nonremovable disk, as opposed to floppy drives, in which you can insert and remove disks. See also *disk drive.*

floppy disk drive   A disk drive that uses floppy disks. See also *disk drive.*

floppy disks   Small, portable, plastic storage squares that magnetically store *data* (the facts and figures you enter and save). Floppy disks are inserted into your computer's *floppy disk drive* (located on the front of the computer).

font   Any set of characters which share the same *typeface* (style or design). Fonts convey the mood and style of a document. Technically, font describes the combination of the *typeface and point size* of a character (as in Times Roman 12-point), but in common usage it describes only a character's style or typeface.

footer   (1) The distance my golf ball travels when I tee off. (2) Text that can be reprinted at the bottom of every page within a document.

formatting   Changing the look of a character (by making it bold, underlined, and slightly bigger, for example) or a paragraph (by centering the paragraph between the margins, for example, or by adding an automatic indentation for the first line).

Formatting toolbar   Provides an easy method within Word for Windows for changing the appearance of text (for example, adding bold and italics).

frames   Small boxes in which you place text or pictures so you can maneuver them easily within your document.

function keys   The 10 or 12 F keys on the left side of the keyboard, or the 12 F keys at the top of the keyboard. F keys are numbered F1, F2, F3, and so on. These keys are used to enter various commands in the Word program.

Grammar Checker   A special program within Word for Windows that corrects errors of a grammatical nature within a document.

graphic   A picture which can be imported into Word in order to illustrate a particular point.

graphical user interface (GUI, pronounced "gooey")   (1) Tar on a hot tin roof. (2) A type of program interface that uses graphical elements (that is, pictures such as icons) to represent commands, files, and (in some cases) other programs. The most popular GUI is Microsoft Windows.

graphics/charting program   A program (such as Microsoft Graph) that takes columnar data and creates a professional-looking chart.

gutter   (1) A leaf, twig, and debris magnet. (2) An unused region of space that runs down the inside edges of facing pages of a document; it's the part of each page that is used when the pages of a book or a magazine are bound together.

handles   (1) Extra fat around your middle. (2) Small black squares that surround a graphic or frame after it is selected.

hanging indent   A special kind of indent where the first line of a paragraph hangs closer to the left margin than the rest of the lines in the paragraph. Typically used for bulleted or numbered lists.

hard disk   A nonremovable disk drive that stores many megabytes of data. Because it is fixed in place inside the computer (see *fixed disk drive*), it performs quicker and more efficiently than a floppy disk.

hardware   The physical parts of a computer (such as the *monitor*, the *disk drives*, the *CPU*, and so on). The programs you run are electronic, rather than physical; they're known as *software*.

header   Text that can be reprinted at the top of every page within a document.

header record   Stores the field names (column headings) for a data file.

I-beam   (1) Godzilla's secret weapon. (2) Another name for the *mouse pointer*.

icon   A graphic image that represents another object, such as a program.

indent   (1) What happens to your bumper when you back up without looking. (2) The amount of distance from the page margins to the edges of your paragraph.

input   Data that goes into your computer. When you press a key or click a mouse button, you are giving your computer input. Data that your computer gives back to you (by printing it out or displaying it on the monitor) is called *output*.

Insert mode   The default typing mode for most word processors and text editors. Insert mode means that when you position your cursor and start to type, what you type is inserted at that point, and existing text is pushed to the right.

insertion point   A blinking vertical line used in some word processors to indicate the place where any characters you type will be inserted. An insertion point is the equivalent of a *cursor*.

intelligent field   Text within a Word document that is updated automatically as changes are made (for example, a date field that updates whenever a document is changed).

jump term   A highlighted word in the Word for Windows Help system that "jumps," when selected, to a related section of the Help system.

keyboard   The main input device for most computers.

kilobyte   A unit for measuring the amount of data. A kilobyte (K) is equivalent to 1,024 bytes.

landscape orientation   Your document is oriented so that it is wider than it is long, as in 11 by 8 1/2 inches. The opposite of landscape orientation is *portrait*.

leader   (1) Someone that aliens are always asking to be taken to. (2) Dots or dashes that fill the spaces between tab positions in a columnar list.

linked object   An imported object (such as a graphic) that maintains a connection to the program that created it, so that if changes are made to that object, those changes can be updated (either automatically or through a command) into your document. A linked object is stored separately from your Word document.

macro   A recorded set of instructions for a frequently used task which can be activated by pressing a specified key combination. Macros resemble small programs.

margin   An area on the left, right, top, and bottom sides of a page that is usually left blank. Text flows between the margins of a page.

Maximize button   An upward-pointing arrow located in the upper right-hand corner of a window; when you click on it, the window fills the screen.

megabyte   A standard unit used to measure the storage capacity of a disk and the amount of computer memory. A megabyte is 1,048,576 bytes (1,000 kilobytes). This is roughly equivalent to 500 pages of double-spaced text. Megabyte is commonly abbreviated as M, MB, or Mbyte.

memory   (1) Something I seem to lose quite often lately. (2) Electronic storage area inside the computer, used to store data or program instructions temporarily when the computer is using them. The computer's memory is erased when the power to the computer is turned off.

menu   A list of commands or instructions displayed on the screen. Menus organize commands and make a program easier to use.

menu bar   Located at the top of the program window, this displays a list of menus which contain the commands you'll use to edit documents.

merging   The process of combining variable information stored in a *data source* with a *main document* in order to produce a series of form letters or mailing labels.

Microsoft (1) A company I wish I had lots of stock in. (2) The company that brought you Word for Windows, Microsoft Graph, Microsoft Draw, Microsoft Equation Editor, and (among others) Windows itself.

Minimize button A downward-pointing arrow located in the upper right-hand corner of a window; when you click on it, the window is reduced to an icon on your screen.

Mirror Margins An option you can use when creating magazine-like reports: when open, the pages of your report would "face each other."

monitor A television-like screen where the computer displays information.

mouse (1) The last name of a little guy named Mickey. (2) A device that moves an arrow (a pointer) around the screen. When you move the mouse, the pointer on the screen moves in the same direction. Used instead of the keyboard to select and move items (such as text or graphics), execute commands, and perform other tasks. A mouse gets its name because it connects to your computer through a long "tail" or cord.

mouse pad (1) Where Mickey and his friends hang out. (2) A small square of plastic or foam that the mouse rests on. A mouse pad provides better traction than a desktop, and keeps the mouse away from dust and other goop on your desk.

mouse pointer An arrow or other symbol that moves when the mouse is moved. When the mouse pointer is over text, it changes to an *I-beam*. When the mouse pointer is over an element of the screen, it usually takes the shape of an arrow.

MS-DOS (Microsoft Disk Operating System) See *DOS*.

newspaper-style columns Similar to the style of column found in newspapers. Text in these columns flows between invisible boundaries down one part of the page. At the end of the page, the text continues at the top of the first column on the next page. Columns can be "interrupted" by graphics (pictures or charts) that illustrate the story being told.

numbered list Similar to a bulleted list. A numbered list is a series of paragraphs with hanging indents, where the number is placed to the left of all the other lines in the paragraph. Used in numbering the steps for a procedure.

output Data (computer information) that your computer gives back to you. Output can be displayed on a computer's monitor, stored on disk, or printed on the printer. Output is the opposite of *input*, which is the data that you enter into the computer.

Overtype mode The opposite of *Insert mode*, as used in word processors and text editors. Overtype mode means that when you position your cursor and start to type, what you type *replaces* existing characters at that point.

page break A dotted line which marks the end of a page. A page break can be forced within a document by pressing **Ctrl+Enter**.

pane (1) What I feel when someone touches my shoulder after I've spent all day at the beach. (2) What Word for Windows calls the special boxes that you use when adding headers, footers, footnotes, and annotations. In Normal View, a pane appears in the bottom half of the document window. (Since it's *part of a window*—rather than being a separate box like a dialog box—it's called a pane.)

paragraph Any grouping of words that should be treated as a unit. This includes normal paragraphs as well as single-line paragraphs (such as chapter titles, section headings, and captions for charts or other figures). When you press the **Enter** key in Word for Windows, you are marking the end of a paragraph. (Note: some computers call the Enter key *Return*.)

parallel columns See *table*.

passive voice (1) Speaking in a whisper. (2) A type of sentence that states what *is done* by (or to) the subject, rather than what the subject *does*. For example, compare "The race was won by Mary Ann" (passive voice) to the same phrase in *active voice*: "Mary Ann won the race."

PC See *personal computer*.

personal computer   A personal computer (or PC for short) is a machine that is small enough to fit on a desktop and is intended to be used by an individual to perform daily tasks, such as typing, calculating, organizing, and filing.

pie chart   A type of chart shaped like a circle, which is divided into pieces, like a pie. Each item that's charted (such as AT&T, MCI, and Sprint) is given a "pie piece," which represents its portion of the whole circle.

point   To move the mouse pointer so that it is on top of a specific object on the screen.

point size   The type size of a particular character. There are 72 points in an inch. Font families usually have only certain point sizes available; if you need larger or smaller letters than your font offers, switch to a different font.

polygon   A multi-sided object which is not a square or a rectangle. Polygons include stars, hexagons, octagons, and open free-form shapes.

portrait orientation   Your document is oriented so that it is longer than it is wide, as in 8 1/2 by 11 inches. This is the normal orientation of most documents. The opposite of portrait orientation is *landscape.*

printer   Most computers are connected to a printer for printing copies of data. The data that comes out of your computer is called *output.*

program   (1) Something you can't tell the players without. (2) A set of instructions written in a special "machine language" which the computer understands. Typical programs are word processors, spreadsheets, databases, and games.

program group   A special window within the Program Manager that is used to group several applications together. In the Word for Windows program group, you will find three icons: Microsoft Word, Word Readme Help, and Word Dialog Editor.

program window   The window that Word for Windows runs in. Close this window, and you close down (exit) Word for Windows. This window frames the tools and the menus for the Word for Windows program.

pull-down menu   A *pull-down* menu contains the selections for a Main menu command. This type of menu, when activated, is pulled down below the Main menu bar, the way a window shade can be pulled down from the top of a window frame.

random-access memory (RAM)   What your computer uses to store data and programs temporarily while it uses them. RAM is measured in kilobytes and megabytes. Generally, the more RAM a computer has, the more powerful the programs it can run.

readability index   A measure of the educational level a reader would need to understand the text in a given document easily. It is determined by counting the average number of words per sentence, and the average number of characters per word. (A good average is about 17 words per sentence.)

rebooting   The process of restarting a computer that is already on. Press **Ctrl+Alt+Delete** to reboot. Also known as *warm booting*.

record   (1) A CD's mother. (2) In a data file, this denotes a collection of related information contained in one or more fields, such as an individual's name, address, and phone number. A record is stored in a single row of a Word data source.

Restore button   A special double-headed arrow located in the upper right-hand corner of a window; when you click on it, a minimized window is restored to its previous size.

Ruler   Provides an easy method within Word for Windows for setting tab stops, indentations, and margins.

scaling   The process of resizing a graphic so it does not lose its proportions.

scroll   To move text up/down or right/left on a computer screen.

scroll bars   Located along the bottom and right sides of the document window; use these to display other areas of the document.

scroll box   Its position within the entire scroll bar tells you roughly where you are within your document.

section   A part of a document that has different settings from the main document (for such things as margins, paper size, headers, footers, columns, and page numbering). A section can be any length: several pages, several paragraphs, or even a single line (such as a heading).

Selection bar   This invisible area that runs along the left side of the document window and provides a quick way for you to select a section of text that you want to edit.

selection letters   A single letter of a menu command, such as the *x* in Exit, which activates the command when the menu is open and you press the key for that letter.

shading   The box of gray which is placed behind text or behind a cell in a table in order to emphasize it.

shortcut menu   A small menu that appears when you point at an object and click the right mouse button. Shortcut menus contain commands which are specific to the object you're pointing at. For example, if you point to a block of text and click the right mouse button, you'll see a shortcut menu for copying, moving, and formatting text.

software   Any instructions that tell your computer (the hardware) what to do. There are two types of software: operating system software and application software. *Operating system software* (such as DOS) gets your computer up and running. *Application software* allows you to do something useful, such as type a letter or save the whales.

Spell Checker   A special program within Word for Windows that corrects spelling errors within a document.

Spike   (1) Something that's done to prom punch. (2) A command within Word for Windows that allows you to copy multiple groups of text to the Clipboard, so they can be placed together within the document with a single command.

split bar   Located on the right-hand side of a document window; when you double-click on this bar, the window splits vertically into two smaller windows called *panes*.

spreadsheet   A computer program that organizes information in columns and rows and performs calculations. If you want to balance a checkbook or last year's budget, use a spreadsheet program. Common spreadsheets include Lotus 1-2-3, Microsoft Excel, and Quattro Pro.

status bar   Located at the bottom of the program window, this displays information about your document.

Standard toolbar   One of the most often used toolbars because it contains the most commonly used commands (such as opening, saving, and printing a document) in button form.

style   A collection of specifications for formatting text. A style may include information for the font, size, style, margins, and spacing to a section of text. When you apply a style to a block of text, you format it automatically (according to the style's specifications).

Style Area   (1) That area in front of the mirrors in women's restrooms. (2) An area that can be made to appear at the far left side of the Word for Windows screen, and which displays a two-letter code for the style of every paragraph in a document.

sub-dialog   A subsection of a dialog box which is accessed through a command button with an ellipsis following its name, as in an **Options...** button.

tab   (1) A drink that's just one calorie! (2) A keystroke that moves the cursor to a specified point. Used to align columns of text.

table   (1) A great place for my keys and all those bills I haven't paid. (2) Used to organize large amounts of columnar data. Tables consist of *rows* (the horizontal axis) and *columns* (the vertical axis). The intersection of a row and a column is called a *cell*.

template   Defines the Word environment, such as margin settings, page orientation, and so on. The template also controls which menu commands are available, and which buttons are located on the various toolbars. Word for Windows comes with additional templates you can use to create specialized documents. If you are using one of these templates, your screen may look different from the ones shown in this book. Also, you may have additional commands available on the menus.

text area   The main part of the document window; this is where the text you type will appear.

text file   A type of file that contains no special formatting (such as bold), but simply letters, numbers, and such. See also *ASCII file*.

toolbar   A bar across the screen that presents the most common Word commands in an easy-to-access form. For example, clicking on one of the buttons on the Standard toolbar saves your document.

view mode   A way of looking at a document. Word for Windows comes with several view modes: Normal, Outline, Page Layout, and Print Preview.

widow/orphan   A *widow* is the last line of a paragraph and appears alone at the top of the next page. If the first line of the paragraph gets stranded at the bottom of a page, it is called an *orphan*. Just remember that an orphan is left behind.

windows   (1) Something I don't do. (2) A box that is used to display information in part of the screen.

Windows   A nickname that's often used for Microsoft Windows, a graphical interface program (see *GUI*).

Word for Windows   Brought to you by Microsoft. Word for Windows is one of the most popular Windows word processing programs, and the reason you bought this book.

word processor   A program that lets you enter, edit, format, and print text. A word processor can be used to type letters, reports, and envelopes, and to complete other tasks you would normally use a typewriter for.

word wrapping   Causes text to remain within the margins of a document. As the text you're typing touches the right-hand margin, it's automatically placed at the beginning of the next line. When you insert text into the middle of a paragraph, the remaining text moves down. If you delete text, the remaining text in the paragraph moves up.

Index

F

Q–R

Installing Word for Windows

Installing Word for Windows is relatively easy—easier than using it, actually. In order to install Word for Windows, you don't really need to understand very much at all. If you've used Windows itself (even just a little), you'll be even further ahead of the game. (If you'd like a quick intro to Windows, read Chapter 3 first.) Feel free to ask a PC guru to help you if you feel at all uncomfortable.

1. Turn on your computer. Look for a switch on the front, back, or right-hand side of that big box thing. You may also have to turn on your *monitor* (it looks like a TV, but it gets lousy reception).

2. If Windows starts, great! Skip to the next step. If instead you get a rather unassuming DOS prompt that resembles **C>** or **C:\>**, type **WIN** and press **Enter**. Now you should see Windows. If you don't, or if you got an error message (such as **Bad command or file name**), Windows may not be installed, so get a PC guru to help you.

3. Insert the diskette labeled "Setup—Disk 1" into drive A or B.

4. Open the Program Manager's **File** menu by clicking on it, and select the **Run** command. If you're using your keyboard, press **Alt** and **F** at the same time, and then press **R**. Congratulations—it's a dialog box!

5. Type either **A:\SETUP** or **B:\SETUP** in the box that says **Command Line:**, and then press **Enter**.

6. A screen will appear, asking you to confirm the name of the directory in which the Word program files will be placed. You can change the name of the directory, but most people don't bother. Press **Enter** to continue.

7. You'll see another screen that asks which type of installation you want to use. I'd recommend **Typical installation** because it's the easiest and it installs the most common options. If you don't have enough room, you can choose Laptop (Minimum) installation, which will install the minimum number of files needed to run Word for Windows. Avoid Complete Custom installation unless you have help. Click on the appropriate button to continue.

8. You'll see another screen that asks which Program Manager Group you want to use (the default is Microsoft Applications). Make your selection and slect Continue.

9. You'll see another screen that asks if you want to install Help for WordPerfect Users (the default is No). Select Yes or No.

There you go! Follow the instructions you see on-screen; you'll be told when to insert the additional installation disks. If for some reason you want to abandon the installation, you can select **Cancel**.